THE B.O.A.T

(Book of Apocryphal Truth)

MYSTERIES OF THE KINGDOM

*Understanding Your connections to the
Universal Mind and how You can Create or Manifest Your life's Events*

Rodh de Sailor

*An Imprint of Thera-Boo Media
theraboo.com
Atlanta, Ga.*

First Published edition release by
Thera-Boo Media
theraboo.com
Email: Rodh17@gmail.com

CopyRight @ 2012

Manufactured in the United States of America
ISBN-13: 978-0615725345 (Thera-Boo Media)
ISBN-10: 0615725341

ACKNOWLEDGEMENT

A good deed never goes unnoticed...

If it was up to me this particular page of this book would be similar to that of an electronic billboard. The hardest aspect of producing this book was completing this page, for I had to be sure to assign credit to everyone who helped make this book possible. I am well aware that once a book has been published and subsequently released to the public it is too late to add more names of those who are deserving. So, I had to make sure and get it right the first time.

Considering all the challenges each of us face in life everyday, I realized that becoming a published author is simply not that difficult to do today thanks in part to modern technologies. No longer do aspiring writers have to bare the prospect of rejection from entrenched book publishers, most of whom literally serve as a sort of gatekeeper for entrance into the industry. There was never any real doubt in my mind that this book would eventually see the light of day, simply because I knew from the start that it was all up to me to get it done (the writing), and just let the universe handle the details.

Without further delay, a sincere thank you goes out to everyone involved with this book no matter how small their effort may have been, it all helped in a very big way towards the final product. The universe conspired on my behalf; as it does for everyone; to make it possible for this book to manifest beyond the invisible conceptual state of my imagination, and into a visible physical reality that others can share.

In terms of individual contributors, I must first give my love and thanks to my wonderful, very beautiful wife and best friend for the past thirty-two years, who has relentlessly hung in there along side me, and actually played a major role in the final editing. As far as she knew there was no guarantee from anyone within the established, traditional publishing companies that would open up venues of marketing and distribution, and to insure that this book would eventually see the light of day aside from my intentional-will. But that's just the way my sweet and beautiful wife is when it comes to giving her support for those she loves and cares about. While she doesn't completely understand all the mechanics involved in the laws of attraction and so forth, nevertheless she is beginning to come around to it in her own time and way.

A very special thanks also goes out to my daughter, who has displayed an incredible amount of love and understanding towards me, she's also helped out from time to time with proof reading this material. Now that the B.O.A.T is released, my wonderful daughter has become very helpful with online marketing ideas and guidance. Together, my wife and my daughter have provided me with much needed moral and spiritual support unlike any I've ever known in my life before. "I love them both!"

Towards the final days of editing and proof reading this book, my niece: Brittany, turned out to be a very skillful and talented illustrator and graphic artist. Considering she's only in middle school demonstrates how good at graphic arts and illustrating she'll become in the years ahead. Brittany is fully responsible for the rabbit logo on the back and spine of this book.

The Laws of Attraction were surely at work for me in the State of Florida as well. I met so many wonderful people along the way who were all to happy to help with this book project in anyway they could. Additionally, I give special thanks and mention to all the free spirits I met while living in the Orlando, Florida area for nearly 5 years. Laura Painter, Terre Miller and her soul mate, immediately comes to mind as they each provided specific needs at the right time. I must also mention with love and good health and prosperity to all former staff members of a Borders' bookstore that was located in Altamonte Springs, Florida for allowing me and my spiritual friends to hold meetings and give classes at the store.

These were truly wonderful people when considering that other bookstores had asked me to leave, since I didn't always make a purchase.

And last but not least, I give special thanks, love and energy to a group of very special women who at one time or another, each volunteered and allowed me to experiment with their minds by way of mental messaging at a distance; better known as telepathy and remote viewing. I will provide their first names only in this space: Joamie, Nicole, Ronnie, Adrienne, Alicia, Sonia, and Sandra. Additionally, special thanks and appreciation goes out to George, Justin and Luis for helping me with the experimentation and research into remote viewing and psychic development training classes that they each participated in almost daily for several months. Everyone mentioned above helped me tremendously without remuneration.

To sum it up, thank you all very much...

In the beginning was the word from the mind activity of God, which brought forth information for the cause of everything to manifest. Reality is that effect.

Contents

Best way to use this Book?
(Getting the most out of it?)

All sections include explanations and commentary as needed.

How should You Read this material?

The best way to use this book and get the most out of it is simply to read it from the beginning, starting with the Foreword and Introduction sections before preceding to each chapter in sequence. Some of you, though, will choose to go directly to a chapter of particular interest to you, such as: Tapping into the Universal Mind, before reading anything else. If you choose this approach there is a good chance that you will overlook some very important information that just might be the key to helping you unlock your full potential.

Just like scenes of a movie, this book tells a story from beginning to end. Each chapter within this book segues into the next one so that the full scope and understanding of what is written is known. So even if you choose to glance ahead to certain chapters, it is still advised that you read through the entire book.

About Information Herein

Information within this book, once it has been collectively consumed by your conscious mind, will set-off a chain reaction deep within your subconscious-mind, this will help you to remember and achieve, by-way-of, manifesting your ideal way of life to be enjoyed in the physical world. The methods and techniques discussed in this book are not new at all, nor, are they rarely known, although at times it may seem that way. In fact, information provided in this book has been around, and is known since the very beginning of time. But it has only been shared amongst a very select and growing host of others who are members of private social groups known today as secret societies.

Human behavior suggests that some people will do anything to keep others in the dark about the content of this book and other information of similar value. In my efforts to bring this information forward I've had to resort to self-publishing just to insure the integrity of content and meaning becomes known by all who apply. As you all know, today's internet technology makes this proposition very much a possibility.

Best wishes to your eventual awakening.....

Foreword

The B.O.A.T (Book of Apocryphal Truth)
MYSTERIES OF THE KINGDOM

At first glance this book reads as if it's fictional, and based entirely upon your religious belief tenets this material just might be interpreted along the lines of being something from an occultist group. Nevertheless, let me assure you my fellow readers that neither is true. This book is not a work of fiction, nor, am I now, or ever have been, a member of any occult. However, with that being said, the topics of this book may not be suitable literature for children of a certain age because it does include matters that are deemed taboo, as far as mainstream society, religion and cultural traditions and values are concerned.

This book includes several accounts of my personal experiences of a supernatural nature including, but in no way limited to the following subjects: God; UFOs; psychic powers; mysticism; out-of-body experiences; remote viewing; energy healing; telepathy; time travel; spiritual awakening and enlightenment; precognition; intentional creation and manifestations of your life's events.

The B.O.A.T as it is titled, is what it is... and each of these matters has been experienced at some point and time in my life. Each event has been recalled from my subjective memory as best as could be remembered, and is written in simple English so that anyone curious enough to read this book, should be fully capable of understanding the nature of the material written herein.

There is always an infinite and seemingly loving and caring force that permeates our being from within and without constantly; supplying us with thought energy; imagination; our emotions and feelings. Most of all, we are continuously supplied with a spiritual intelligence and inspiration, and an abundance of life sustaining elements.

There is something very magical and mysterious about all human beings; there exist some sort of infinite, caring and loving power within and outside each of us; which influences our lives in every way imaginable, and unimaginable. Could this omniscient, omnipotent force be the entity known as God all over the world?

Acknowledgment of the existence of a very powerful force known as God does not imply in anyway, as some would have you believe, that we have no control of, or say-so in our own individual lives, or that in some manner our fate has been predetermined. This is not the reality of the realm we occupy.

As you will soon discover in this life or the next, once the mind-control technologies you've been subjected to all your life begins to wane, that there is always a choice to be made... that you do have the final authority over any circumstances that pertains to your particular life. This is known as FREE WILL! Whether or not the decisions you make exercising your right to choose is a subconscious response, or a conscious one, the final outcome is always a choice that was originated by your use of free will. Free will, although this is just a generic phrase to some, is the most powerful aspect of being human. Exactly where does this awesome power we have within us come from, it has been highly debated since the very beginning of mankind's ability to reason.

What is known for certain about the power of free will is that all other known laws of existence; such as the law of attraction, etc., by comparison, all yield to the law of FREE WILL. All of our achievements, both individually and as a collective, stems from our use of this very powerful law.

There are a number of taboo matters mentioned in this book, because as disturbing as some of these subjects are to the human psyche for some; in particularly to those of a religious persuasion; the reality of it is that all of these matters are a natural aspect and actuality of how the mind functions. This implies that no matter what the nature of the event or subject matter may be, all are interconnected in some way, and yet, interdependent in some unknown fashion to everyone alive and has ever lived.

Such revelations about esoteric matters has kept many scientists (philosophers and quantum theorists, alike) awake at night trying to make sense of it all. This was also the final scientific project ensued by the late Albert Einstein's unfinished book---just moments before dying.

Like most inquiring minds, you are probably wondering: what do UFOs, psychic powers, energy healing, telepathy, remote viewing and any other aspects of the supernatural have in common? And the obvious answer to that question is that each play an equal role in the Mysteries of the Kingdom.

In my opinion, these topics are one and the same, especially questions pertaining to Aliens and UFOs, which are as real as you and I. But, for some reason or another there has been so much deceptive tactics thrown about denying their existence with carefully orchestrated covered-ups over the years, maybe even centuries, to the point that a great number of people simply do not know truth from fiction. Fact is, at some moment in your life you'll come to the realization that we are not alone in the universe. Never have been, never will be because there are more variations of life in existence than there are possibilities of DNA combinations...

One thing's for sure, as you read further into the content of the B.O.A.T you'll most likely become more knowledgeable of metaphysical, esoteric and supernatural matters in a personal way and, you will to some degree or another, attain a certain peace of mind in knowing that there is a way, a very sound way of discovering for yourself that which is truth from that which is simply a case of propaganda by those who rule.

And another thing; as a result of reading this book is that you will never see your life, nor that of others, from such a narrow perspective again.

In that sense, you too, will have changed...

Please be FOREWARNED that once you mentally consume this material your life and the way you see the world will forever change.....

Introduction

It was nearly 26 years ago when I first began what is known within the new-age community as a process of awakening. Then about 10 years afterward, I accidentally stumbled upon a book at a local Barnes and Noble bookstore located a few miles northeast on the out-skirts of my hometown of Atlanta, Georgia.

Why I just happened to look downward, onto a bookshelf that was well beneath the level of my knees when returning from a run to the men' restroom still mystifies me to this day. This enigmatic book which caught my eye, and immediate attention was titled "Children of the Matrix," by Author David Icke; a British born, ex-jockey turned writer of alternative history and speculation topics. Eventually I picked up this book and began reading through several of its pages while sitting inside an upstairs' cafe until I became compelled by inner emotions and enough concern about the subject matter outlined in this book to make a purchase.

Children of the Matrix had become such a total shock to my belief tenets at the time. I just couldn't believe all the negative things that were written about some of the most important people in the world today, and that this guy (a virtual unknown) had enough nerve to write about it. According to the author (David Icke), the world as we know it, and history itself, is one great BIG LIE!

Author David Icke wholeheartedly believes that there is a worldwide conspiracy where a controlling race of non-human (reptilians) entities from another world or dimension, that has projected a false concept of reality into the collective consciousness of humanity; an illusion of sorts; with the use of an advanced form of mind-control methods and technologies; which he has dubbed the matrix. Bear in mind that the matrix analogy had become the underlying scheme of a major blockbuster movie years earlier. Not only were such allegations of bad conduct and outright criminal activities against humanity being openly written and thrown around about world leaders past and present, but Icke went on to name names of some of the most recognizable figures on the A-list of whose who--such as former president Bill Clinton and former first lady Hilary Clinton, former president George H.W. Bush, former president George W. Bush, former vice president Dick Cheney, Queen Elizabeth and the entire Royal Family, former defense secretary Donald Rumsfeld, former president Jimmy Carter, former vice president Al Gore and many other well known and successful people in the world of entertainment, business and politics, just to name a few. Since the release of his book, David has gone on to publish an updated version and follow-up that lists more conspirators and mind-control manipulators of humanity; which includes current United States President, Barack Obama.

Now, before completely writing this guy off as a self-serving, total lunatic, you should know that he has a growing number of believers around the world who'll gladly pay big bucks for his research and opinions. And within this following are some well known leaders, researchers and business magnets who've come to respect his work.

It would be several years later after that first reading of David's book, along with other books seemingly congruent with David's findings, when I began cross-referencing David's views with that of other writers' books that can be found among the backroom bookshelves of most bookstores, and are listed under various speculative and societal taboo matters along the lines of religion, psychic phenomena, government cover-ups of UFO sightings and landings, conspiracy theories, human-hybrid aliens, the Illuminati and other secret societies, that I began to take notice of and see for myself that not all was what it seemed to be in this world.

As the affects from many years of being under mind-control methods, along with the rest of society had begun to wear-off, the illusions and truthfulness of reality began to really sink in and reveal things about my life that I had once taken for granted. You see, I had to wake-up from my own self-imposed, nightmarish dream in order to realize that there are some very important facts about humanity's existence being denied to us continuously by those who are in control. But, it would take the tragic events of September 11, 2001, the so-called terror attacks on the world trade towers, with use of skyjacked commercial airliners, resulting in the loss of nearly 3,000 lives that really opened up my inner most faculties. Ironically, these events had been foretold, theoretically at least, in David's earlier books.

Since that time, I have become highly spiritually awakened and enlightened to a whole new way of seeing life and experiencing reality that is so very different from that of my upbringing. While I do believe some of what David has alleged in most, if not all of his books are somewhat true, I am not ready to fully embrace all of his views on a wholesale basis about all world leaders, past or present, as belonging to members of a hybrid race of beings who are all something other than human. The main reason for my dissent is that I realize that all humans beings are hybrids of some sort. And just as I was blind in the beginning of my life to what reality really is not, there has to be many others in this world who are holding onto very similar views to those I once held.

Beneath the main vibrational level of humanity's collective consciousness ideology, I have intuitively sensed plenty of evidence in some instances that would suggest that there are certain members among world leaders, as well as leaders at the local levels of state and municipalities across the country who are self-serving and up to no good. And, that many of these people are actually intoxicated with the power they feel when manipulating the minds of those who lack real knowledge and historical perspective of what's really going on in this world based in part on competition and the pursuit of power, aggrandizement and individual wealth.

I am not speaking about monetary gains, because some of the things that these people do are in fact rituals of some sort for initiation into secret societies, or, as members of unknown occults. And some of these people do things for simple bragging rights so

17

that others can bear witness to what they can get away with. It seems that fear is a driving motivator that is used to open people up to the effects of mind-control technologies. In retrospect it is no wonder all newscasts in America, and for that matter the world begins every broadcast with a leading event of fear. Fear not only opens up certain vibrations within the subconscious level of mind, it also translates into increased viewership which means more advertising revenues. This is not to say nor imply that everyone working as a TV news reporter is in on the conspiracy.

Furthermore, I have witnessed on a number of occasions some very good and extraordinary events that were manifested by some of these very same people mentioned by David Icke as being in on the conspiracy to control the soul of humankind, which has been very beneficial to so-called common folk, too. To me, such acts of kindness only demonstrates that there are good and bad tendencies within everyone, regardless of their place of origin. It all comes down to a matter of choice among the individual beings as to what their underlying intentions really are. After all, life is life, regardless of where it may have originated in the universe. All life should be cherished.

While David Icke's book in my opinion, seems to be focused mainly upon the power that these people of non-human origins hypothetically retain over that of earth born human beings; the focus of this book is centered around the powers that all human beings have within themselves, but for one reason or another do not make use it. Everyone has the ability to break free of their falsely constructed reality with the help of what I am referring to as their very own mental or psychic powers.

It is also my intent and hope of highlighting the hidden talents that lie within and around all human beings regardless of whether there are, or are not, non-human entities living among us, controlling our very thoughts and reactions, and are manifesting a false sense of religious hope and redemption from a made-up deity based entirely upon the vibrations and emotions of fear, which is suitable only for their needs and purposes. I simply want humanity to WAKE-UP!!

I believe that we are all individual spiritual beings, who were created in the image and likeness of what is collectively known worldwide as God, can finally choose to exercise their uniqueness of free will and become the sole authors of their own interconnected-interdependent life experiences. I am totally convinced that this is the only event that can and will change the trajectory of humanity's collective future.

One things for sure, there are many things happening right now in this world that are both seen and unseen that would defy acceptable logic and reasoning. And it has become my life's mission to help as many as I can, one by one to awaken the *nous (Greek: Spirit)* of their inner guidance system; also known as the genie within; so that they too can learn ways of experiencing the mysteries of the kingdom in a better light the way that I have learned to over the course of many years of relentless research, practice and meditation.

Repeatedly, I have asked these very same questions over and over, again and again, telepathically in my mind: what was it that really caused me to awaken in the first place? Did the UFO sighting I witnessed in April of 1997 after watching Tiger Woods win the first of four Masters golf tournaments that he's conquered have anything to do with my initial awakening process? Or was it the large triangular shaped, virtually translucent UFO that I witnessed at a close range, hovering silently about 150 feet above my head shortly past midnight on September 13, 2005, while walking my dog (Bogey) that would eventually lead to my acceptance of the paranormal as a reality? Or, was it reading through many pages of David Icke's book, and then witnessing the event of 911 live on TV that finally opened my mind and eyes? Or, could it have been the miraculous event of hearing the voice of God within the silence and stillness of my mind, externally, in the darkness of my bedroom on a cold wintry night for the first time do it? Or, was it suddenly seeing the image of, and then communicating with the late Princess Diana in a subdued vision shortly after her untimely departure from life?"

While there are certainly a host of extremely and spectacular events for me to choose from as that eureka moment. Wholeheartedly I believe and conclude that my spiritual awakening and subsequent enlightenment had come about as a cumulative effect of life-long events that were so full of adventure and unexplained manifestations of things into reality that finally allowed me to sense, feel and experience the world, in a different way than at any time I had in my life years before ever coming across and reading David's book. Admittedly, his book could have provided the final spark which ignited the flame of curiosity deep within my core.

To begin sensing, seeing and knowing that at least half of life's existence, if not more, is invisible to physical sight and senses, and theoretical ideas about how invisible sub-atomic particles are consolidated into matter from nothingness, and that they somehow manifests into the vibrational frequency of the physical realm is truly something of a miracle in and of itself. This means that miracles are constantly happening all the time much faster than the speed of light is estimated to be, every split-of-a-split second of each moment, every day. From purely a scientific and hypothetical view, I believe the so-called theoretical big-bang effect never happened at all. Instead, what is happening is that somewhere within the unknown regions of space a major event of creation occurs all the time. And that this means that life itself is not an anomaly in and of itself. And that something of immense power and intelligence had to intervened, and continues to do so.

Notwithstanding, there are some very well meaning people who'll willingly take offense to anyone claiming to having had a direct and personal conversation with God. To those who harbor a strict interpretation of their religious foundation, this sort of admission, especially from someone who does not display any inclination towards adhering to any religious doctrine, nor hold a church membership, is akin to blasphemy.

And to anyone brave enough to admit publicly of having paranormal experiences, such as seeing ghosts, talking to the dead, or seeing UFOs, you might as well pack your bags too, and begin living in isolation on an island.

The funny thing about all of this is that there isn't anyone living in the world today, who has not had at least some kind of supernatural or paranormal experience of some kind, or at least having engaged themselves in a private conversation with God every once in awhile. If so, will they please stand up and be recognized as a liar!

By the way, isn't belief in God, spirits, angels, devil and demons, also a paranormal thing?

The honest truth of the matter at hand, is that there is absolutely no one living on this planet today, able to make the claim of being truly innocent from experiencing any form of a supernatural matter simply because life itself is a supernatural event generated by the powerful activity of God's mind. I will also say this, in actuality there is really no such thing as a paranormal event or activity. Everything that exist here and happens here, also exists elsewhere in existence, whether visible or invisible, and is therefore, simply natural.

With all that has been written, I am not making any outrageous claims nor, am I seeking any acknowledgment of others for what I now know to be true. It is what it is. One things for sure, though, since you've read this far into this document your higher self (subjective mind), that part of you which maintains a direct link with your true self existence, (or if you prefer, the mind of God) has begun to unleash and awaken a part of you that has been idled for a very long, long time.

The time is near when all of your most inner powers will become self activated, when this happens, you too, will start seeing and knowing things like never before without a logical explanation to back it up. I call this occurrence, "the event." But it is more widely known throughout the new-age community as the AWAKENING!!!

There is a great distance between knowing something and believing in it.

About this Book and Title

The B.O.A.T has been researched and written for the express purpose of helping to right a wrong that has been acknowledged by the great philosophers, prophets and luminaries of both the old and new ages. It is my attempt at providing real, meaningful and time tested information that everyone should have access to. One things for sure, if you are not creating your own life experiences, then someone else is doing it for you. Difference being, is that it just might not be to your overall benefit to let others manifest your life the way they see fit. In short, this book is written to bring you the truth.....

Use of the acronym *"The B.O.A.T,"* for this book is simply an easier way for readers to grasp its' full phrase, which is: *the book of apocryphal truth*. According to the latest edition of any *New World Dictionary*, the word *apocryphal* when used in this context defines a book that is written by an unknown source, and is therefore deemed unreliable by the powers that be. Historically speaking, based upon its' Latin roots, the word *apocrypha* was often used to described texts of the lost gospels, according to some scholars, predates the canonical gospels of Matthew, Mark, John, and Luke.

Most apocryphal texts, and/or, scriptures include alleged sayings of Mary Magdalene, Didymus Judas Thomas, Enoch, and many other such notables whose writings were hidden in the desert a long time ago for the purpose of protecting these religious documents against those wanting to destroy them. Such works, or texts, labeled apocrypha, holds an entirely different version from that of biblical antiquity, beginning with the story of creation, to the life and times of Yeshua ben-hur (the real name of Jesus), and other luminaries appearing before him.

The one thing that each of these books known as the apocryphal texts have in common, is that they were all banned from inclusion in the Christian Bible, and as such were hidden and forbidden from public knowledge until they were accidentally unearthed some time ago, and thus reintroduced into the collective consciousness of a curious society. While there have been numerous attempts by well meaning authors, theologians, scholars and researchers over the years to tell a more accurate story of what is written in the pages of certain forbidden and banned religious works, we are still faced with the fact that many of the more detailed pages, containing some of the most insightful and beneficial information to humankind, is simply not there.

If you are a person given to inquiry, research, and eager for knowledge as I am, you'd have to be curious about the whereabouts of all of that missing information from the likes of Jesus, and Leonardo da Vinci, and others, especially information pertaining to their prime years of life. What happened during this unique time in history has been open to speculation the world over. At the earliest, some of the most ancient and forbidden scriptures (books and texts) were hidden by the Pharisees, their high priests, priestesses and scribes from falling into the hands of ordinary people. It is no secret that the rulers of Sumeria and the pharaohs of Egypt maintained their rule over slaves and those they conquered by keeping them ignorant of reality, and by encouraging the worship of false idols and religion. To this day and age, blueprints, traditions and practices laid out by earlier rulers of society are alive and well in places like the United States, Europe, Russia, Canada, Australia, Asia and South American countries. Obviously, such efforts were well thought out and planned, the attempts to keep information privy to certain members of secret society has been in practice a very long time.

An earlier prophecy of Yeshua clearly stated: 'the Pharisees have received the keys of knowledge and has hidden them from the people. They did not go within, and those who wanted to go there were prevented from doing so.' Such sayings attributed to Yeshua is an early indication that *Mysteries of the Kingdom (which refers to the mind)* were being withheld from the knowledge of ordinary people during the heyday of the biblical era, which means that this information is still a secret. Instead of allowing humanity to move forward, unimpeded to the next level of its eventual evolution, those who are in possession of this knowledge have simply chosen to keep it amongst themselves.

Here's a question often not asked, what is the real meaning behind celebrating December 25, when it is clearly not Jesus' birthday?

Answer: December 25, is the continued celebration of Charlemagne's recognition as Emperor of all of Europe, which occurred post Rome, in the year 800.

For more than five thousand years humanity has been kept in the dark about its true origin, nature, power and capabilities. Each individual has the ability to summon forth from within themselves, all the help ever needed to navigate whatever obstacles that might occur in their life.

The ability to program the minds of millions of people into acting or thinking a certain way is an awesome display of power. This kind of power can only come from one source, and we collectively recognize this source as being that of God. Please remember, that god doesn't judge who's good or who's bad, god simply delivers to those who understand how to access the power, rather on purpose or accidentally, the answer is always yes. This is the unknown message of all sages and prophets ever to walk the earth. Others have come to know this source as the *Universal Mind*, or Spirit. One things for sure, the name you decide to call upon when addressing a higher power is not that important, it never was, or will be. What seems to matter most are your inner most feelings and belief held at the core of your being when you choose to summon forth help.

The powers that be has always had a number of ways available to them for keeping the most secretive information away from the rest of us. One such method has been by controlling how words are defined in all dictionaries, in each language, worldwide. You see, the key is to use simple methods and/or technologies that no one suspects. Such technology is right out in the open, so much so, that most people would never suspect, nor believe that a dictionary wields so much power and can be used in such a strategically, undetectable way.

In modern reality, a dictionary is one of the most useful and effective technology ever devised, it is very good at preconditioning perceptions in brainwave thought patterns and vibrations of both laypersons and the most educated professionals, alike. Take for instance, the word: apocrypha; there is such a broad meaning for this word in the way it is defined and applied in most modern-day *Dictionaries,* so much so that it can be used for a number of situations within the construct of a sentence. It can be defined as information regarding religious content, as it is mostly applicable today. It could also be routinely used to denounce certain works of art by those considered as being fringe members of society.

Think about it for a minute! If someone is willing to put forth that much effort into keeping the real, original meaning of particular words within a dictionary encrypted in secrecy, decipherable only by certain members inside the loop, surely means that there are some very powerful, and possibly character damaging information that certain people of power simply don't want others to know, ever. Thus, some encrypted efforts hidden from the consumption of mainstream society requires a grasp of Latin and ancient Greek language skills and perspective in order to define its original, intended use, just to arrive at a meaningful understanding.

Sometimes, the encoding and re-coding of words and their definitions are placed in plain sight without any attempts to hide them. Take for instance, one of the most highly insensitive, deplorable, and disgusting word to be used openly during slavery, and well into modern-day society: "*nigger.*" This word's original definition was used to describe an African from the country of Niger. It also meant "*ignorance;*" which by the way could apply to anyone, any race.

The word *nigger* was so openly used by the aristocrats to the point that during America's and Europe's slavery past, many uneducated and illiterate people of the times were wrongly led into thinking

26

that this word applied only to black African slaves. Keep in mind, the aristocrats of Europe initially used this word interchangeably to describe those who were economically, politically and socially disadvantaged, and lacking a proper education, and knowledge of certain skills such as reading, writing and comprehension. The word "nigger" was also commonly used to define indentured servants, of which, even though they were mostly white, Asian or other, nevertheless, were still considered slaves by the upper class and those who ruled society.

If you were to research this word today (nigger), its original definition would be very hard to find, even *amongst elite scholars*. You'd have to consult with an etymologist because the term defined in most modern dictionaries has been changed to reflect harsh realities of its more common use today, which is, by the way, to mentally harm, and to imply inferiority of dark skinned people.

Now, lets look at a very common name: Charles, as an example. Although there are many people living in America and Canada by that name, this is not so for those in Europe. Of course, there are Europeans with that name, but historically speaking the name *'Charles'* meant king. That is why most royal male members who became kings where often times named Charles I, Charles II, Charles III, Charles IV, and so on. You only need to look at the royal families of European ancestry to see this proof. Some time ago these families decided to use another coded name; thus, Edwards, James, and Williams were added to a long list of encrypted words within their highly secretive culture.

Charlemagne, was ruler of western Europe as king/emperor for nearly 48 years, and was born under the moniker of Charles. Later his name was change to reflect the size of the kingdom, which during the years of Roman dominance was known as an empire. If you haven't figured it out, the *Charles* aspect of Charlemagne was kept.

By the way, here's something most people still don't realize, is that the royal families of the world don't have last names. For the purpose of keeping matters under wraps and away from public scrutiny, royal families have been encouraged to select, only as a convenience, a last name. In actuality though (their), last names are not needed, because like the days of old, everyone knows who they are... We just don't know anything about their true origins.

Perspectives of a
Free Thinker

Obviously, this book discusses a lot of unbelievable things that deals with religion, the paranormal, psychic phenomena, metaphysical and mystical topics of today and yesterday, as each applies to the physical realm.

Personally I don't believe any supernatural ability should be isolated and kept hidden from anyone and, that each phenomenon is interconnected in someway or another to all others simply because, all are from the one mind, a unifying field, which is the underlying basis for all forces that exist in nature.

Since I have personally experienced most, if not all commonly known psychic phenomena at one time or another, it's a little odd placing any of my experiences aside as if such abilities are unrelated.

Telepathy, for instance, is considered to be a phenomenon only because its presence is greatly misunderstood by most scientists and laymen alike. However, such misunderstandings doesn't negate the fact that telepathy is a part of our DNA, and everybody put to use this innate gift every moment of the day. In short, telepathy is as simple as breathing, and we must breathe in order to live. What if I told you that within this book lie the keys to using telepathy? Well the basic keys to telepathy are listed here (see Telepathy).

It is virtually impossible for anyone not to make use of this very basic skill; and here's why...telepathy comes in mainly two basic forms:

1. intentional,
2. and unintentional.

For instance, as I was writing this book with the use of a computer, my mind was focused mainly on the words I had to type, while simultaneously, each of my fingers are seemingly moving at the speed of my sub-conscious thoughts at the right moment and time, striking the appropriate keys necessary to convey my train of thought, so that this book becomes readable by others. Movement of my fingers along the keyboard is a form of unintentional telepathy, which simply means that I have consciously communicated to my subjective mind, a desire to move them. In fact each cell, each organ in the entire body functions in this manner.

What this means is that all along we have been multitasking our whole lives because of telepathy. Everything that you do with any part of your body, including something so simple, like the vital act of breathing, or the pumping of blood by the heart, is a form of telepathy executed unintentionally, subconsciously by your mind. What I am saying is that your mind communicates with your body telepathically, and vice versa.

I am not alone it this opinion, even quantum physicists and other academically trained professionals of the sciences are reaching a conceptual hypothesis that the mind and body use some sort of telepathy, of which most prefer the term 'unified field' as a way of saying that we are fundamentally, one. So it is with such frame of mind that I present to you my inner most thoughts on the matters at hand.

One might ask, why then, would I include the subjects of UFOs, ET, religion, the occult, secret societies among other socially taboo topics along with psychic phenomena in the same book? And the answer to the question is that I've thought long and hard about each topic in the process of writing this book, and it was decided at the very beginning that all should be included.

After all, this book is titled the Apocryphal Truth, which means nothing should be withheld, even at a cost of turning away some potential readers. With that being said, I am completely comfortable and willing to go on record in stating that each human being possess within them the aptitude of a genius. And that some, if not all, have the abilities known to be associated with such non-physical skills (esp) as those who have demonstrated them to notoriety in the past and/or present.

And, if they so choose and are willing to accept these powers from within themselves—be fully capable of applying the techniques and methods mentioned herein to learn how to tap into and, then put to use these long forgotten skills that they were innately born with.

Wisdom of Free Thinkers

Today, we are expected to believe ancient Greek philosophers, alchemists and mystics are wholly responsible for creating the world's knowledge base even though evidence has always strongly suggested otherwise. I've mentioned a few ancient and spiritual minds beforehand simply because they have helped me to understand many mysteries--by way of telepathy while meditating and focusing on their image and likeness, what we consider as new to us today, is in fact not new at all simply because everything repeats itself, eventually.

For instance, no one has ever asked how or why early European scientists (alchemists, astrologers and sorcerers) such as Giordano Bruno, Nicolas Copernicus, and Galileo, were able to view the skies far beyond the atmosphere of earth's protective halo, and glance outwards into the darkest regions of deep space with such precision and clarity. Their ability to observe the physically unobservable regions of the universe without the use of modern telescopes or satellites was truly a miraculous feat in and of itself. The reasons why is quite obvious to me; these free and spirited thinkers had use of what we now known as remote viewing, which allowed them to expand the consciousness of their mind beyond the confines and restrictions of their bodies, into the vastness of the universe. I'm sure that one day in the future all of this information will be forth coming.

Even famed European scientist Isaac Newton, displayed a certain amount of extra sensory perceptions and remote viewing skills. Newton is on record for predicting the year the world will end. According to Newton it will expire in the year 2054. Newton was also among early adopters of those who believed that the Bible has a hidden code among its scriptures, which has become known as the Bible code.

Certain methods deployed by European scientists to obtain information about the universe were often non-conforming (or mysterious), and quite frankly many of them hid such matters out of concern from within their own rank and file.

These revelations have been systemically overlooked and continues to be til this very day among historians and scholars alike in favor of aspects that were both physical, logical, and acceptable to the standards of academia and European royalty. Today's societies owe a tremendous amount of gratitude and credit to the so-called dark arts from an era long ago for our entire base of knowledge and advancements that we have attained as a modern society. Even though no modern governing body will ever admit to it publicly, every aspect of physical and metaphysical knowledge used in science and all of its disciplines today, owes its origin to information received from an invisible source. It should be easy to see or understand by now that all knowledge comes first by way of an unseen nature before it becomes visible and known in reality.

Telepathy

As far as telepathy goes, it has been proven under very strict laboratory conditions and testing to be real. Research has also revealed that telepathy can be used by anyone with a minimal amount of preparation and understanding. In fact, one doesn't need to know how it works, just that it does.

While many scientists agree that telepathy is real, the overall knowledge and procedures for using such skill has not been released for public consumption. The mere act of acknowledgment of any kind from a recognized official body of intelligence, about the validity and existence of mind-to-mind talk at a distance, also means that there are no more secrets to be kept. In other words, the world's governing body will no longer be able to hold society at bay by simply withholding vital information from them.

Kingdom of heaven is within all things of this world..

MYSTERIES OF THE KINGDOM
(Acknowledging The Divine Source Within Yourself)

Please Note:
The material you are about to read is all true from a certain perspective.

There I was, floating high above my lifeless body. Looking down at this physical shell, was a concerned little Jewish boy named Brody, who watched tentatively at my side, weeping, frantically calling out to me, saying: coach! Please get up, coach! You can't die on us! Come on coach, get up!

Hovering over my body, and witnessing all that had transpired, I was somehow magically capable of doing literally anything that I imagined in my mind instantaneously. For instance, if I thought of you during this time, I would suddenly end up staring right into your face, almost as if you and I were one. But, the thing was---you just couldn't see or hear me. Somehow, up until that moment, my entire life, from birth until death, begin flashing onto my mental screen as if I was watching a movie. Everything happened so fast that it is difficult to assign time to it. Soon realized that I was able to travel back and forth across the universe in the blink of an eye, defying time and space. At one point I had traveled so far into the deepest regions of space that I came into contact with a darkened wall of unknown origin and size. As weightless and nimble as I was, I still couldn't get around this wall, or climb over or go beneath it in any direction. Each time I tried to move beyond this wall, it seemed to expand in the direction of my movement. And after awhile, I just stopped trying and decided to return to the scene of my lifeless body. Once the decision was made to live again, all I had to do was imagine seeing my body. When I eventually returned to where my body was, I could see that the emergency crew had arrived on the scene, and was checking my vital signs. The paramedics apparently reached a consensus and soon put a sheet over my body. Before reentering my body I decided to look in on my wife and our daughter, just to see how they were doing. They both seemed happy, going about their normal day, even though they were at least 300 miles apart at the time, I was able to visit them simultaneously. Suddenly, I had the urge to be with them again, and realized that in order to be with them physically, I had to live. In a sense I simply wanted to hug and kiss them both, and tell them how much I truly love them. I could sense their deep love and respect for me, and how horrible the notification of my sudden demise would affect them emotionally once they received the news. My love for my wife and daughter was very strong within me. Much stronger than the love I had for myself while living.

From out of nowhere, a voice from within began talking to me. I couldn't tell exactly where this voice resonated from, but it sounded much like that of mine own. When this voice began speaking to me, it said: if you want to return back to your body, think about it first, then visualize it, and imagine seeing your body being fully reanimated, returning to life, and it will manifest. Immediately I began following the instructions given to me from this voice of wisdom without delay, and shortly thereafter life baring energy began slowly returning to my once lifeless body, a region at a time, until I had regained all physical sensations and movement entirely.

Suddenly, I became alerted to the sound of people standing nearby and talking around me, as I begin to revitalize and move my once lifeless body. At first, I regained the ability to see, as my eyelids which felt heavy at first, opened slowly and the light of day filtered in. Then vital life energy began to flow into my arms and legs. When I finally got up, everyone seemed startled. I heard someone say: look at that, he's not dead!

What you have just read is based upon a true account of a near death experience I incurred during the summer of 2010 while I was living in a southeast Georgia coastal city. Take from this event what you will. I know what I've experienced, and I now know what happens when we die. What I experienced during that last NDE/OBE episode doesn't mean that everyone will experience exactly the same things the way I did. I believe, based upon other OBE/NDE accounts that I've become familiar with one way or another, is that there will be a moment of past life reflections of some kind for most, if not all who undergo such an event. Since each life is different, so is the experience.

Based entirely upon my understanding, when someone dies, they will simply transform, and live on as a pure form of intelligent energy. Some call this energy, spirit. I don't believe it matters what we call it.

In the spirit realm religion means nothing at all. What you believe in when you physically depart the realm of earth, you will initially hold that belief to be true, because, you do retain your ego mind and subjective memories about your life. All the love you held for others while you were living, suddenly becomes magnified. All your hate, misconceptions, and prejudices seems to fade away. Most likely you'll be inclined to look in on those you have immediate concern for. In this state of being that medical doctors still refuse to acknowledge, you can see and hear the ones you love simultaneously, where ever they may be in time and space, for time and space becomes totally irrelevant. And only the ones who are adept at sensing pure energy generating from the astral realm will be able to feel or sense your presence.

Note:

Obviously there is a lot of information I was able to retrieve from this spiritual journey. This entire book is based upon; in part, that which I am able to remember, research and demonstrate to a certain degree.

Every human being exists simultaneously in two dimensions, and carries within and around them a divine presence, a source of light that guides them in both good and troubled times, a light that shines when and where no other source of light is available. The kind of light that I am referring to is known by many names around the globe, but for the purpose of this book it will be referred to often by a name used many times in the past by none other than Yeshua himself, who often referred to it as the Kingdom, and sometimes by the phrase: kingdom of heaven.

For those of you who are steeply programmed into religion; it really doesn't matter which doctrine that is; you may find the following revelations hard to accept, or read. You see, a long, long time ago when the powers that be discovered that religious beliefs could not only be used to condition the way people behaved towards authority figures, it is also a very good method of deploying subtle mind-control technologies aimed specifically at your subjective mind. The fact of the matter is...is that reality is far more stranger than the overall perceptions and expectations you've become accustomed to. When I experienced that last OBE in the mist of writing this book, I gained the ability to see and know things that I never would have known or seen by any conventional means.

For instance, I was able to come to the realization that Yeshua (Jesus) once lived and walked upon the earth, and that he was here to teach us how to access what he termed as the kingdom of heaven from within our very own mind. I witnessed intuitively as a conspiracy developed among priests, politicians, and owners of slaves who all felt threatened by Yeshua's innate ability to attract people from all walks of life. And it was for this reason alone; his ability to attract people like a magnet; that he was killed. So in conclusion, he did not succeed. But his efforts of freeing your mind with truth has been continued by others who have taken up the cause, and they too are being systematically killed. In fact human history is littered with the blood of those who tried to make a difference by revealing the truth about the true nature of all humans and their connectedness to everything that exist.

This is a list of those who were killed trying to reveal true nature of being. In actuality this list is both long and is continuously growing:

1. Buddha
2. Joan of Arch
3. William Wallace
4. Gandhi
5. J. F. Kennedy
6. Martin Luther King Jr.
7. Malcolm X
8. Steve Biko
9. Benazir Bhutto

Obviously more names could be added here. However each person listed above were highly magnetized and gifted with the ability to mentally induce and attract lots of people to their cause, even in death. This is what scares the powers that be most, which is contrary to what most people believe. It has never been about their ability to defy logic and perform miracles, because people are still manifesting miracles today. In fact, we all have this ability.

Additionally, authors of the bible conspired along time ago, they put together a very special book of laws for you to abide by, and surrender your personal intellect to that of authority. This book of laws, which was designed specifically to dissuade your thoughts and feelings away from new age information which eventual leads to your awakening to truth into believing before hand that certain beliefs or actions of those who discover forbidden truths are the work of devil worshipers, and are blasphemes toward God. They named this fictional book: Deuteronomy, of which they claim was authored by Moses. But along the way it was somehow over looked that Moses purportedly received a total of 613 commandments, of which 365 were negative. Isn't it a convenience that this number coincides with the number of days in a year?

What does all of this, if any has to do with the way you act or think about who you are? Everything...Because what information you read, feeds your mind. Your mind is the only thing that actually exist. Mind, soul, and spirit are one and the same, all are of the essence of God.

Keys of Knowledge

Although your psychic-based senses are somewhat unknown as a part of your being, they are your primary senses. The five physical senses you take for granted are actually a set of imaginary functions good only for use in the physical matrix. Your other senses originate from your spiritual being.

Side by side comparisons of the physical and spiritual senses:

1.	Sight	Mind
2.	Smell	Instincts
3.	Hearing	Intuition
4.	Taste	Feeling
5.	Touch	Emotions

Spiritual senses originate from spiritual energy, which we know as the mind. Prophets and psychics were taught, or discovered in some cases, how to activate these other senses through the use of their pineal glands; which is of the material brain, and is located slightly between and above the eyebrows about two inches inside your head. The pineal gland appears as if it is surrounded by water, and suspended in space. Many psychics have become quite efficient at using their pineal glands as a sort of mental video. Using the mental video technique makes it easier to use the powers of the mind to manifest things or events into the material realm.

Prophets, Psychics and Prophecy

Prophecy is an ability to hear and speak to God from within the silence and stillness of your mind; which is very similar to the conditions of space. Within your mind you are able to sense and feel the signals and forces of nature as they originate.

Consciousness, soul, and spirit, along with all other forces of nature, combine to form the mind. This is the main reason why the human mind is not only in the brain and body, it has a presence in every sub-atomic particle, atom, cell and molecule within and without. The mind encircles your body like a donut hole around your finger. This pattern is known as the torus.

Psychics (prophets) are those who have learned how to activate the pineal gland while they are in the physical body, and this allows them to communicate with a higher source; be it a spiritual entity or God. Many of them (psychics or prophets) have developed their ability to interpret what they hear or see from the other side into logical information that we understand in this reality. Its seems that information from a higher source is not always literal, it sometimes requires interpretation.

The Jewish Bible contends that there were at least 55 Hebrew prophets; and of these Malachi is thought to be the last prophet of Israel. Since that time, there has been Joan of Arc, Nostradamus, Martin Luther, Edgar Cayce, Jean Dixon, and countless others who are known to possess the gift. One look at the names of those mentioned reveals a pattern of truth in the following statement: The world has plenty of psychics, or prophets to go around because they are born, not made.

Some people spend their whole lives in search of the keys of knowledge in their attempt to gain information and understanding about the unknown, the unseen and the future. It is the application of knowledge that leads to power, and to know with certainty the meaning of life. Knowledge and information eventually breed confidence in the minds of humankind.

For those who are able to clear their minds of all thoughts and noise, and are versed in the art of prophecy, all events of the past, present and future become known to them, except for where such laws are prohibited. No one, even Jesus, can see things of the present or future beyond the choices they make. Meaning, if we can keep an unbiased nature when we tap into the powers of the mind, we can gather any form of information we seek. That is another reason why psychics are needed, and a growing number of people from all walks of life are open to getting a psychic reading. Even high powered world leaders use psychic readings on a daily basis.

They just don't want you to know about it…

Key attributes of mind power (spiritual Energy) are:

1.	Astral Projection	Imagination
2.	Blood-stopping	Manifesting
3.	Channeling	Precognition
4.	Clairaudience	Prophecy
5.	Clairvoyance	Remote Viewing
6.	Clairsentience	Telekinesis
7.	Healing (Psychic)	Telepathy

Spiritual Energy

Basically, we can sum up all of these abilities with one phrase: Spiritual Senses or Spiritual Power. But the best and most accurate description for this phenomena is the term: Spiritual Energy.

Everybody has the use of spiritual energy available to them everyday whether they are aware of it or not. You see, we can't live without spiritual energy. The best way to demonstrate spiritual energy to you is to use the mind as an example. Spiritual energy and the mind are one and the same. You can't see your mind, or stop it from functioning, ever. That is because the mind extends and connects us to everything in the entire universe, and to the uncreative source simultaneously. The mind keeps your heart beating and your lungs breathing while you sleep. The body cannot live without the mind. Science has come a long way in terms of medical technology, they are able to keep a heart functioning, a lung breathing, transplant almost all major organs of the human body. But they can't duplicate the power of the mind.

Genesis: A Journey
of Spiritual Beings

Everything has a beginning, including God and the spirits which sprang forth from it. We may never discover the exact origins of the source overwhelmingly known as God. Relatively speaking, as a species, we are somewhat closer to discovering the origins of mind than we have ever been. But what if there was no beginning, nor an ending, and the big-bang was simply an event which still occurs to this day? Unthinkable!

Since God is the only uncreated source, then mind/spirits must be the first effect (creation). Taken this statement literally, mind and spiritual guidance via meditation has allowed researchers to peer into aspects of existence not known before. I have written this hypothetical article about the Journey of Spiritual Beings to narrate the metaphorical visions seen during extended hours of deep meditation, of which you are about to mental digest.

Genesis of Creation

Note:

Spirits existed long before the advent of the universe came into being. They were created in the likeness and image of God, which means Spirits have the ability to summon all of existence into action with shear will. Spirits provide God with the ability to experience creation everywhere simultaneously. And as such, spirits actually expand God's creative master piece: the universe.

In the beginning of time, there existed a very powerful force, a core level of consciousness which began to express itself in likeness. During this moment there was darkness all around its presence, for there was no light. There was no sense of up or down, left or right, nor was it needed. There was only stillness, silence, a void. There was no heat or cold temperatures. There was simply nothing at all; except an inner whispering of vibrational energy, which became a subtle voice, gently conceptualizing within itself, its auditory: "come forth and multiply into my likeness, an infinite number." And with these words spoken authoritatively, with potentiality, compassion and love, the presence of an infinite number of spiritual beings were created everywhere within the darkness, instantaneously. And then, that same subtle voice spoke inwardly again, it said unto these newly created beings: "you shall all be called spirits, because, you were inspired into existence by me, the original spirit. I am, that I am. You have the intelligence and authority to create all things as you desire. You have the powers to command potential energies into existence at will, and put it into motion, any actions within your thoughts, imagination and visualization of thine own mind, because you are the purest-form, a source of energetic creation. Whatever your mental forces conceive, will be. All the powers and abilities I have, you have also, even greater than I do, for you are many, and I Am, that I Am. Now Go forth and become co-creators of all that will become, fill this void of darkness with light, fill its skies with satellites, and fill them with animate and inanimate matter. I give unto you my likeness and my image, the light of my being is you, for you are the illumined ones from within me. Go, command all of creation at your will, command all forms of energy into visible matter." And with these spoken (intuitive) words, a source of intelligence had duplicated itself into an infinite number of spiritual beings.

Eventually the darkness we know as the void became structured into three dimensions, and then a finite space was formed, we call this finite space, the universe. The universe suddenly began teeming with spiritual beings everywhere, and together these free-willed beings began the acts of creating an infinite number of parallel universes, star clusters, galaxies, solar systems and planets, and eventually life. Science has come to recognize this phenomenon as of late, they know that everything big is composed of an infinite number of smaller things. We now know that consciousness came first, then structure. Sacred geometry provides proof of this....

Creation of Humankind

After eternities had long ago passed since the creation of universes, a select group of spirits began creating a dense form of intelligent life upon numerous planets existing throughout multiple universes. And finally, a select group of spiritual beings entered into what is now known as the blue realm (earth), of which they had previously created. They saw that this realm was barren, they begin speaking among themselves: (Genesis 5-6 mentions), "let us create human beings into our image and likeness, as we were created into the image and likeness of our maker. Let these humans bridge the gap between the invisible and the visible realms. For these humans are our vehicles to experience the physical realm, so that we may interact in the light. Let us animate their bodies with our essence, therefore we can guide them from within. Thus, when they are done here in the physical, if they chose to, they can return to the source and become whole, for eventually all will become one again, or they may choose to experience physicality again, and live perpetually.

These were the first acts of creation throughout existence, which brought forth the actions of consolidated energies from the core, eventually creating the lands, mountains, oceans, seas, rivers, lakes and springs of each habitat. For in the beginning, the blue-realm was void and empty. It was basically consolidated energy without a purpose.

Before humans could bridge the gap between the two realms of existence, the blue-realm, had to have a of source of infinite heat, this led to the creation of sun stars in each solar system, as spiritual beings began creating a super star in the center of grouped planets, for the sole purpose of providing a source of constant heat and light within each newly formed solar system. Solar systems and their planets were formed in the same manner, all with spin, like a gyro-scope, which means that each planet, similar to that of stars, generate their own internal source of power from within. This arrangement allows each planet to spin on its own axis, eternally.

The self propelled gyro action draws its power directly from the source. In fact scientists are beginning to understand that everything in existence spins. Spin creates energy, and in the case of universal bodies, this energy recirculates back and forth into the bodies, never losing any amount of energy. This same action is what creates gravity.

With the addition of an atmosphere, which serves as a protective shield for the fragile bodies of humans against harmful heat rays provided by its nearest star (sun), the blue-realm suddenly began teeming with all sorts of visible life forms. On the surface of the blue-realm, the spirits created humans on almost every mass of land near and far. The reasons for this was obvious; humans were part physical, and mental. Human bodies were ideal vessels for spirits to experience what they had created.

When spirits enter a newly formed body, they seemingly became ignorant of who and what they are for a number of years. This was not a problem for those spirits who manifested as adults upon visiting the blue-realm. To solve this issue, adult humans (spirits) began to teach the newly formed humans, or newborns, a way of life.

Initially they were taught how to fish for a source of food and how to gather edible plants directly by spirits, so that their physical form would be sustained. They were also shown how to construct water irrigation channels, and farming technologies, making it possible to live more inland and away from coastal areas. From such early technological advances inspired by the spirits intervening in human affairs, people began to accumulate in large masses, and organized societies were eventually formed.

Water irrigation, farming, storing of foods, were the core technologies first taught by the creative spirits that are still with us today. These early technologies have a long lasting effect on the survival of humanity. And today, scientists insist that mankind evolved from the seas and oceans as the result of a single celled organism that was forced to adapt to a surface environment. The science community as a whole just can't bring themselves to the realization that although religious texts such as the Bible don't tell a complete story, neither does the theory of evolution. Even so, some aspects of religion are true from a certain perspective.

Other aspects of humanity that were influenced by spirits at the beginning are the main reason why societies place such a high premium on almost every coastal land area in the world. People spend billions of dollars traveling to islands of the Bahamas and other destinations located in the oceans without knowing about the deep rooted cause of why they value such annual excursions to these places. Areas such as southern California, Florida, and increasingly the coastal regions of Texas and Mexico continues to draw millions of water seekers every year, regardless of economic conditions. I call this type of programming, ideograms. But then, that is another story......

Recognize what is in front of you, and what is hidden from you shall be revealed. There is nothing hidden that will not be revealed.

Matthew 4:22

A Great Awakening
(Apocalypse)

The awakening and apocalypse are basically the same thing; which means a revealing. In short it says, that which is unseen, shall be seen by all. The awakening, or apocalypse, is a process that involves all of humanity, and collectively includes the earth and all of nature. While the religious expectations of the *Apocalypse* is filled with doom and gloom according to scriptures written in the new testament's book of Revelations. Christians believe the skies will open-up and fall in, and that the earth will suddenly come to a stand-still, everything will climax with the return of Jesus and his army of angels, waging a final war against Satan and his demons. Of course, every practicing Christian expects Jesus to prevail in this war to end all wars that will be fought at the ancient city of Megiddo, the site of many historic battles. To Christendom, Megiddo is identified with the Biblical Armageddon. Upon conclusion of this great last battle for the soul of humankind it is believed that peace will reign a thousand years.

As a teenager, I often thought about the day the world comes to an end coinciding with the returned of Jesus. I often harbored vast images of dark clouds filling the skies, as gravity defying chariots with flame throwing angels zipping around the earth's atmosphere while stamping out the wicked, and making room for the righteous. At one point in my life I just couldn't wait for these events to begin, that way it would make the world a much safer place. You see, although I am not religious, I grew up in the bible thumping-belt of the deep south, and, there was almost always some god-fearing Christian-minded adult readily available to reinforce my mind with more doom and gloom images about the apocalypse and end of days. Let me tell you this, it was no way for child to grow-up, fearing God and the eventual end of days, all the time..

New-age Thinkers

New-age spiritually based thinkers generally consider the awakening as an affirmation, a sort of revelation of the spirit that dwells within themselves, of which, according to many self-styled gurus, represents a moment of clarity in the overall understanding that a greater reality exist beyond the physical plane. Most spiritually minded people believe that God does exist, just not in the sense of religious myth. They see everyone as an individual aspect of God in both image and likeness. In short, the 'Awakening' will most likely have a different effect on everyone.

When will the awakening Occur?

It could be that you've already begun to experience a version of the awakening that is uniquely your own. In this chapter I will discus what an awakening means and how you can recognize the signs. Also, this concludes my comparisons of the Christian Bible Apocalypse and the New-age awakening. While I personally find the Bible filled with fear mongering, there are some good things within its scriptures, too. I just wish, for humanity's sake, that religion would place more emphasis on the positive aspects of the Bible and less, far less on negative ones.

Ironically an awakening occurs when one realizes that he or she has an alternate existence, a spiritual version of themselves that is capable of expressing itself independently and is infinite within time and space. And that they may call upon their uncreated likeness, and its godlike powers in times of need or want, to manifest or co-create an ideal way of expressing life in accordance with universal laws of harmony.

This in my view, is what an awakening means. As you can see, the awakening is an individual event of which everyone alive will participate at some point in their lives. And truth be told it doesn't matter one iota if you are religious or spiritual, atheist or agnostic, an awakening is still within your future.

Five stages of the Awakening

Of course this is not exactly the way things are but, from my experience I believe that there are basically five stages to an awakening, which precede a much greater level of awakening. The greater awakening is the fifth and final stage of the process. Each stage of the awakening is slightly different than the next but they all play a vital role towards the greater stage.

Stage One Awakening:

The first stage of the awakening will most likely occur as a culmination of your life's experiences. You may begin having dreams of past life experiences in very rich details. For instance you may realize that certain aspects of a previous life has carried forward into your present one.

In my case: I realized that I'd once lived in Paris, France some time during the 1400's era, and then again in Ireland before finally being re-born in America. When I entered the fourth grade level of elementary school, French became my second language, according to my teacher she'd never seen a student learn a new language so quickly. And, about thirty years later ended up speaking a form of Gaelic during a dream. I later discovered that I have a fondness for Celtic music and customs even though I'd never been there. All of the events were obvious signs of my awakening at stages one and two. Your own experience may include habits from each of your previous lives that you may somehow seemed to overlook. But you should know by now that everything is connected. Once you start recalling aspects of your previous lives is when you begin to synchronize with your inner guidance. Although you may not tell anyone at this point in your life, the voice within you (subconscious level of mind) will become more active in helping you to direct your life. It will say or bring about things with subtlety, guiding your thoughts toward whatever resolutions you are seeking. These solutions could be in the form of a better job with more money, a new car, or finally meeting someone that you believe is your ideal soul mate. This is were many become side-tracked about the powers of their inner guidance, thinking that logic or luck is responsible. And in doing so further awakening becomes stalled.

Stage Two Awakening:

During this stage of awakening you may begin taking notice of the subtle things happening around you that you haven't before. Your sense of smell, for instance, becomes more sensitive. You may even be able to smell things miles away and know exactly what it is that you are sensing, almost animal like. Your physical sight will be far better, too. If you are in need of eye-glasses, you may find that your sight has improved significantly. In fact there may come a time when your use of eye ware is no longer needed. Your body may become healthier and less likely to become ill. You will begin to realize that it is not your body that becomes sick, only your imagination. You'll finally realize that if you imagine better, you'll be healthier.

You may also develop a sudden urge to seek knowledge of subjects that were once off-limits to your intellect; such as reading books about ghosts, magic, occultism, and global conspiracies. Your view about traditional religion may become more of a challenge and, a bit confusing will set in. At this stage the stream of information flowing into your conscious mind from your subjective levels can seem overwhelming at times. Normally this is about the time many people begin to notice the existence of UFO's entering the earth's atmosphere and zapping in and out of view like magic. You may even begin dreaming about them. Then you'll realize that there are over 5 million UFO reported sightings in America alone each year by people from all walks of life, including politicians, peace officers and the like, and that they all can't be crazy! Neither are you...

Typical Stage Two experiences:

These are typical experiences that many people will experience before they begin to realize that they are in a process of awakening to a level of consciousness much deeper than their normal physical senses provide. Although not exact, such series of events will take place for everyone. It's just a matter of when, not if, these things happen. For the record, now that you have found this book, and have read this far into this chapter is also an indication that you have begun the process of "Awakening." For its the process itself that has caused to you to own this book. Remember, everything is connected....

Stage Three Awakening:

At some point in time; each one of us alive or dead; will experience a sudden and unexplained ability of non-local awareness, or, most commonly known as psychic phenomenon, when these powers are suddenly thrust upon you from out of the blue. At first, you might think that you've lost your marbles when this happens. You may suddenly have the ability to read another person's thoughts without trying to do so, or, you could experience foreknowledge of upcoming events hours, days or even weeks, months and years in advance of actual events. Such events may appear to be a re-occurrence of a dream that you've had, or it could simply be passed off as a case of deja vu. And suddenly, you may know if someone is truthful, or, if they are simply lying to you. Some people may even experience the ability and power of healing others, just as Jesus did. And, most importantly of all, your views of reality will begin to shift towards a world filled with love and probabilities.

Stage Four Awakening:

As you begin unlocking the mysteries of the kingdom you will see through the veil of mass illusion that is projected onto this world collectively by all of us, but controlled by those who lead.

Together we will seek out others with similar experiences as that of our own. At first, it'll become somewhat difficult pretending that nothing in your life has changed, and soon enough you'll begin searching for answers to what is going on inside of your mind; which has suddenly allowed you to see, feel and know more of the truth. The truth is that you are not what you once thought you were, but, in fact, you are much more than you've ever imagined. And finally, you are beginning to understand that you are the author of your life and its' experiences. And, just as mysterious as these strange and unexplainable powers occurred, they somehow may suddenly vanish without warning. This my friend was your wake-up call... The awakening.

The awakening, as it is called by those who've realized a great and unexplainable change within themselves and the world around them, along with the incredible things that they are now able perceive and do without much explanation, is something that everyone will experience at some moment in time. For some people, it could happen in this life time or the next, but, one things for sure, though, it will eventually happen.

Some of you will have all known powers associated with this experience, and will be able to call upon these abilities at will if and when the need arise. For others, these skills may become somewhat limited in use. But nevertheless, all will have them (special powers) in due time when they unlearn, what they have learned in a reality based strictly on that of the physical. These new powers are popularly known as psychic powers, or ESP for short.

Stage Five

The Greater Awakening

The great awakening occurs when everyone of this world comes to realize that we (humans) are not the only form of intelligence in all of creation. In fact, we may not even be the youngest life form to exist. As we move closer towards the greater awakening, we'll began to experience a reality at a higher frequency, simultaneously, as events of the universe fills us with a sense of oneness with all that exists. Humanity is destined for only one thing, and that is a return to wholeness, from which we each descended.

As a people, we must take full ownership of our negligence in the role as stewards of earth. There is a system of governance in place around the world lacking continuity, fairness and treatment of most inhabitants of this planet, built upon a mountain of historical fabrications and professional dis-information agents who are spreading propaganda to hide truth. Least we forget that it was Pope Urban VIII who established the world's first college dedicated solely for the spread of propaganda. This school of dis-information didn't just go away over the years, instead, it simply duplicated itself as part of every nation's education system.

While there is enough blame to go around, we are all guilty of hurting someone or some thing. Could it be that everything that exists is a part of the greater awakening that we will soon face? Since we can't see beyond the future choices that will be made, we can anticipate the probabilities based upon the possibilities before the future unfolds. This is not to say that humans are incapable of seeing into the future because this has been proven time and time again to be true, at least by me. What it does mean is that the ability to see into the future is a difficult task and it all comes down to correctly interpreting information received. The greater awakening just might unite humanity into finally acting as a single unit when it comes to understanding what lies ahead.

One things certain, as the 21, December 2012 begins to unfold more and more people will begin experiencing signs of prophecy as well as other psychic phenomena. People will begin a new level of tolerance and understanding of people from diverse cultures than ever before. No longer will the color of a person's skin be used against them in a negative way.

Technology will also be a big part of this movement worldwide as previously witnessed throughout the oldest cultures in the world. This may sound like a campaign slogan at first, but the events occurring in Africa and those of Japan are connected, although there are some who would prefer that we see these things as separate and isolated events.

I truly wish that it were so...

Is December 21, 2012 the beginning of the ending of the world as we know it? Or is it the simply start of a new earth cycle, one that will bring great physical changes to the planet such as pole shifts, global warming, more earthquakes, flooding, public unrest and mass hysteria? Will we finally witness UFO sightings and landings on a global scale? As my very lovely and wonderful wife often asks me: what will become of us?

There will be plenty of scare tactics leading into and up to December 21, 2012. While I don't believe the end of the world is at hand on that particular date and time, I will tell you that in the year 2013 the earth will still be around. But that is not to say that change is not forthcoming, cause it is. Revelations from a remote viewing session that I conducted upon myself, the earth is still here in January 2013. What I did see during my remote viewing visit to south Florida (somewhere near Miami beach), was a very clean and pristine beach front, absent of any man-made structures such as buildings in the foreground. My conclusion is that the earth had somehow cleansed itself of air pollution along the eastern coast. As for as 2012 is concerned, I believe it is a beginning of a cycle that occurs about every 26,000 years or so. What happens, and astronomers know this to be somewhat true, is that all solar systems and galaxies within the universe will suddenly align themselves to a point where all of creation first occurred.

This could also mean that an infinite amount of energy will be channeled along this galactic or universal alignment in such a way that is only reminisced of creation itself. It could be an event to end all events, starting over.. So the question and concern on the minds of everyone should be: what if the Mayan calendar calculations are correct, and these events do take place, will creation itself survives intact?

Since this cycle has occurred in a distant past, several times as far as astronomers can discern, mankind, or rather life on earth has prevailed. Life, in my opinion will go on for everybody since there really is no such thing as death, at least consciously. When it comes to life, we have all been subliminally programmed to think only in terms of our current physical life.

But there is life beyond our physical bodies, simply because we all have lived many lives in the past, bringing to each subsequent life experience what was learned. Some spirits choose not to return here on earth or any other realm with an existing life form, while others may reincarnate into other life forms or even parallel universes. Just as there are more variations of life forms on earth than there are strands of DNA, there are other versions of what we call earth. Life itself, all forms of it, simply goes on... Always has and will be.

This is what, under ideal conditions, *the greater awakening* could mean. It means an end to all forms of suffering to humanity, because collectively, the ability to stamp-out all forms of diseases now and in the future has always been a reality. It also means an end to starvation everywhere. Food clothing and shelter would become everybody's task, since there would be no egos in the way of progress. Most of all, it would mean an end to all wars since the myth of limited supplies for energy and other scarce material would no longer prevail. And since religious doctrines will be replaced where it counts, within the minds and hearts of an awakened people, no one will ever again die believing in a false deity.

In short, a greater awakening is when all world conflicts are resolved because we will have learned how to amplify the likeness and power of god to uplift everyone, including the planet earth to a frequency high enough to evolve as a species to the next stage of evolution.

Noetic Knowledge
(Adventures into the Mysterious Mind)

Psychology means science of mind; and psychologists are those educated in the field of psychology. Truth is, psychologists know very little, if anything at all, about the inner workings within the complexities of the most advanced laboratory in existence: the human mind. Psychiatry on the other hand literally means the medical treatment of the soul, which today is translated as the science of diagnosing and treating mental disorders. As a discipline, psychology and psychiatry, both an offshoot of philosophy, has been around nearly 500 and 200 years respectively. And yet, for all of their theories and storied history, neither are closer to knowing the origination and capabilities of mind.

Schools of science and medicine are still insisting that the brain of both humans and animals (to a lessor degree); somehow encapsulates the mind by producing some type of electrochemically based fluids, of which, as theorized, are then connected to, or builds a network of neurons that instructs specify organs via the cerebrum-spinal nerve system. Furthermore, they postulate, that with each sustained thought resulting in a clear and precise image in the theater of the mind forms a complete neural connection within the physical brain itself. They go on to speculate that each time an established belief or idea held inside the mind is rethought, that it also results in disconnecting all associated neural connections within your brain in order to construct a set of new ones. While this may be true among the brain's many biological functions internally, this theory still falls way short of explaining the mysteriousness, evasiveness of mind. Noetic knowledge; which pertains to the mind; seems as elusive as ever to all philosophers and scientists alike when it comes to fully understanding the mind.

Scientific hypotheses reinforce and highlights acceptable theory only, that mind and brain are interchangeable words. Essentially, what they are saying is what many have been taught to believe in the first-place: that mind and brain are one and the same thing. That both mind and brain are simply a physical organ housed in the body. Their thinking lends credence to the belief, 'that if the brain dies, so does the mind and body.' This line of thought is in sharp contrast with what many folks have witnessed throughout time, especially when a loved one has died in the eyes of medical science, basically meeting all the qualifications of a physical death, only to suddenly revive themselves without aide of any medical staff intervention, hours, sometimes days later. And, why then, in light of such overwhelming evidence having been collected by trained, educated medical providers themselves, who have seen people come back to life after being pronounced as deceased, are simply being ignored? An open and honest mind would simply realize without reservations, that something is definitely going on here. That the system itself has been designed in such away that it wrongly encourage medical professionals into covering up the truth in favor of protecting the status-quo.

To laypersons from all walks of life, who have been witness to a near death experience episode, what occurred was nothing short of miraculous. To most new-age spiritualists this could be a sign of truthfulness, confirming that human beings are much more than flesh and bones. But, when you bring religious doctrine into the equation, things all of a sudden have the tendency to become more complicated than it should. Which in my view redirects truth into a narrower path full of self doubt and fear. Such activity serves one purpose only, it allows the church to claim ownership of your soul, while the medical profession declare themselves rulers of your body. Needless to say that so-called mind experts can't seem to find an explanation after nearly 500 years of their existence, at least to any credible degree within their own ranks. The existence of reports taken from thousands, perhaps millions of people, complete with eyewitness accounts world wide about such events continues to cast doubts.

There is no wonder why most ordinary folk believe the very same ideas as those being embraced by the so-called mind experts. If the experts believe that the mind and brain are one and the same, then why should Joe six-pack and his family believe differently?

In this day and time it all boils down to money, it decides who gets to be heard above the noise of everyone else; which means that someone with a background similar to that of mine, who has the self motivated inclination to question and challenge established thought, to think out-of-the box, and come into possession of very compelling information from observance and experience. Who has the audacity to write about such things, and is willing to make this information public, somehow finds it very difficult collecting an audience.

Since I have spent nearly 26 years or more studying various aspects of the mind alone makes my opinions no better or worse than that of a psychologist, or any other medical practitioner when it comes down to examining research data that I've personally accumulated over the course of several years working on this topic. Which just might mean that I'm on to something that could add value to the overall knowledge base of humankind.

Historically, there is nothing in my background academically or otherwise that would lend or suggest any scientific credibility to what I have personally experienced, observed and researched--as difficult as this may appear at first glance, is true. On a subject so mysterious as the mind, you may have reason for some concern about where and how I received this information, and conducted research. But, I believe, that while others, more conventionally trained researchers have failed to advance there knowledge base about the workings of mind, I have succeeded.

As far as my credentials are of concern, they are far superior to those of all ancient philosophers dating as far back as ancient Greece with the likes of Themistoclea; Pythagoras; Socrates; Heraclitus; Plato; Hypatia along with many more who's names are forever listed and linked in the annals of time. In fact, my academic background far outweigh the likes of that received by Michael Faraday (1791-1867), who as a self taught physicist of chemistry and electrochemical science, never received a formal education prior to discovering the truth about certain principles of electromagnetism, and as a chemist made the discovery of benzene. Many engineers still make use of a technology known as the Faraday cage when testing lightning. Automakers design the frame of their vehicles using these same principles, which helps to prevent lightning from striking passengers while they are in cars. Some people foolishly believe to this day that such protection against lightning strikes is provided by the rubber compound of automobile tires, which insulates and protect vehicle occupants during a thunder storm. But this assumption is wrong.

My credentials, by the way, includes a PhD. in metaphysics and applied theory from the university of source.

The point that I'm making with all of this metaphysical talk is that anyone, at any given moment in time, who has the inner inclination to think like a genius, to become creative enough to make a contribution to the whole of society, should be allowed to do so even if they are not an educated physicists who happens to be recognized by mainstream academia.

The point of the matter is, there really is no such thing as a dumb person in the entire world because, as you will soon realize one day--as I have, is that there is only one mind in all of existence, and that there are only those of us, for one reason or another, who just do stupid things. But then again, that's all a part of human nature. If we didn't do stupid things from time to time we may never learn how to do the things that we do right.

Your Non-physical Mind and Physical Brain

For centuries, all of mankind has been held hostage to an idea which defines the mind as being something of a physical matter. Basically, this materialists view means that the mind, just like the brain, is thought of as being a mechanical attachment to the body----as is the case with all other organs of the human body. Even among the high ranking and file members of medical schools and their offspring establishments, this materialistic view of the human mind still remains prevalent. In my opinion they are right in their assumptions about the brain; which according to many scientists, is just an organ (a muscle-like organic computer) that sits centered inside the skull and, its primary area of responsibility and function is for creating and distributing electrochemical based impulses throughout all regions of the body, via fluids and possibly some form of telepathy. So by this limited explanation and definition alone, it is acceptable for everyone to conclude that the brain, be it human or animal, is something of a physical bridge, a biological communicator between the mind and the body. But this acceptable theory in and of itself still falls short of defining the mind.

When it comes to the mind, I believe that by its very nature, it is assigned the task of supplying our physical body with a flow of consciousness and an awareness of itself, and, as being of a separate entity apart from other humans and animals. In other words, consciousness flows in existence as the mind on an individual level, one person at a time. And through the portals of the mind we are allowed the constant miraculous feat of instantaneously recognizing each other as separate beings.

The complex mind of humans is also charged with the powers of storing memories both short and long term and retrieval of such information in complete details for later use, and generating our thoughts into and from the subconscious levels of mind. But, in no way is the mind confined to any one particular area of the body within, or outside, it just seems that way since the brain organ plays host to many neurons in a finite space. Considering all that we do know about the mind, it is still a mystery to us, so much so, that it lends itself to all sorts of speculation; both pros and cons, to a wide range of would be new-age gurus, occult leaders, and religious fanatics alike, about its origin, power and capabilities.

Over the years since becoming a self-taught spiritual practitioner, and a more purposeful meditator, with awakened psychic senses and recognized healing powers, I have read more than a lion's share of new-age and esoteric books and articles from a variety of authors, credentialed researchers, and/or writers, whom sincerely believe that they have come to know and understand the mind. In more ways than not, I believe each has come into certain noetic knowledge via observations from experimenting as best they know how. As such, the knowledge gained still doesn't begin to cover the full scope of what the mind is able to do.

But still, I am quite certain that many of these people are possibly in possession of some long-lost secrets; which were re-discovered in the act of examining various aspects of the mind in action. But, for one reason or another, such secrets do not appear within the pages of their books and/or articles released for public consumption; this I do not understand.

In this chapter, and the chapter of Tapping the Source, I hold nothing back from you; in terms of what I have personally observed during my research into this matter. In the end, what you believe is up to you....

Levels of Consciousness
(Getting to know Your Inner-self)

There are overlapping responsibilities between levels of consciousness because there really is just one.

Quantum physicists, self-taught new-age and spiritual gurus, and independent researchers, seemingly agree to a point that the conscious mind of intellectual life (humans); although it is a non-physical entity, is somewhat layered, or is somehow divided into varying vibrational levels of consciousness. While this theory pertaining to consciousness may not be exactly the way the mind is structured in regards to intelligent life, however, it is currently the best model available. I personally believe this theory to be true with a slight departure from the consensus. In my opinion there are at least three levels of the conscious mind inherently available to each human being. In order to make full use of all three levels of consciousness one must become familiar with the mechanism and protocols of access.

Seek first the kingdom of God and all things will be added to you

Matt 6:33

The following are basically a theorized model of how individual levels of mind consciousness are formed, it is assumed that there are three levels chiefly believed responsible for the makeup of the human mind. They are commonly described as (in order of ascension):

1. Superconscious (core, universal mind, cosmic consciousness, or God),
2. Subconscious (subjective mind, inductive mind),

65

3. Conscious (ego, reasoning, logical, deductive, conscious mind, individual mind).

Superconscious Level of Mind
(Universal, God Level)

In theory, the superconscious level of mind is the only thing in existence that really exist, and it is uncreated. It is considered by many as the mind of God, the core; aka, the highest or deepest level of consciousness there is. At this level of mind, without exceptions, is believed responsible for causation of all there is and will be, ad infinitum, and that individual levels of consciousness available to humans is mysteriously filtered downward, upward, sideways or whatever, to what is described by many as the subconscious and conscious levels of mind. If this conceptual view of superconsciousness is correct, it just may explain why there seems to be a sort of temporary blockage in the flow of conscious streams flowing back and forth between the core (root) and other levels within the conscious mind of humans.

We know this temporary blockage of consciousness exists because it is the best way of explaining why some people are able to access the superconscious level and while others have difficulty doing so, unless they are shown how to do it. This also explains why some cultures ancient and modern turn to drugs, because some drugs allow a faster connection to the superconscious level than by simple meditation or other means of safely altering ones' state of mind naturally. In a sense, this is why some people become addicted to certain types of drugs. Freedom from the cycle of pain and suffering of the external world is what actually attaches them, once they've been to nirvana, its hard for them to return to reality and let go of the experience.

In my humble opinion, superconsciousness is the highest level of consciousness attainable, it pertains to all matter, animated or inanimate...This is the place where god dwells within all things. The source is solely responsible for creating and releasing sub-particles of energy into the universe by way of black holes. Called quantum particles by Einstein, we see the visible effects of this natural phenomenon in the form of light radiation. And science discovered that light can become both a particle and a wave, which in and of itself seems to be conscious, because these particle also display a reaction to observation.

Many believe that the core level of consciousness becomes accessible to everyone each time they enter into a deeper level of sleep. The probable reason why most folks don't remember much about their adventures into this realm of deep sleep is that for the most part, there is a lack of expectations, and most haven't been trained consciously how to become more aware of the experience. When it comes to exploring the superconscious (core) level of mind, experience is the best teacher, this hypothesis has been proven time and time again to hold true by all the great prophetic luminaries of old.

Throughout human history there have been those born into this world who were highly adept at accessing the core level of consciousness at will. As a result they seemed gifted with such unlimited powers and abilities over matter, they could perform miracles and manifest or change reality as they deemed necessary. Such people of renown, have become so worshiped and venerated over time that they are seen by untold millions as being those who were sent here by god itself, to deliver a message to all of mankind. The ancient grounds where these extraordinary people once lived and walked upon the earth are forever held sacred by mainstream religions. We recognize two of these luminaries by the names: Moses and Jesus but, there have been many more since their departure, and there are still people living among us today with like abilities.

Research shows that there has been an untold number of people born into this world throughout time, as humans, who were gifted with extraordinary powers of the mind, and, that all of these people fall within the category reserved for prophets, but, for one reason or another, seem to gather less recognition from the church.

Acknowledgment of the superconscious level of mind as the causation and effect of all matter, large and small, seen and unseen, of all actions and events, collectively and individually humans experience as life, means that information about the past and future can be accessed under the right conditions. In fact some intuitive people do have this ability.

From time to time I have experienced the ability to see into the future with incredible attention to details. Only when the foreseen events come to pass that I realize the accuracy of the information received. Since the future can be foreseen, does this mean that the life is predetermined? Not at all, because we are constantly setting and rearranging the future with every decision made, followed by action. The future then become the past as both are simultaneously recorded at the core, which constantly uses the forces of mental feedback the release of electricity and other forms of energy into the universe in order to fulfill the task at hand.

Just imagine, if any of this is true, we finally know where electricity and all other forms of sub-atomic particles of energy originate.

This concept also explains to us whether or not opposites, such as dark energy and dark matter exist. And most of all, it would finally put to rest long held questions about the true origin of human beings. No one knows for sure, but what we do know is that everything had to originate from somewhere, and, I for one, do not buy into the big-bang theory of the universe, nor, do I buy into ideology of a blond-haired man in heaven, who is overlooking all activities of humans, because, this is obviously a theory of man-made religions. However, I do know that something started it all, and that creation occurs somewhere everyday in time and space, if not, it seems like an awful waste of space. I truly believe that something, is responsible for creating it all, it was unlikely an explosion; which hypothetically occurred some 15 billion years ago out of nothingness, nor was it a man. Basically, what all of this means is that life itself, is not coincidental. It also means that there is a purpose of being human.

By the time you are done reading this chapter your assumptions about the consciousness, mind and brain will have changed. It is obvious that the brain of humans is like that of other organs in the body; simply a very complex organic means for the distribution of electrical impulses to other internal organs and exterior parts. It is now known that the actual electromagnetic currents are generated (originated) from somewhere outside of the body and brain, most likely from a source whose origins are unknown. And, that these mysterious electric signals occur in all areas of the body, its organs, down to its molecular structure and corresponding cells, simultaneously. Knowing that the mind originates elsewhere other than the brain and body is one explanation why there are millions of people from all stripes of life, races and cultures, who have reported to medical personnel worldwide about out-of-body, or near-death experiences.

If scientists were to ever isolate the superconscious mind somehow, they might discover that it stores every event that occurs in the universe as experience, or an expression of itself. This means that the superconscious mind; in one aspect; learns from the activities of not only humans, but every other aspect of existence, it then acts as a sort of super-sized, infinitely powerful memory chip. This may be the reason why humans are able to recall events that have occurred in a previous life time while undergoing hypnosis, events that they can't possibly remember otherwise. Many new-age gurus past and present have collectively dubbed this phenomenon: the Akashic Records. It was stated by the Edgar Cayce as the place where information of all that was and will be is permanently keep. I believe Cayce spoke metaphorically about this rather than literal. Nonetheless, Cayce was right.

Practitioners of spirituality believe that there is only one mind that exist in all actuality, and that this one mind is considered to be that of a universal mind. Which means, in my opinion, that there is one level of consciousness to the mind, and that the so-called separate layers of consciousness that most new-age spiritual gurus speak about are no more or less, an increase, or in some instances, a decrease of vibration in the fabric of space. And I also believe that the superconscious, subjective consciousness and consciousness levels collectively forms what we know as the mind. Which means that humans are the event horizon...

Since it is a literal scientific fact; that the physical brain itself is actually suspended in some type of bio-fluid within the center of the skull; which means, the brain does not touch the bone structure of the skull at all.

In fact, some theorize that the two hemispheres of the brain do not make physical contact, either. But all agree that the brain does vibrate constantly, slowing down as we sleep, only to vibrate faster when we are awake and fully conscious. What this means is that we all share an aspect of one universal mind and its infinite powers. If this is the case; and I believe that it is; it could explain a lot since everyone has the ability to dream, and, while in a dream state of mind, you can do anything that you desire and imagine, even defying the laws of gravity and traveling at rates much faster than the speed of light (sorry Albert)!

Notwithstanding, is the ability reported by many people who are able to see into the future with astonishing detail and accuracy. Yet, there still remains one glaring problem when seeing the future; you can't seemed to observed the timing of such events; which provides skeptics with room to refute results but, in actuality it goes to show that the illusion of time is a real one. Time after all is simply an agreement among humans.

While I do posses several theories and secrets as a result of research conducted on my own; nevertheless, I am willing and natural inclined to share this body of knowledge with any of those who have preceded me into explorations of the mind. In my opinion, the mind of human beings is the Kingdom of heaven, the event horizon so often spoken about throughout biblical antiquity from the likes of Abraham, Moses, Enoch, Noah, Jesus and other prophets mentioned in the context of religion, the mind itself has always been and will be the focal point and source of non-traditional information and miraculous manifestations of reality. The parting of the Red Sea by Moses, at the behest of Pharaoh's army, Jesus' ability to heal the sick and raise the dead, were such an awesome and incredible display of mind over matter, that these events are still the subject of debate among scientists and non-believers to this day. I for one, believe they happened....

What you are about to discover or re-discover is that there really is only one mind, of which all things, large and small, seen or unseen, evolved or manifested from. And this means that at all times we are being observed, not by some imagined old, white-bearded, white-haired and balding male figure, but, from the same point of view that we ourselves are capable of monitoring and experiencing activities far and wide each and everyday without thinking about it.

We are the ultimate observer....

If you take time to reflect upon this inherited ability that you have, then you'll know it to be valid in so many ways. Consider this, before a word is ever verbally spoken by anyone, a thought occurred first. And with each thought, we imagine and visualize what it is that we are saying, even to the point of its intended effect on others and reality.

We do these things within ourselves (the mind) around 10,000 times or more an hour, all day long, and we continue to do these things even more as we asleep. Just think about it for a moment! No one ever leaves home; whether going to work, out to play, or simply a night on the town, without some thought, imagination and visualization occurring first. Its absolutely impossible to do so, because first off, your body is simply a bio-mechanical suit, a reactionary tool, or vehicle for the mind. It serves as a bridge between two realms of existence; which are both mental and physical.

In layman's terminology, the body is the only way for human beings to inter-react with others who also share this world. Without a body to physically move about at the will of your thoughts, you might as well be a ghost.

In conclusion, the superconscious mind (the core of existence) is the ultimate power, the infinite living force you know as God. And all things we know of originated within...

Subconscious Level of Mind
(aka subjective mind)

For hundreds, thousands, perhaps millions of years ago; no one really knows exactly how long because time is irrelevant; indigenous cultures of the world have been privy to seeing miracles made possible as a result of someone accessing their subjective level of mind. For instance, many have seen the human body; as frail as it is; recover miraculously from various injuries and diseases that had once taken the lives of their loved ones. People today fail to realize that during the era of the great black death, a plague that took the lives of untold millions in Europe during medieval times, also revealed that there were a lot of people who were virtually immune to the disease. In fact, the same holds true today as modern medical scientists are still scrambling to understand why millions of people are immune to HIV, the virus chiefly believed to responsible for causing aids. If history has taught us anything it should be quite clear that the power to heal, and restore the human body back to good health is mainly the result of manifestations brought forth when the subconscious mind changes reality. There is no longer a debate about what the subjective level of mind can do, the argument remains in how does it accomplish the things it can do.

Your subjective mind is not yours alone. Because of this characteristic, it is constantly open to suggestion while in certain states of consciousness.

Only in recent times have we begun to understand some of the abilities emanating from the inner workings of each human being is also a by-product of their subjective state of mind. For instance,

73

there are more theories floating around about the powerful forces of the subconscious mind than there are about any other level of consciousness. As a result a lot has been learned about this level of consciousness from an abundance of information gathered over centuries from prophets, mystics, scientists, and researchers alike, and yet, there seems to be so much more to discover.

Here's what we do know about the subjective level of mind:

1. There is only one subjective mind in all of existence, which is sometimes referred to as the subconscious mind.
2. This means that you and I are connected at this level of consciousness along with everyone else. This is what is meant by the phrase: We are One.
3. The subjective mind serves as a bridge between the superconscious core level of mind, and the conscious mind.
4. Which means the subconscious mind is directly responsible for the dissemination of all information between the core mind and the event horizon, aka the conscious state of final awareness.
5. There are no limitations to the power of the subjective mind. Which means it has the ability to cure any ill conditions manifested into the body, it can even reverse physical death.
6. It is the source of all paranormal experiences.
7. It is the source of all psychic and prophetic powers.

The subconscious mind exists simultaneously everywhere within all realms of existence, and similar to the core source, it is unaffected by time or space. In fact, you may even suggest as some are beginning to speculate that the subjective mind is the space, because they argue, the subjective mind is both omniscient and omnipotent, and there is virtually nowhere that it does not exist... Just like space. And yes, what I am saying here is that the subjective mind is endowed with complete authority to carry out its responsibilities, even if this means it has to change reality to do so.

However, the limitless power of the subjective level of mind does come at a cost. One apparent downside of the subjective level of mind's infinite power is that the subjective mind is strictly non-logical, and is constantly open to suggestions or requests as it rests in an altered state. This is especially true of such techniques and methods like hypnosis and other subliminal mind-control programming.

The reason for this so-called downside aspect of the subjective mind appears to be a sign of strength, too. For the subjective mind is inherently by very nature, inductive only, which means it does not have the option of rejecting any information it receives because the information is perceived to be right or wrong, irrespective of how the information is impressed unto the subjective level of mind, for it is not open to logical thinking, reasoning, nor debate. In other words the subjective mind never analysis commands given to it by your conscious-mind or otherwise, it simply obeys; the way a sponge absorbs water; it then goes about finding ways to perform the assigned tasks without ever questioning the authenticity of the source.

Note:
Now here's the one thing that mystifies many theologians, scientists, and spiritualists alike: is that there seems to be only one subjective level of mind in all of existence, and that everyone one alive or dead, in this world or another, share this same subjective mind.

What this means is that you really are your brother's and your sister's keeper, alone with everyone else'.

The mind is a bridge between the material and immaterial realms. It makes reality possible.

Responsibilities of Subjective Mind

The following revelations will make many of you stay up late at night trying to figure out whether or not, the following statements are true or false about the various responsibilities of the subjective mind.

The subjective mind is where all the long and short term memories of everyone who lives, and has ever lived are stored on a permanently basis, this includes memories of animals too. Your subjective levels of mind records and store everything that's happening simultaneously around the world and the entire universe. This infinite and ubiquitous database of knowledge covers every minute aspect of even the smallest non-physical, sub-particle matter. This includes all impressions ever recorded by inanimate matter and the environment as well. And it doesn't matter what form the information arrives in, be images, sound, body movement, or the explosions of a dying star, it will be stored by the subjective mind. This particularly all important attribute of the subjective level mind is what allows wireless communications possible, and yes, this also means that telepathy is real.

But, the most critical function of the subjective mind is that it keeps your heart beating, your blood flowing, and your lungs breathing without your conscious awareness, even while you sleep. For the subjective mind really is the chief mechanic of all that exists. In terms of the human brain and nervous system, the influence of the subjective mind can be witnessed there too. For instance, science now realize that memories of humans, and for that matter animals, are not stored in the brain. The reason for this is based entirely upon the ever growing volume of data quietly being recorded about near death experiences.

Millions of eyewitness testimonies from various cultures can't all be lying when it comes to what actually happened to these people, and in some situations; I can think of several off-hand; people were dead much longer than Jesus before bringing themselves back to life again. When a brain cease functioning, and people still return back to land of the living, and are able to recall not only the experience they had, but can also describe everything that occurred around them during that time should be evidence enough that memory is not confined to the brain.

Psychic Powers & Paranormal Phenomena

The subjective mind is the underlying cause or force behind all paranormal phenomena, including psychic experiences, extra sensory perceptions, out-of-body experiences, NDE, ghosts and poltergeists, mental telepathy, astral projections, precognition, and remote viewing. In a literal sense all things are manifested into the physical realm by the subjective level of mind, for it is the power that springs forth all illusions into the material world.

The subjective mind is able to manipulate physical objects kinetically; size not withstanding.

If you were to assume that the subjective mind is also the mechanism responsible for creating all types of energy, then you might be right cause, there's just no sure way for scientists to know. However, it is my personal belief that energy is manifested at the superconscious level of mind, where it is then summoned into action by the subjective mind, and sometimes this request is made by the conscious mind. Then again there is good reason for these assumptions, but, apparently others within this field of research have expressed differing views. My findings, however, are based in part on my personal experiences and observations from years of independent research, in addition to reading reports and articles of others.

Your Conscious Mind

After reading the previous chapters there should be no doubt in your mind about the purpose and nature of your conscious mind.

Basically your conscious level of mind plays the role of captain, it has complete authority over the subconscious levels of mind but lacks the power to act or make changes entirely on its own. Make no mistake about this crucial, most important distinction, because your conscious mind holds the power of free will, and visualization, without which the subconscious levels greatly depend upon for correct interpretations of spoken languages into images, which, other than the vibrations of musical tones, just happens to be the preferred language of the subconscious levels of mind.

Your conscious state of mind is what allows you, well... To be you. In other words, your conscious state of mind is uniquely that of your own, which means all that you have learned since you were born; all your activities and thoughts; has played a major role in your life's events, both good and bad, this has become your reality (the unique way in which you alone view the world).

Additionally, the conscious mind is where you store your random access, or short-term memory. Your long term memories; as you recall; is the role of the subconscious levels of mind. Even though there is a limited, somewhat restrictive role of your top conscious level of mind; especially when compared to your subconscious levels of mind, your conscious mind is both master and commander of your soul, for it is ultimately responsible for everything that occurs in your life, because this where your free-will resides within you. Which means that everything begins and ends at the conscious state of mind. Learning how to control your mental forces begins and ends here. Do this and you'll gain complete control of your life's events.

To learn more about your conscious mind, and how it summons the subconscious levels of mind into action, you should read the chapter: Tapping into the Source for a better understanding.

How Consciousness Ages Your Body

The more you learn about the abilities of your consciousness, the sooner you can begin taking control of your journey through life. When your subjective levels of mind responds to a command from your conscious mind to influence or bring about a physical change to body, it does so by communicating this command for change (in this case) to the smallest particles within your body, first. From there, the process begins to flow upwards until every part of your body is in full compliance. This hypothesis holds true for both healing and aging. After all, how else would you explain why some people look very old at 30, 40, or 50 years of age, whereas some look very young at 60 or older. There is only one explanation that can account for these differences: consciousness. And when it comes down to it how you think really does matter.

Role of Microbes

There are basically two types of microbes found within the cellular structure of the human body: alkaline and acidic. On the surface, each microbe is separate in terms of their functions. Scientists theorized that alkaline microbes are constructive in nature, while acidic microbes are destructive. But, there are occasions where each microbe combine with the other to become either constructive or destructive as a force. The effects of microbes on aging the body, or the task of healing a damaged body overall are profound.

Note: *For those of you who are scientifically literate, the event of subatomic particles combining to form microbes are omitted for reasons of simplicity.*

Acidic microbes are formed into viruses, or bacteria of fungi. The effects that these microbes have on the human body are well documented by research microbiologists. What isn't that widely known is that in almost every event, these microbes somehow reacts to vibrations, or rather frequencies originating from the subjective levels of mind. What this means is that any negative vibrations (stress or illness related) with enough strength will be received by your subjective mind, and that this frequency will eventually manifest in your body, showing up as a physical negative.

In the activities of aging, all negative signals eventually become acidic microbes in nature. It's a well known fact that aging is caused by a slow, albeit minute, acidic action (negative vibration) within cells of your body. In other words, the previous scenario is what causes your body's tissues and organs along the path of decaying. Essentially, this is nature's way of preparing the materialistic body for re-entering into the realm of subatomic-particles within the core. In layman's term, this is what happens in a physical death.

Other means of aging the body comes from the type of food being consumed. Live foods, such as vegetables and fruits, resonate at a positive frequency, while dead foods, such as animal flesh and complex man made foods, resonates at a negative frequency. You could argue that this is because slaughtering animals for the purpose of human consumption is excruciatingly painful to the animal, which the act of killing in and of itself generates negative energy. Others might go on to argue that eating animals is the number one cause of all illnesses and diseases plaguing humans. For a very long time this has been my inner most feelings about eating the flesh of animals. Knowing what I now know there is good reason to believe this assumption is right.

What we do know for sure is that dead food becomes acidic in nature, and that this type of reaction (negative in nature) is what causes the body to decay more rapidly, more than it normally should. In layman's terms, a slow decaying body is a body that is becoming older, much sooner than later.

What Can You Do to Reverse Aging?

Now that you know and understand more about the real causes behind the aging process of your body, the question then becomes, what if anything, can you do about it? Well, for starters, you should consciously monitor the type of mental signals being emitted into to your subconscious levels of mind. As an example, instead of saying how old are you when asked this question, you should respond by saying how many years you have been on earth as it travels around the sun within the solar system.

I have become quite a fan of the Latin culture as of late. Spanish speakers basically have a unique way of stating this question the right way; for instance: when asked how old they are, the response isn't: "I am 20 years old," but rather, "I have 20 years (anos tengo 20)." To an English speaker, this may sound a bit silly at first, but if you notice how young looking on average the majority of Latinos look compared to their actual age, then you'll sooner or later agree with me that they are probably onto something.

Secondly, I know you've heard this one before, start eating more fruits, vegetables and nuts, and less meat as possible. Edgar Cayce, the best known psychic and prophet in America's most recent history, has been quoted in saying: "eating less, or no meat at all will improve your psychic functioning." So, truth be told for all who are seeking the fountain of youth, know this, you've been looking in all the wrong places. For the fountain of youth has and always will be found within the consciousness of your mind.

Simply stated, from within you lies the location of eternal health and youth. But you can only access this fountain of eternal wellness and vitality within your mind. For this is the promise of the uncreated source of nature.

Consciously Reverse Effects of Aging

1. Make it an effort to re-program your subjective mind by sending positive statements like: "I am" getting better and better everyday, I am younger and younger, I am healthier and healthier. Say to yourself telepathically: "I am better and better," etc..

2. Remove these words: old, getting older, in regards to your age from your subjective vocabulary, and replace them with more age neutral words.

3. If not already, start meditating for at least 5 - 15 minutes daily. Regardless of how busy your schedule, make time for mind time (see how to meditate).

4. Regardless of what happens during your day, always go to bed happy.

5. Change the types of food you eat. Eat to live, instead of living to eat. Consume more live foods.

6. Pursue a moderate exercise regimen. The human body is designed to move for a lifetime, which should be between 150-200 years. Inactivity is the worst thing for your body. For everything that exists in nature is in constant motion; you can't always see this with your physical eyes but, this is the state of being. Movement is good, non-movement is not.

7. And learn to heal yourself and stop your dependency of all drugs, including vitamins (unless they are attained in foods).

If you adapt this plan, not only will you feel better and reverse aging of your body, but you'll also maintain an ideal weight for your body type without trying to do so. I know that many of you reading this chapter might conclude that the methods mentioned herein are way too simple to be effective, or that they will not work, etc... As my daughter's generation would say: "don't knock it, til you try it."

As for industries that stand to lose a boat load of cash if society suddenly begins self-correcting itself and consume less meat and drugs, I say to you: "everything changes, its only a matter of time before real change affects you personally. Instead of complaining or filing a lawsuit designed to shut me up: Get on board the B.O.A.T."

Attachment to matter gives rise to passions against nature. Thus trouble arises in the whole body; Be in harmony... If you are out of balance, take inspiration from the manifestations of your true nature.

Yeshua

Forces of the Mind

The mind (consciousness) is key to all things in life and beyond. When combined with the elements of energy and matter, the forces of mind becomes inextricably interconnected to everything within the universe in ways we may never fully understand. The Forces of the mind is what controls all aspects of the physical and metaphysical nature of all life forms and the environment they live in. And yet, there is still another more potent forms of energy known to exist. One of these so-called forms of energy has become the most important of all, in that it literally seems to enhance your experience of being human in ways unimagined. This form of energy has come to be known as psychic or intuitive powers.

As stated previously; I believe that there is but one mind in all of existence, and we are all aspects of it. We all know of this one MIND by various names which has been assigned to it by different cultures throughout the years of humanity's time spent on earth. In the western hemisphere (basically Christendom), this one 'mind' is known largely as God. In most areas of the middle east it is referred to as Allah. The Jewish community uses the name Jehovah, while the new-age or new-thought communities often refer to it as the source; the creator; causation; or simply the universe or nature.

Whatever name one chooses to use when addressing this awesome, very powerful and intelligent entity of love, compassion and awareness is really not that important at all, simply because it all means the same thing whenever and where ever it is called upon. In a strange way, I believe that it is the vibrational level of each person's tonal voice that determines the actual meaning behind all these varied names being used to address this very powerful and obviously intelligent source simply because the world's first spoken languages were tonal based. This could explain why the Dogone tribe on the southern most part of the African continent, and those of early native Americans in the north and south still use such tonal languages today when speaking directly to their particular entity known as God.

Vibrational or tonal languages is nothing new, animals use a form of tonal or pitched language when they talk among themselves verbally, or when they speak to humans. When you think about it, we can tell by the pitch (vibration or tone) level of a dog's bark whether or not if man's best friend is vicious or harmless.

So in a nutshell, since it is covered in other sections of this book more than once, the Forces of the mind are as follows: 1. Thought, 2. visualization, 3. imagery, all of which is an aspect of consciousness at every level.

Dark Side of Mind Power

Within almost every western nation on earth lives a dark and unspeakable secret, of which no country's leader will ever openly talk about or admit to their common citizens. All the world's major powers: the United States, Europe, Russia, Japan and China, have been secretly conducting tests into what is known as the dark powers of mind for at least the last 100 years. This also takes into the probabilities that each of these nations have collected a treasure trove of extremely invaluable information combed from ancient records and national museum archives that span the globe; and that such findings have provided a very high level of tangible evidence on how to access powers of the supernatural, mostly for nefarious reasons. Keep in mind though that publicly none of these aforementioned governing bodies, who have made use of ancient knowledge of mind power will never admit to it, nor release any of their findings to the public.

On the surface, these mighty and powerful nations of earth had done all they can to foster an image of sharing what information they have uncovered among ancient ruins with all of humanity. Of course, they each openly deny the use of such knowledge detailing the powers of mind, or proof of the existence of God. And until UFOs or the existence of other worldly beings began landing their multidimensional space-crafts on the lawns of each nation's capitol, you shouldn't really expect any governmental-sponsored revelations about such matters to be forthcoming.

Major nations of the world, over time, have each managed to appoint the role of deity to the domain of religion. In return, religious leaders, along with their desire for controlling humanity's access to God, and their constant thirst for increasing the size of their respective congregations, while constructing ever larger houses of worship for their parishioners' amusement, still owe their entire right to exist to that of an earlier political action committee that harbored a willingness to enact policies which would eventually force-feed all religious belief systems, basically fostering an environment that allowed them to prosper and grow.

The bottom line is that religion and world governments have been very successful at deploying the very thing that they portend to be against; at least publicly; the dark side of the forces of mind.

Censoring Truth

From within the hidden backrooms of power, policies of the new, old and ancient church and politicians brought forth a world-wide bounty, which started the unofficial hunt for psychics and others who practiced the art of witchcraft, sorcery, spirituality and self-empowerment of any kind, by means of unleashing powers within their own minds. These people were systemically hunted down and killed without a trial, they were mostly accused of being associated with demonic forces. After all, religion had given rise to a thought-form that became an enemy of God; an ex-angel who was reportedly banned from entering heaven ever again, and was sentenced to reside forever in a place called Hades (Hell), this ex-patriot of heaven over centuries later became known as Satan.

In Europe alone, a very deadly biological agent was unleashed unto an unsuspecting population of commoners through means of sexual transmission, by way of ladies of the night. The spread of this virus nearly killed a third of the nation. This event became known as the 'black plague.' Only when it had become evident that those of upper social status and kingship also sustained losses from this epidemic did a sudden and mysterious end manifest. The cure for black death turned-out to be a very simple solution known as soap and water. Of course, if historical perspective is recorded and controlled by those who ruled, they got to tell a version of this great tragedy in human history in a manner that absorbs them of any role in its eventful manifestation.

Ironically, the black-death plaque epidemic in Europe had given more power to the church than it ever had before. More and more people; by the millions; became followers and were inclined out of guilt, induce into believing they were all sinners in the eyes of God, and encouraged to turn over their possessions, along with their heart and soul to the Vatican. Needless to say this event helped the church to become the most powerful institution on earth, and it remains that way even today. I am still amazed that most people don't realize that the Vatican, a nation and country unto itself, answers to now one.

You might be inclined to ask, what does all of this have to do with understanding abilities and powers of the Mind? My answer to you is: EVERYTHING! You see, in a world of mind-controlled subjects, FEAR of the unknown is a great motivator. It was fear of meeting a very horrible fate at the hands of an unknown killer-virus like the black-death, which, eventually drove both the population into granting both unprecedented and unparalleled power of authority to the church and its clergymen over virtually all of Europe, and later allowed expansion and influence into the new territory of the Americas.

Media headlines lends the impression that biological warfare is a modern-day war phenomenon----even though we now have a better understanding of how biological weapons are deployed, the machines of war has used such technologies a very long time. Biological warfare technologies can also be found in the Bible.

Early European scientists had known about man-made biological viruses since uncovering information about such use and deployment of made-made biological assaults that had occurred during the biblical era. As it turned-out many key battles were often fought using the rotting corpses of dead soldiers in battle as a weapon. Remains of the fallen were thrown over enemy walls to spread diseases. Strange as it seems the same source that provided information on how-to create a deadly virus was the same source that also provided information about its cure. Scientists were well aware of these developments early on. To them, such advantages over their enemies was worth the loss of life among commoners.

All modern wars were fought using technologies discovered from so-called dark powers of the mind. Upon further research one might be safe to include all wars ever fought in human history were aided in some way by higher intelligence. This includes all wars of the last century such as World War I and II, the Korean war, the Vietnam conflict, the Soviet war in Afghanistan, the US war in Iraq I and II, the US war in Afghanistan, and the most recent upheavals of countries seeking a regime change of leadership such as, Egypt; Syria; Libya; and Yemen. And soon to occur: Saudi Arabia; Iran; North and South Korea; and of course, North and South America face similar events.

What is a Psychic?

There is no standard definition on what the word psychic means, or for that matter what truly defines a person who is psychic. In antiquity philosophers used the word 'psyche' as simply a way of expressing the soul or spirit of person. At some point in time the word took on an additional component as the spelling changed from psyche to psychic.

The Greeks ended up shortening the word psychic (psyche) to PSI (pronounced sigh), which just happened to be the 23rd letter of the Greek alphabet. Maybe it was this event; which was simply academic that caused most people over time to wrongly assume that those with demonstrated psychic abilities were a phenomenon whose origins were Greek. Keep in mind that the oracles of Delphi were known for their psychic powers all over the world. Psychic skills describe a subset of nonphysical senses or abilities that some (a very small percentage) people who identify themselves as psychic are able to do repeatedly for personal gain or to help others on a ready basis. We are referring to a set of skills beyond those of your normal five senses. Except in cases of blindness, or any other condition that restricts any normal sensory input.

Today, the term PSI can be used interchangeably with the words: psychic or psyche. But in general, PSI represents an entire range of Godlike abilities that have been available to all spiritually sensitive people. For the purpose of this book PSI refers to any and all powers of God as those manifested within the mind, whether they are animated or inanimate, makes no difference. And with that being said a psychic person refers to anyone with the knowledge and skills to apply such powers using one or all of the following skill sets: telepathy, energy-healing, astral projection (OBE), remote viewing, remote mental influence (telepathy), prophecy, dream interpretations, post cognition, or medium. It doesn't matter what tools a psychic choose to use as an aide to help her focus mentally. This means that the reading of tarot cards, staring at water in a bowl, or even a crystal ball, as long as the psychic feels that it helps, its completely okay to do these things. The end result is as long as it works, the method of attainment shouldn't matter.

What this means is that everybody psychic in one way or another whether they accept this notion or not, nonphysical senses is a reality of human abilities.

Secrets of Psychics

Again, as previously mentioned, when discussing PSI, it is important to remember that we are talking about the secret mysteries used by psychics to gain access to an infinite *Source* or origin of power. And to a lesser degree we are talking about levels of human *Consciousness*.

Tapping into a *Source* within yourself for whatever reason can only improve your life. In other words, if it works to your satisfaction, who cares about what they call it. Well, apparently a lot of people do care about their choice of words as this has been shown throughout history. It has been proven time after time that words do matter. The list of known abilities attributed to PSI continues to grow as more people are trained to use their hidden skills, or discover on their own that they are already psychic.

Who is Psychic?

Who is psychic can be answered in the book of *Genesis 1:27, and Isaiah 43:7 which states: 'everyone that is called by my name, and whom I have created, whom I have formed, whom I have made.'*

Human beings, as well as all other intelligent life forms throughout the cosmos are a by-product of the uncreated. The uncreated of course is God, he has always existed and is the origin of Source from which we draw upon constantly. It doesn't matter if you believe in the Source, or if you don't. Your very existence still depends on it and it never lets you down.

Although you've heard of these terms before it is best to remember them as an aspect of PSI:

Laws of attraction you invoke this power based upon how you think, act, feel, and the words you say. This function of PSI is always working on your behalf – good or bad, so be careful of what you think about, which most times become the words you say. The Laws of Attraction are the most widely used function of PSI – simply because all that is needed is your mind, which is all spirit. Everybody has one, because we are all are psychic.

Intuition Awareness/knowing/ instincts. The best way to explain what this is all about is to tell you a story about what happened to me a long time ago when I was a soldier serving time in the US Army.

In late summer of 1980, I was temporarily assigned to the Army's intelligence training school – located at Ft. Huachuca, Arizona. On one particular day around noon, I was driving along a very dusty, unpaved road through some rough desert terrain in a US Army issued vehicle (jeep). Riding along with me was my mentor and boss: Colonel Walker. Colonel Walker had earlier instructed me to make a right turn onto an upcoming, unmarked road. And as instructed, I made a right turn and continued driving down this road for the next two miles when suddenly, the Colonel realized that we had entered into a live artillery impact zone that was being conducted by the Arizona Army National Guards. When live artillery rounds began exploding all around us, Colonel Walker hastily ordered me to keep driving straight ahead until we were cleared of the explosions, and out of the artillery's gun range. I drove as fast as the vehicle would go, back then the maximum speed limits for all military vehicles were 45 mph, tops.

Nevertheless, the Colonel and I were in imminent danger, I floored the accelerator as quickly as possible, nearly pushing through the floor of the jeep. All of sudden, and without explanation, while still imperiled by exploding bombs all around us, somehow and inexplicably, I became very calm and relaxed. In fact, there must have been a smile on my face because the Colonel commented: "you won't smiling for long if a round were to hit us. While still driving down this road as fast as the vehicle would move, and without another word spoken, I suddenly applied the brakes, bringing the jeep to an abrupt and complete stop. The Colonel then asked me: "why did you stop?" I immediately pointed out to him that the road ahead of us was not there.

Approximately three feet in front of us was nothing but the bottom of the Grand Canyon. To make a long story short, I turned the Jeep around and drove back the way we came.

In hindsight, it was my intuition – or if you prefer, my inner genius which intuitively warned me of a pending danger in the road ahead. I stopped the vehicle without logically thinking about it. I simply reacted to an inner voice that was inside my mind, instinctively. I shared this true event with you for a reason. What it shows is that sometimes there are things happening around us, away from our normal senses, that we just know about or react to without any logical explanation. By the way, from that moment, on the recommendation of Colonel Walker alone, the US Army granted me a top secret clearance, and the colonel kept me around as his personal and most trusted assistant. As a result of such actions I moved up the ranks very quickly.

The message here is: learn to hear the small, still, silent voice inside your mind, your life will only improve if done right.

Clairvoyance, Clair-audience and Clair-sentience

These three skills are equivalent to your physical abilities of sight, sound, and smell, except that in a psychic sense, seeing, smelling and hearing is not limited to that of the physical.

Clairvoyance, allows you to see into the past, and or future, as if it were all happening at once, because the past and future are happening in the here and now.

Clair-audience is the ability to hear things beyond that of the physical plane; such as, an ability to hear spirits talking. This skill is more common than you might think.

Clair-sentience is the ability to feel things, which is also more common than you think. If you've ever heard the phrase: "I feel it in my gut," then you know what Clair-sentience means, and is about. In the movie 'Star Wars,' Skywalker was constantly reminded to always trust his feelings, no matter what, because they won't betray him. This something that we all can do with a little more practice.

Remote viewing is the ability to project your mind anywhere in space and time, while maintaining consciousness (see chapter on remote viewing). Remote viewing is also more common than some would have you believe.

Out of Body Experience is the same as a Near Death Experience, or (NDE), and are very similar to remote viewing (RV), except that in the case of an OBE and NDE that are reportedly experienced by millions people around the world everyday, they are basically involuntary and spontaneous.

Over the years I have learned how to bring about an OBE on a regular basis, at will. Besides the usual flying up towards the edge of the earth's atmosphere, or floating around my home town looking in on the folks I know and love, there are moments where I see into the future with quite a bit of accuracy. Lately, I've been able to project my mind at will to anywhere I want to go, or at specific events I want to see. The functions of OBE, NDE and remote viewing are very much similar., of course, those who specialize in selling remote viewing classes to the public for huge fees may disagree with my assertions. But this is my opinion, and I've experienced in this area.

In my view the difference between remote viewing and those of an OBE or NDE are two things: 1. Remote viewings are an intentional event, while the those who have experienced an OBE or NDE seems to do so accidentally, which doesn't mean that either can't be an intentional, it just implies that the bulk of reported events have been unintentional in nature. 2. The protocols (methods) used to access these *Sources* differ, (also see Astral Projection).

Precognition Seeing into the future.

Post-cognition Seeing into the past.

Telepathy Mind to mind communications (see chapter on Telepathy).

Manifestation The power to manipulate or alter reality to suit your needs or that of someone else. While I've seen this in action, and have lucked upon its' wonderful powers on more than once, the exact protocols of manifestation remains a mystery. Because of what I have seen and done, I am most certain that there are those living among us in the world today, who know the secrets of how to make this ability work extremely fast. They are so advanced in their knowledge and understanding of PSI that they are capable of doing anything they want. Chances are that you may never meet such an individual in person simply because they prefer it that way. In a sense, manifestation and telekinesis are the same thing. They both include the ability of mind over matter and mental influence.

ESP (sixth sense) – Just another definition for what is already known about PSI.

Magic Is the ability to change reality, a PSI function. It is also known as manifesting. Basically, what you are beginning to realize is that all of the abilities mentioned above are a function of the mind, and the mind is a function of consciousness. There is only one *Source* that we all derive our abilities from; whether it is realized or not. Praying, meditating, or chanting with a focused and sustained single thought or idea, will eventually manifest something into reality. It is the law! You may choose to call such things a miracle, or the work of God. But, the truth is a combination of both a miracle and the work of God, brought forth by one thing, the power that lies within you that is a part of your divine nature supplied by God. Psychic powers are no more or less, the intentional will of an

98

individual, or group, that is focused on a giving matter to bring about an effect. It doesn't matter if you believe this or not, it works the same for everyone. For non-believers the results will always be less than suspected, and for believers the results will always be more than expected. The days of debating whether or not such things as psychic abilities are real should be behind us in light of all the evidence from millions of people around the world. There is no need for debating anyone about these truths anymore. Such efforts are fruitless because only in due time will non-believers ever see the truth.

All that is born, all that is created, all the elements of nature are interwoven and united with each other. All that is composed shall be decomposed; everything returns to its roots; matter returns to the origins of matter.

Jesus

Psychic Powers and Prophecy

I have decided to come forth with information that experientially I know to be true about human potentials. You see, I've always been blessed with a wide range of psychic powers and skills that were virtually unknown to me earlier in my life. Only in hindsight did I realize that these incredible gifts have always been there within my grasp, connecting me to a far greater knowledge base and power known as the universal mind, or in a more direct way, the likeness of God. These special abilities were always waiting to be summoned to the forefront of my conscious mind, and despite of it all, I am still just a regular guy, a human being, who is trying to provide for his family by honest means. The mere thought that I would someday be able to do the things that I have done, and can do, has simply made a true-believer out of me. Make no mistake about it...I am psychic, and I can see the future, but guess what? So are you!

Since the realization of what I now perceive as a real spiritual awakening and subsequent enlightenment, I have been witness to a plethora of unexplained phenomenal events of a spontaneous and intentional nature. Which has collectively served to strengthen my knowledge base on how the subconscious levels of mind operates in relation to the way things really are in life, and that the mind alone can create and change reality. Let me just say this as plainly as I can: "Nothing in life is exactly as it seems; but, and a big one at that...things are always exactly as we mentally project them to be, for every life is more mysterious than we'll ever know."

Here's the thing, we are as a species, known as human beings. Which means that we are much more than a consolidated collection of flesh and bones, whose advent of being created just happened to be coincidental, or some by-product of a universal anomaly. According to theoretical speculation: we are nothing more than cosmic soup, a phenomenon which no one of science can even begin to explain fully and keep a straight face. As such, scientists have resorted to constructing endless theories upon old ideals as to how and why they believe such things happened at the beginning of creation. They even go about creating imaginary mathematical calculations to support their concept. The problem is, as with all assumptions of its kind, is that their theories are just plain wrong.

Even the great physicists Stephen Hawkins has fallen victim to this practice. According to Hawkins we are all going to be swallowed up inside the Milky-ways galactic black hole. Obviously Stephen is a very intelligent human being, but not even he will admit to being wrong about black holes, which are at the center of every galaxy in the universe. Intuitively I know that black holes are a portal of creation rather than a monster of destruction as most scientists believe.

We might as well face the truth, human beings are the event horizon, a singular and timeless entity created at the precipice of a black hole, which has spiritually existed long before the advent of the universe and cosmos came into being. This reality has become quite evident by all the strange and unexplained phenomena occurring on a regular basis around the world everyday, even as you read this book, such unusual happenings as the recent UFO sightings at a major Chinese airport in Mongolia. Reportedly, this event occurred on a regular basis for nearly four months in the summer of 2010, causing problems for airport traffic controllers who had to hastily re-route the landing of incoming air crafts for hours. Unlike Americans, Asians are quite open about their belief of UFOs, paranormal events and even magic. For more information on what happened in the China UFO event, simply Google: China's airport UFOs.

Those of you who have discovered that you have spiritually awakened to truth all of a sudden will attest; that the universe is us (our soul, mind and spirit) on a collective level of consciousness that we may never fully understand. If we cannot accept the nature of reality as being a very mysterious and complex matrix that we've subjectively constructed, then as a species we won't graduate to the next stage of evolution. Since there is virtually only one of us here, we must still confront that same nagging, underlying and deeply seeded question within us: if there is only one of us here, why do we feel like separate beings? Think about it for a minute! Imagine being told that you are virtually the same age as a newly born child! Or that you are sharing the same mind and space of Einstein even though he has been dead for at least 54 years! Can you imagine being told that you were somewhat responsible for allowing all of the world's most atrocious events in history, such as the holocaust which claimed more than 12 million lives? And before that event allowing the slave trade to exist?

Even though it appears on the outer surface of your skin as if you are a person of African, European or Asian descent, historians tells us that we ascended from the continent at one point in time. This ideology is totally based upon DNA testing and hypothesis. If scientists are capable of tracing the entire human DNA genesis to a single source, why can't they come forward and tell the truth about the origin of God. DNA is basically the frequency that brought forth all intelligent life, where ever such intelligence exists. I do realize that it is so easy for me to sit back and say that all life is a product of one uncreative source (God), but it is equally difficult for a person of science to make that assumption because of a professional peer review system and their lively hood is at risk. As so the system itself keeps most of them quiet.

As human beings we all reside in a realm (an illusion), which is a projection of our own individual and collective subjective mind. Consciously, we perceive individual awareness of our other selves (other people), and even though we appear as separate entities, in reality there is just one of us. Our mind, or consciousness, or spirit, is the most powerful force in existence that still maintains a connection with the *Source*. Because the mind precedes and supersedes the physical body, we simply cannot and will not ever die, cause, we are all spiritual entities experiencing life as human beings. It is time that we realize "Life, is the ultimate Gift!"

Because of the knowledge base that I have attained, my personal experiences and psychic abilities spoken about earlier in this chapter, it is my deepest and most heartfelt belief that everyone in the world has some amount of psychic powers residing within them. The thing is, not all of us are willing to accept the fact that we have this kind of power.

"Free Will, means that we have the power of choice. You can't have it any other way"

It is a free and intentional will of mind, which is an aspect part of God that resides within us all, that provides the freedom of choice and gives us power to manifest our sustained thoughts. In other words, simply because you believe something to exist doesn't mean it does, unless you are intentionally willing it into being with the power of the universal mind. Contrary to popular beliefs, the mind does not reside in your brain alone; as those in science and academia would have you believe; for the mind consists of an energetic substance unknown to science that surrounds and permeates our entire body, including all its organs, molecules, cells, and atoms. A proper way to understand this is to realize that your body exist inside of your mind.

The mind is what connects us to everything and free will of intelligent species is an attribute of our being that can only be found within and produced by our objective mind. As for the physical body, it is merely a projection (mental frequency) of light manifesting as consolidated matter. We see it as flesh and tissue surrounding a skeletal frame of bones. This illusion (a perception), along with self awareness, causes us to sense separateness within each other. If you take away the aspect of the body, we are basically unborn in nature. We simply exist.

As for those who enjoy and practice any form of meditation on a regular basis can attest to, we are but one entity of immense mental powers and imagination, and, without fully knowing why, we are somehow able to consistently project reality into existence. And many new-age quantum physicists have reached a similar conclusion about our aspect our being, albeit, theoretically. And many of them are beginning to come forth publicly about this information.

Accordingly, they (new age thinkers) believe that your mind is a non-local entity, and is not bound by either space or time. Because of my very own experiences, I know this to be true, simply because I have displayed such abilities in the presence of others, and I have successfully healed numerous people from various degrees of illnesses including cancer, high fevers, bleeding, and clogged veins, using only telepathic energy at a distance. In each instance of healing, I possessed very little information as to what was wrong with the ones needing to be helped. The end results speak for themselves. Additionally, I have discovered a number of meaningful ways of deploying psychic powers on a daily basis to help improve my quality of life, significantly. In terms of life's deeper mysteries, I believe that I am now better prepared to deal with whatever manifests into the physical; good or bad; as the result of someone's ill thoughts. These things I have learned and can do with the power of my mind alone, you can do also, even to a much greater level than I can.

The younger you are when you discover your inner powers; the stronger, more powerful and deeper your abilities will become. The reasons for this belief of mine is simple, the younger you are, the less reconditioning your subjective mind will need clearing due to systemic programming.

The fact of the matter is, everything big is made up of very small things. And everything within the material world and spiritual realm are a manifestation from source at the request of a sorcerer (or the ultimate observer). If all that exists emanates from the mind activity of God, then we should all strive to live and experience our own ideal way of life as we want it to be, and not let others design it for us. For instance, if you seek to be rich and/or famous, think mentally alone those terms and surround yourself as best you can among people and things that remind you of being successful in that field of choice. The key here is to remember, if its on your mind all the time, sooner or later it will happen (in your life) if you continue to think and act accordingly. If you are sick and in poor health physically, know this, it is only the imagination of your mind that is sick and in poor health. Simply correct the problems that plague you by focusing your mental imagination and visualization forces more inwardly towards a positive outcome and you'll soon enjoy good health and prosperity. I know it sounds simple, but, it really is that simple, because God is pure love without exceptions.

Remember: We all have the gift, it's just a matter of self realization which allows it to come forth from within consciousness and manifest in the moment. Reality is that moment, or real time. So be very mindful of your thoughts, always!

Prophecy

(The ability to perceive future information)

At times I am able to see future events unfold in America that goes far beyond the anticipation and imagination of most people. I see these events as if they are happening now...

In a distant past; especially during the inquisition period; possession of this book alone would be more than enough to get you burned at the stake, or even hanged by the neck until you are dead. If lucky, your trial would have been swift and simple. Your judge and jury are one and the same; that of your accuser(s). Thankfully, in this time and era such events are no longer practiced, at least that is, out in the open. Since I am able to speak freely about such things that were once whispered in private, I feel that it is an honor to disclose this very important information where all of humanity may benefit.

The material written in this chapter is for all to read and render their own, independent judgment as whether to believe it or not. I have no fear about the possibility of reprisals from some religious zealot one way or the other, simply because the entirety of the human race is shifting towards a revealing of the truth. Although this ongoing shift in human consciousness seems to be moving at a snail's pace, it is nevertheless, underway and steamrolling in the right direction.

Since the very beginning of time the world as a whole has been in the age of information. We are now moving beyond that stage and into the age of knowing. What this means is that suddenly, without explanation, people will just know things, of which, under normal physical senses that they shouldn't know at all. The age of knowing has been evolving for a very long, long time. At first, there were only a hand full of people with the powers of foresight; the ability to talk to God and spirits of the astral realm; the gift of dream interpretation and the art of healing people. Some of these people who displayed such miraculous gifts became known as prophets, which was based in part on the original meaning of the word: prophecy, which simply meant the ability to hear the word of God. Adam was obviously the proverbial first prophet on earth if you believe the time line provided by the bible, and Ezias was last. Now, I realize that this information doesn't sit well with bible enthusiast who insist that the first prophet was Abraham. But I ask this one question: didn't God speak to Adam and Eve? Reverting to the original meaning of the word prophet should be the end of that argument. Now while the profits of old were mostly gainfully employed by kings the secret societies of their times, it is not the case for modern prophets who must put their talents on display for public approval.

Prophets of today must also deal with skepticism at the hands of religion, politics, and science, each of which has managed to hindered the course and pace of humanity's evolution into the age of knowing by simply denying that the art of prophecy even exists. The role religion ensued was slightly different than that of politics. Through the church, and with political help at the point of a blade, the church has managed to set themselves up over the course of history as being the sole authoritarian on the matter of prophecy, and who can become a prophet. In other words, only the church is endowed by self decree, the ability communicate with God.

Even though I am well aware of the existence of the source; of which, some of you may prefer to use the name God; I know very little of its true origin. And before you ask the question, I do use the words psychic and prophet interchangeably. To me they are one and the same.

Ironically, everybody has psychic abilities born within them but, not everyone is willing to accept this notion. And in my opinion, this is the reason why some people stand out above the norm as being exceptionally different. You see, we all have the gift, but that is not enough. You must believe in your psychic abilities for them to work, and you must also be open to receiving none traditional information from sources beyond this realm. If and when you make that leap of faith your psychic powers will rise within you to the forefront of your conscious mind. With a little bit of help from methods mentioned in this book, you'll soon become the sole author of your life's events.

Past Prophecies

A funny thing about the art of prophecy is that anyone can do it, if they are familiar with the nuance of how this ability works. Just like a particular sport, some are better at it than others, but with a study practice ritual a novice can eventually become more efficient than a professional. All it takes is time and patients.

It was in January 2007, during the airing of a Super-Bowl commercial, when I first took notice of a young senator from Illinois with a strange name: Barack Hussein Obama, who at the time, was teasing with the audience as he appeared ready to announce his candidacy to become the next president of the United States. Even though he did not let it be known at that time, intuitively I knew at the time that I was looking at the first African-American who would become elected president. Before that appearance on national TV, I had never before even heard of this man.

In the closing months of the 2006 NFL football season, I'd foreseen that not only will there be, for the first time ever in NFL history, a team will be coached by a black man in the big game, that both the American Football Conference and the National Football Conference would each feature black head coaches. The significance of this development assured that the a team coached by a black American would also hoist the Lombardi trophy at the conclusion of the game. And because of ability to see into the future before it became a foregone event was like having the best seat in the stadium for free.

The Superbowl of 2007 was indeed a historic moment in sports for all fans. Since both teams featured head coaches of African-American heritage, virtually eliminated all the possible talk of racial divisiveness that had occurred during the playoffs between the Chicago Bears and the New Orleans Saints, and again with the Indy Colts and New England Patriots. While the experts overwhelmingly believed that the Saints and the New England Patriots would be the ones to face-off in the big game, I knew better because of prophecy. The question is, why and how could I know the outcome of the playoffs and who the eventual winner of the Superbowl would be months before the game was ever played?

Back in the days of Biblical history people with such abilities as mine were known as prophets, or seers. Today they are known as psychics. Since that time I have come to a realization about how powerful the human mind can become once it accepts and acknowledge from within its unlimited potential.

The Great Economic Debacle

I foresaw the greatest housing debacle this country has witnessed since the great depression. During the summer of 2005 I warned family members and friends alike, by sending out thousands of email newsletters warning about the coming crisis ahead. In 2008, when the economy and housing debacle was acknowledge by government officials, a friend of mine, now living abroad in Indonesia emailed the original newsletter dating back to 2005 back to me, saying: "you hit that on the mark.."

It was in July of 2008 I told a friend of mine and anyone else who'd listen that the price of oil per barrel was about to crash. At the time oil per barrel was selling somewhere around $147.00. I said the price per barrel would drop below $35.00 when the so-called experts were predicting higher prices, still.

Well, prices per barrel did drop below my prediction that summer. As I had foreseen the oil cartel reduced production to less than half, which has caused prices to rise again.

My previous list of foresights goes on:

January, 2007: Tornado that killed at least 21 people in Lady of Lakes, Florida.

2009: The Gulf oil spill disaster.

2012: Reelection of Barack Obama to another term as US president.

2012: Superstorm that hit Northeast US seaboard.
2012: Gaza conflict.
12-21-2012: World will not end!!!

Future Prophecies

Now this is the page that most will want to scrutinize just to see if these insights come to pass. As mentioned before, and I must confess again, I have a problem with seeing the timing of my prophecies, unless it is quite evident during the actual visions. For instance, the Superbowl of February 2013 will feature the Atlanta Falcons and the Houston Texans. And the winner is........

It was purely accidental that I discovered that I have these abilities, especially the ability to see into the future. I don't know how far ahead I am able to look, but I do know that I can see things one or two years out. Over the last seven years I have indirectly solved a few high profile murder cases using this ability.

So let's cut through all the suspense, the following events are forthcoming in the very near future. I have foreseen these events as clear as seeing the sun rise in the east and setting in the west each day.

Prophecies continue:

UFOs

Soon the skies all over the world will bare witness to an extraordinary event as UFOs fill the skies over every major city, large and small towns. No longer will there be any doubt whether other worldly beings exist. These space-crafts shall land indiscriminately in open spaces, some people will voluntarily board these crafts and will be transported elsewhere. This is all that I will say about this event. Anything else would be purely speculative. I have seen this vision time and time again. It is always the same, and now others are beginning to share the same insight. There is no doubt in my mind that this will manifest.

Deluge

The Florida peninsula will become inundated by flood waters unlike any time in its history. The city of Miami and nearby municipalities will no longer be there. Florida's land mass will literally be cut in half due to the waters forth coming. Only those who fail to comply will perish during the deluged.

Frozen Cities

Portions of New York City, Detroit, Saint Paul, Indianapolis, Ohio, Philadelphia, Virginia, North Carolina, and Washington, DC. Will become frozen coffins for many unfortunate souls. These cities will suffer unprecedented cold temperatures, snow and freezing rains, followed by major power outages.

There will be a late winter storm in 2013 to hit southeast cities of Atlanta, Columbia, and Birmingham.

Assassination Attempt

There will be an unsuccessful assassination attempt on President Obama's life in or near the White House lawn by a trusted insider along with others, in late winter or early summer of 2013. Obama will survive, but he will be wounded and hospitalized from a gunshot to the back area.

Earth Changes

Significant earth changes will occur both from the inside and outside of the atmosphere. Soon there shall appear two sun-like objects in the night sky whereby all can see. Expect a huge earthquake to rock Mexico City, killing hundreds of thousands.

Japan will sink beneath the sea, as will parts of Indonesia and Hong Kong, China.

The Next President (2016) of US

The next elected president of the United States will be a woman. I can, but won't provide a name of this person. But I will tell you this: she will be a white democrat, but it won't be Hillary Clinton.

The Republican party will disband by the end of the next decade due to infighting, a dying electorate, and racial overtones.

About Art of Prophesying

There are many books floating around about what is to come; a few of these I find very creditable and I believe the authors are gifted with the art of prophecy, while many others are well off base. When it comes to prophecy few are willing to be more detailed about the information they give. This could be out of fear of being ridiculed, publicly. You see, everybody has the gift of prophecy, but not everyone understand the art of prophecy. A lack of information is the culprit, whether it is because of those with the knowledge refuse to share with others, or simply because some people choose not to believe. Belief is the key to all things in nature. Without it nothing happens...

Meditation: Doorway to Prophecies

There are so many reasons to make meditation a part of your daily rituals, and fortunately all of them are good. But before I begin laying out for you information that I have seen about future events, and that is basically what seeing into the future means (another source of information), I want you to know by what mechanism I am able to do this. Most of you can do this too, maybe even better than I can, simply because there is no monopoly on the art of prophecy but, there is a monopoly on information showing how to go about achieving this task.

Meditation is a doorway to prophecies because it helps you to open up your pineal gland, or third-eye, and for that reason, among many others, is why I meditate on a regular basis. Meditation also helps me to deal with life's issues, it keeps me healthy and safe from negative vibrations. At times I am able to receive information about things I want to know that are otherwise unknown to me. There is no need to go further into the art of meditation other than this brief introduction because there is a full chapter dedicated to meditation in this book.

Energy

Energy is a mystery in and of itself. Additionally, it's the most abundant resource available in the entire known universe, and, as far as anyone knows, this holds true for all of creation. Energy can be found and accessed everywhere, anytime, even within the deeper regions of space, there is some type of energy present. Here's the thing about this mysterious force known as energy.... no one really knows exactly where energy comes from, where it resides, or how it is made? Ask any scientist: "where does energy come from?" He or she, will most likely say: energy is the one thing that can't be created, nor destroyed, it can only be used or transformed.

In physics, energy is simplistically defined as an ability to do work. This explanation is often expanded to include these words: power and force. But, even within the previous definition there is no mentioning of where it comes from. Therein lies the enigma. The origin of the word energy (energia; pronounced: inner he-yah); like almost that of every scientifically based word, has both Latin and Greek roots, respectively, which continues a time tested tradition amongst research professionals' egarness for assigning a Latin or Greek name to the things they know very little about. Today, energy has become closely associated with, and is thought of as being attainable from one of the following resources found in this world; such as oil, coal, nuclear power and natural gas, all of which, once converted produce electricitity, heat and/or motion. There is also renewable or green sources of energy generated by wind, water, and solar radiation. Obviously these types of energies are used and designed to make life more comfortable by controlling home and work environments, and transporting people from one place to another.

Renewable energy sources offer the prospect of clean air and a pollution free environment, but, these alternative use of green power still foster a controllable mechanism in the hands of national governance, oligopolies, multinational-corporations and/or local governments. Economically speaking, this is very unfortunate for the rest of mainstream society. While the afforementioned types of known energy remains dominant and prominently in the hands of few, there is also other, less known, rarely mentioned forms of energy that is growing in demand. But even these forms of energy will likely fall into a dubious categaory known as pseudo-energy, mainly because they are less understood and controllable by a few well placed operatives, and are based almost exclusively on bio-energy, and are not recognized by mainstream science or academia for that purpose. Also, researching or backing controversial forms of energy carries with it a certain amount political and professional risks.

The point being made here is that there is an unlimited, alternate source of energy available for myriad purposes, that's freely available and accessable to anyone willing to explore its use. And yet, perceptions about there being a limited amount of resources , especially pertaining to energy persists in the mind of many.

What is Bio-Energy?

Many people have come to think of energy only in terms of something that can be physically measured by some type of instrument, stored and then processed using oil, electricity, coal, and this includes renewable energy like solar, wind, water and plant based ethanol. While each of these types of energies are unquestionably possible in terms of mechanical and technical know-how, they still fall way short in potentiality when compared to that of human generated energy, which unknowingly, comes in abundance and is only dependable, but very powerful, too. Bio-energy, also known as human generated energy, is the greatest untapped resource, which is infinitely abundant and available in human history. The only problem with this source of energy seems to be a lack of knowledge on behalf of everyone, with few

116

exceptions for those who have unintentionally discovered how to tap into it.

Metaphysically speaking, bio-energy (human energy field) is best defined as an invisible force of vital power that facilitates the conditions for life to exist, be it by way of a vibration, or soundwave frequency, that eventually cause matter to clump together, among other circumstances, allowing work of some kind to be done. When deployed in a healing capacity, this vital force of energy has been known to manifest miraculous recoveries from some of life's most deadliest diseases (see Healing Powers).

Human Energy Fields

Another type of energy not mentioned at all by some of the most prestiges medical programs in the United States and select European universities is the existence of what has been described by some new-age physicists as a human energy field. Nevertheless, there is a small, but growing cottage community of registered nurses and other medical professionals, who have began applying their knowledge of traditional treatment with bio-energy, better known as human energy fields, are among a list of options being offered to patients. The existence of the human or bio-energy fields and its possible applications for use has wide spread potential for a number of industries unrelated to the medical profession. There is now a concerted effort by a few scientists to do more research into this natural and abundant energy resource. The problem many of them face is that their findings are still met with organized skepticism from the rank and file members of their respective profession.

One such academically trained professional, the late medical doctor and psychiatrist, Dr Shafica Karagulla, author of Chakras & the Human Energy Fields, conducted a series of experiments into human energy fields and virtually came away convinced of its effectiveness in healing conditions and diseases once thought untreatable. Of course, there are other research professionals, of late, who are involved at the moment examining the efficacy of human energy fields, but, and a 'BIG' one at that, not at the expense of becoming ostracized by their peers and losing one's livelyhood.

While there are enough books on the subject matter readily available on the open market, along with the efforts of psychics and Shamans to study this growing phenomena to validate earlier findings by a courages few, the problem facing widespread use of this abundant source of energy still remains the same...a lack of acknowledgment from mainstream academia. As a result human energy fields (bio-energy) remains a mystery. But one things for sure, everyone has one.

Chi-energy

Chi-energy (spelled and pronounced Qi, in Asia) represents a vital force that sustains all life forms. Chi-energy is very powerful, it can be repurposed for various tasks, and yet, it is least understood by all except a fortunate few. Acupuncturists use their knowledge of chi-energy when placing needles at strategic locations on a patients body for treatment. In China, the practice of channeling Chi-energy to perform a variety of tasks, including strength building and healing has been in use for at least 5,000 years (depending upon whom you ask).

In some regions of Asia, practitioners of Chi-energy are said to be able to stop bullets with their bare hands, set things afire without an igniting source, and do incredible martial-arts type stunts that would make any special effects coordinator envious. Personally, I view Chi-energy as primordial, an uncreated force of nature, demonstrable in the hands and mind of those who have gained a working knowledge of its existence, and know how to tap into it.

As a young man, I began using Chi-energy as a means of demonstrating my ability to withstand physical pain, and to break bricks using my bare hands or head. I also defied gravity at times by jumping over the heads of several people at the same time. While such feats made me popular at school and among friends, not once did it ever occur to me that the greatest use of this energy was in healing the sick and/or wounded. Now that I'm much older and a little wiser, my use of Chi-energy is more strategically applied.

Case in point. The story you are about to read is based entirely on truth from my perspective. Take from this what you will.

The year and exact date of this story is being with held out of respect. It all began when my wife and I were staying overnight at the house of a close friend, who had just become engaged to marry a guy that she had a long and intimate relationship with. Since my wife and I were in town vacationing and I agreed that we would spend more time with her close friend, and this involved staying overnight and sleeping in a spare bedroom.

As in some situations that starts out well, people tend to celebrate good news while also drinking alcoholic beverages, and this occasion was no different. Since I have never consumed alcoholic beverages, and my wife drinks socially, it is safe to say that the two of us were very well mannered when we decided to call it a day, and turn in for the night. At some point in the wee hours of the morning, my wife and I were suddenly awakened from a deep sleep by the soon to be groom as he burst open the bedroom, running across the room and into an adjacent bathroom. Shortly there after, enters the bride to be, naked and crying out loudly, with both hands clutching a .45 magnum handgun. She then pointed the gun at the closed bathroom door where the groom lay hidding, firing off two rounds before quietly leaving the room.

Luckily for the groom, the bride to be was a terrible shooter. Not one round that she fired-off made contact. As such, he soon reemerged, entering a hallway leading toward the part of the house where the bride was waiting to take another crack at him. And once again, his actions put both my wife and I in harms way as he ran toward us, and away from his temporarily deranged bride. All three of us began desparately trying to pry open a nearby window to escape possible gun fire. The enraged bride began firing off more shots, but this time a bullet hit my left lower leg, bouncing off of it before finally falling to the floor.

Note:

Recently I discovered that humans can summon enough electrical energy from within themselves to re-charge a battery, size not withstanding. I do this feat myself when my remote control batteries need replacing. The thing is, it doesn't matter if the batteries are re-chargeable or not, they'll still take a charge from your inner Chi-energy. This has now been confirmed by European scientists, but is still doubtful among American scientists. Just imagine being able to re-charge all of your electronics without buying more batteries!

Energy Fields

Energy fields are invisible, nonphysical structures that exist everywhere through out the universe. We don't readily see these energy fields with our naked eyes but, they are detectable with our nonphysical sight or third eye, which is believed to be aided by the pineal gland.

Energy of some sort surrounds us contantly, permeating and penetrating the molecular structure of our entire body. Energy fields makes it possible for all communications technologies such as wireless cellphones, radios, televisions and satellites to work.

This is why NASA is able to send space crafts from earth to the far regions of the solar system and beyond, maintaining control and communicating with these unmanned crafts. Unbeknownst to many is that the agency has discovered a way to make use of energy fields to supply its unmanned space crafts with an unlimited source of fuel. No one has ever asked how can a space craft travel to the end of the solor system on one tank of fuel, while vehicles here on earth can't travel 500 miles without running out of fuel? If you think about it for a moment, the existence of energy fields typifies what is true and observable since everything is interconnected to everything else. I believe this is the reason why telepathy, or the ability of mind-to-mind communications among humans and animals are real. The existence of energy fields of some kind is why psychic phenomena has a far reaching impact on our very existence, no matter how many times such powers are denied by scientists and are debunked by skeptics. It is time that we look beyond those in denial and move forward.

Books of Deception

(How Deep and How Wide is Your Rabbit Hole?)

There are basically three books of mass deception that permeates all countries and cultures worldwide. I have chosen for reasons of simplicity, familiarity and my comfort level to focus mainly on the Christian Bible and history in general. With that said, we will discuss other religions where needed because this situation applies to all historical books and vital records pertaining to humanity's origin, this include the most widely accepted dictionaries.

Although it was the first book ever produced by Johannes Gutenberg (born: 1398, died: February 3, 1468) with the advent of his invention; the world's first printing press; it still enjoys a status-quo as being the world's perennial best-selling book with well over 100 million plus in sales each year. Exactly how much of that volume is from actual sales versus that given away to charity remains a secret. The book that I am referring to of course, is non other than the holy bible.

The Holy Bible; as its most affectionately known; speaks volumes about all sorts of miraculous events that were called into action by numerous prophets of old, who were somehow endowed with very special powers to manipulate reality, and mysteriously enjoyed a direct and personal relationship with God, of which no one alive today is capable of doing. And since that time basically all of humanity has been taught, directly or through indirect channels, into believing that such activities alone, is now a reserved domain of a privileged few (the oligarchy), even though people of all cultures have been talking directly to God without the intervention of a middleman since the very beginning of intelligent life.

If biblical scriptures are to be taken literally (and this is the case for many converts), and placed into proper perspective, then the most amazing, prominent story of all times is that of Adam and Eve, which illustrates an incredulous event involving a three-way interpersonal relationship between a deity and its subjects, which all takes place in a mythical garden called Eden, at a geographical location still unknown to this day. But, lets say for the sake of simplification, that the garden of Eden refers to the earth itself. If so, this issue is resolved because you know earth is no myth.

According to the late Zecharia Sitchin, author of a series of books known as the Earth Chronicles, Eden was most likely a reference to a laboratory on board an advanced race of beings' spacecraft. He and German author Erich Von Daniken (Chariots of the Gods) ideas are somewhat similar, in that each believe humans are the result of genetic manipulation by other worldly or inter-dimensional beings, who just happen to be far more advanced than we are.

The Bible used as a historical reference manual, even quoting scriptures from it is not absolute, for there are numerous versions of the Holy Bible in circulation which means that all of them claim to be the authoritative one.

The Old Testament (the Pentateuch or the books of Moses), consists of 39 books written mostly in Hebrew and Aramaic 1000 BCE and 100 CE. The New Testament, written mostly in Greek consists of 27 books and includes books from the Old Testament.

The word Bible is Latin from Greek *biblia*, meaning books. Most Christians consider the Bible as the world's oldest history book. Even though there are many contradictions inherent in the old and new testaments, and plenty of reasons to doubt the authorship from Moses to the gospels, and there are many that believe in every word ever written in the book known as the Bible, literally. The problem with such blind faith is that no matter what new evidence that comes forward which casts a doubt on numerous aspects of the Bible, such diehards are too programmed to absorb any worthwhile updates.

Genesis

Genesis (the beginning), among other things, records the story of Adam and his second wife, Eve (Lilith was Adam's first wife of record, according to the apocryphal texts), Noah, Abraham, Isaac, Jacob and Joseph. Purportedly the story of Genesis traces human history from the very beginning of time, the advent of the universe, the making of the stars, galaxies, solar system, the sun and planets, and lastly earth. Genesis is strictly told from a Christian's point of view, as being a literal account about something quite extraordinary and unique.

Lets just say for the purpose of simplicity, that the garden of Eden story is a true account of humanity's beginning, that it is literally the actual location on earth. Where humans (both male and female) were created by God--according to the book of Genesis, which was, by the way, purportedly written and authored by Moses himself. Advancing further into the story of Adam and Eve to the episode where Cain murdered his brother Abel, we learned that the end result of Cain's aggression transpired into his being evicted, rather, he was forced out of paradise and exiled into unknown lands existing elsewhere. But then, something miraculous occurred, instead of being cursed or reprimanded, Cain was blessed with the companionship of a woman, who just happened to be living on lands outside of paradise. Later it would be revealed that there were hundreds, perhaps thousands more humans living and flourishing in these strand and uncharted lands. You have to ask yourself this question, where did these people come from?

Now for those who hold words written in the bible as being inspired by God, then story of earth's first inhabitants accurately describes without fault exactly how humans came into existence. But, for inquiring minds this is the first inkling where the storyline of the bible completely fails to deliver, mainly because there are simply too many questions that go unanswered. For instance, there is no actual record edged in stone anywhere inside the pyramids which specifically corroborate the Adam and Eve story.

Considering the fact that archeologists were able to discern a treasure trove of information from hieroglyph inscriptions found on the walls inside the temples and pyramids. These image based writings were said to have been created by the God named, Thot. According to the belief of the Egyptian people who lived during the time the pyramids were most likely built. For instance, we know how they lived and died, we know what foods they ate, we know how they dressed, how they loved, who they worshiped. But, and a big one at that, we still don't know who built these great monumental displays and for what purpose. By the way, did you know that the word hieroglyph means, God's word?

The greatest unknown fact about the Pyramids, regardless of their location, is that they were somehow built from the top down-to-ground first, well over 10,000 years ago at a time when humans were clearly not that technologically advanced. And when you realize that the wheel had not yet been invented, then the question beckons to be asked, how did they manage to build these things? What I'm saying is this, based upon where the pyramids are, in relation to where the stones where manufactured, there's just no way Egyptians or any other culture for that matter, could have built them, let alone lift them into place using slave-labor, ropes, trees. Where talking about a task that not even today's engineers would be challenged to duplicate or build pyramids to rival the ones already before us. And then the question becomes: what were they for?

Reverting back to the story of the world's first family makes you realize is that it simply has too many large holes in it to provide a complete understanding. For instance, where did the woman whom Cain would eventually marry come from, especially since the bible states that there were only four people living in the world at that time, which consisted of three men and one woman, and one male was later killed?

As a child, who was so eagerly in search of answers to many questions which seemed so obviously lacking in substance from the stories being read to me, actually resulted in getting me banned from Sunday school services. So, it was at an early age when first I came to blows with the first rule of an imperialistic society.

124

Imperialism is the best way to describe what is known nowadays as the NEW WORLD ORDER. Whether you believe in conspiracy theories or not, one rule governing body for the entire world is already here...

Now, if the story of Adam and Eve seems somewhat suspect to you too, it doesn't end there? When you scrutinize the story of Moses, given his upbringing, of being raised as an Egyptian royal family member, which most likely meant that he spent his youthful years as one of many privileged students who were being taught and trained in deep secrets of the universe by priests and priestesses in the mystery schools of Egypt.

The mystery schools of Egypt would eventually become known as Universities. Because the core curriculum for their students were steep in alchemy, the cosmos and the true nature of human origins here on earth, and about the sun gods, spirits, reincarnation, alternate realities and much more than historians are inclined to comment on. Knowledge gained by these students are not a part of any public, nor private school teachings anywhere else in the world today, except for the schools being run by secret societies; which by the way, are not known to even exist by the general public.

Getting back to the bible, there is one glaring glitch in the assertions given the time-line of Genesis, the problem is that the bible's attempt at detailing a positive spin to Moses' prime years, growing up as a teenager, basically omits about 18 years of information. The math just doesn't add up!

Granted, all that we are told about him when reading the bible is that he was drawn from the waters of the Nile, and raised among the Pharaohs as if he was one of them. Suddenly, as the story goes, Moses becomes a young adult, and sometime shortly thereafter he falls out of favor with the ruling powers of Egypt when he kills a task master to save the life of a Hebrew slave, Joshua. And so, the story of Moses begins and ends very mysteriously.

Various cultures outside of Europe and the African continent, such as the Mayans, Incas, and the Australian Aborigines just might posses a more lengthier and richer history on earth than any other culture. But, as in most instances of abuse, world history, including that of religion, is a view imposed upon the rest of society by a very powerful and dominant minority, and is simply force-fed to everyone else by means of covert actions and fear. In fact, most laypersons reading the bible failed to realize that the account of Adam and Eve, as told in the bible, is the story of one family, as measured in linear fashion. This doesn't mean certain aspects of the story did not occur, it simply implies that if you were to look beyond all the rhetoric, then the most widely accepted book of Christendom are based around words written in the bible, which was clearly sanctioned by both politicians and religious clergymen of its time. This is reason alone, why inquiring minds will always have reservations and many questions as it pertains to religion doctrine and religious based books in particular, and that such questions will always remain unanswered.

Quite simply, the bible, as well as other religious texts of the same era were not meant to fill the intellectual appetite of those who think outside the norm, no evidence suggests that such works were from the start targeted toward a society of low intelligence.

Whatever your religious persuasion may or may not be, it should be noted that no one (religion) has a monopoly on God's ability to respond and manifest miracles on behalf of those who may not even be religious at all, nor believe that God exist. God is god to everyone or thing without exception or expectation. If this weren't the case, then no one would ever have reason for hope, redemption, and forgiveness.

Deep down inside everyone of us is an undeniable belief in something, a source much higher than that of ourselves...we don't know what this source is, or even care to know, but we all feel that something is there. Even people of science sometimes find this instinctive knowing to be very confusing within their ranks.

Even so, at the behest of academia, their profession and peers, many in the world of science are taking a leap of faith when going public with such personal revelations about what they fell is the true existence of a God presence, which permeates and resurface time and time again during many tightly controlled examinations. What this says to the layperson is that God has been found to exist in the laboratory of some of the world's foremost think tanks. Exactly why that is, remains the greatest mystery of all time.

Personally, I have always known that deep within me, something is there. To me, that something is way more than plain ole' luck, or intelligence based upon logical reasoning. That something has helped me to overcome many obstacles that were placed in my path. Keep in mind, I am not saying that certain challenges will never occur again in my life, because, after all I am still human. However, what I am saying is that whatever unknown circumstances are placed before me, I'm prepared to handle... Because finally, I've come to the realization that each obstacle before me, is a creation from within my own train of thoughts, and I take full ownership of them...

Religious Experience

The following scenario happens repeatedly somewhere in the world, almost daily. I've had first-hand knowledge of what you are about to be introduced to---just in case such an event has slipped your consciousness.

Imagine meeting a total stranger at some shopping mall. The first thing you notice about this person is that there seems to be a glow about their face. Indeed, this glow sort of reminds you of a halo, sort of like those depicted around angels. In your mind, you liked this person right away. The two of you connect and exchange pleasantries, eventually striking up a conversation during which you soon discover that this person had a religious experience, or awakening. As the conversation continues you notice how happy this person seems to be when telling you about their former life of crime, or hard-times, and that since they are now reborn and saved by Jesus, and now they plan to spend the remainder of their life serving the lord (strange still, is how little many of these people know the true definition of the word: Lord).

Suddenly, this person's life has changed for the better, as they now spend a great deal of their spare time spreading the gospels to anyone who'd lend an ear. Sincere in their mind, they have become experts of biblical scriptures and the word of God. One can't in good conscience, help but feel very good for people like this, simply because deep down inside all of us, lies the vibrations of love. But then comes one eventful day, about a year or two down the road, when you run into that same person again. Only this time, you realize that there is no longer a glow about their face. Further inquiry later reveals that this person has reverted back to the ways of old, and no longer preaches the word of God to people they meet. You gotta ask within the silence of your inner self, what happened?

Speaking strictly from a point of observation, some people have experienced such a bad life, for whatever reasons there may have been for this to materialize in their life. So, all of a sudden they have reached a breaking point. A moment where reality and all its illusions seems to become crystal clear. When this happens, several options are usually considered:

1. they give themselves totally (mind, body and spirit) to a religious experience, and are usually reborn again into a certain faith,
2. or contemplate suicide,
3. or simply give up hope of a better life altogether.

A great number of people who find themselves in a similar situation often choose the first option, but, not even this choice becomes permanent, as you will learn. Sometimes after declaring themselves born again Christians, the tendency is to also believe rightly or wrongly, thinking of themselves as the only authority on the matter of God and religion. At that moment, in no way do they realize that no one has a monopoly on God, and that religion itself is a creation of man. For many of these people, what they've experienced during a brief moment of conscious clarity and inward bliss, should hold true for everyone else yet to undergo such a revelation. And, while all of these people mean well, they also fail to realize that such an event is somewhat different for everyone who undergo a similar religious experience. In other words an awakening will be different for everyone.

Reading/interpreting Scriptures

Reading biblical scriptures has become a daunting task, even for theologians and seminary students. What meaning these words hold for those of us today requires quite a bit of insight and continuous study. It would be quite foolish of me to omit information referenced in the bible specifically about the metaphysical, esoteric and spiritual matters, especially any sayings purportedly uttered by Yeshua. But this seems to be the case among many scholars and historians. Misquoting Jesus is a common abuse that I find most unsettling as it pertains to biblical scriptures, which more often than not allow for a wide range of interpretations even among theologians and others who spend a lot of time reading, studying and researching not only the bible, but other religious documents as well.

For instance, misinterpretations and misquotes of bible scriptures were often used to justify slavery and inhuman treatment of non-whites in America, Europe and South Africa. And to some degree, even though its frowned upon publicly, is no longer practiced in plain-sight anymore, such teachings are still encouraged within certain religious sects and secret societies around the world.

The point I am making here is that the bible can be and is often misused against low information types for selfish reasons by anyone with an audience and is willing to do it. So then, it is what it is, after nearly twenty-six years of conducting independent research into the nature of the mind, metaphysics and psychic phenomena notwithstanding; and attending various lectures around the country, engaging into endless conversations with virtually anyone tuned into the mysteries and nature of consciousness, and life in general.

I have formed this hypothesis, rightly or wrongly so, that the kingdom of heaven (which is basically consciousness or mind) does indeed exist, and that its miraculous powers are always within reach of everyone, if only they knew how to access it. For the truth be told, the kingdom of heaven is not a geographical location on earth or some other planet, nor is it a universal region to be found somewhere in space or time. In fact there never has been, nor will there ever be such a place of purely a physical existence. But rather, the kingdom of heaven does exist as an alternate state (or realm), that can only be found within the infinity and vastness of each individual mind.

References to the kingdom of heaven and its exact location can be found within the teachings from some of the worlds oldest and continuously practiced religions (Hinduism-20,000 years old) which was established eons before the advent of Judaism (4,000 years old); Islam (1,400 years old); and Christianity (2,000 years old) combined; all state that kingdom can only be accessed from within the individual self, not without. Only upon the founding of Islam and Christianity did heaven become a physical and specific location other than that within the mind. Might I remind you that even to this day and time, nearly 4,000 years later, the bulk of devout Christians and Muslims alike, have no idea as to exactly where that is. For if they did know, it is very likely that human suffering would have ended a very long time ago. In fact humanity would have long rid itself of competition based economics for the control of energy and other natural resources that are incorrectly deemed as scarce.

From my perspective, now that I have dedicated the remainder of my physical life to practicing spirituality. The kingdom of heaven can only be found in one place only, and that place is within the mind of each individual being, but, its not just within a human mind that I am talking about, for this ideal includes a universal mind. This means that the mind itself is an omniscient, omnipotent and infinite entity of eternal means. And with this new found belief, knowledge and acceptance, I have begun a process of discovering and understanding more about the mysteries of life and reality than all of my previous years combined, while at the same time collecting more data about truths, possibilities and strength, of an infinitely powerful force that lies within deeper regions of my being. Even though I've grown a lot spiritually there still more to learn. A much deeper knowledge and understanding of humanity's purpose would seemingly explain the intricate relationships and, the interconnectedness of mind to all things within space and space-time continuum. In a sense, it is the allusiveness of the substance we call space that should intrigue us the most. Of space itself, we know least about it, what role it plays in the grand scheme of things that we believe and think of as reality? Think about it for a moment! Is there any place or thing where space doesn't exist?

At this point in time, since you are obviously still reading this book, maybe your intellectual curiosity will allow you to go much deeper into this content. For the sake of humanity, it is my hope and dream, that at some moment in time, within the immediate future, we can finally shed all invisible barriers that are holding us back, convincing us to believe in such fabricated historical untruths for the purpose of political and/or religious gains, that we'll simply tune-out truth in favor a false ideology of God, the universe and humans ability and role altogether.

Documentation

Many of the very same people who believe authenticity of the bible would find it hard-pressed to learn that there is more physical evidence supporting the existence of extraterrestrial beings and UFOs than there are in support of what is written in the bible, especially as it pertains to Yeshua ben-hur (Jesus' birth name). And yet, we are told to have faith in what is represented in the bible in regards to its truthfulness and validity, that religious scriptures have not been compromised by man, and biblical scriptures were inspired by God, and authored by prophets of the old Hebrew Pentateuch and disciples of Yeshua thereafter.

Numerous documents like the Dead Sea Scrolls, were unearthed within the last 100 years; which purportedly provide an indication of Yeshua's presence during the time frame mentioned in the bible. But these documents are only made available to those of a certain stature or secret membership for an up close examination. The public at large will never be allowed to scrutinize such specimens, nor review other findings without viewing them through the lens of a glass enclosure. Take for instance, a recent announcement by Karen King, a Harvard Divinity school trained scholar, released to the press the discovery of a papyrus; which seems to confirm what new-age gurus have said all along, that Yeshua was married, which also means that he enjoyed earthly pleasures just like everyone else... Within a week of Karen's press release to the world, the Vatican pounced upon her with a full media bliss from all corners of Christendom in an effort to discredit the findings.

There is no doubt that Karen will face the wrath of the church. Most likely from this point forward she will never again attain another research grant to continue her work. Why? Because such revelations indicates that Yeshua was human after all, but in no way does this negate the supernatural aspect of his abilities. I, for one, believe that Yeshua was the most gifted psychic to ever walk the earth. But I have always intuitively suspected that his life's story had been taken over by the powers that be in an effort to continuously withhold the truth.

Neither you nor I will ever get a chance to examine any of these findings up close, which means society must continuously depend upon the integrity of those who rule from the shadows of darkened rooms to interpret information pertaining to religion, human history, and the real nature of God. This is something I will never come to terms with.

As I began closely examining history books and religious scriptures with a scholarly effort, I soon discovered quite a few startling facts, which seems to be continuously overlooked by many who profess to know and study human history and biblical scriptures regularly.

The following questions are front and center on my list:
1. who actually wrote and authored the following books of the bible: Genesis, the Gospels, and Revelation?
2. Why is King James I name featured on the Christian bible?

3. Based upon the evidence, why is there no acknowledgment of UFOs in the bible as well as other religious books when they were clearly referenced in them?
4. What role did politics have in authoring the bible?

5. Why did authors of the bible conspire against women, characterizing them as being witches, or involved in sorcery, even prostitution? Why do other religions encourage inhuman treatment of women?
6. What impact, if any did alien intervention have on worldwide catastrophes?
7. Why doesn't the bible account for Moses and Yeshua's 18 missing years?

The story time-line formula for both Moses and Jesus sounds very similar; even though they occurred centuries apart. From birth to approximately age 30, their whereabouts are virtually unknown. Hmm! Look at it this way, two of the most important figures in bible history, representing freedom from oppression and a promise of ever lasting life, and no one seems to recall anything about their youthful years... Go figure!

Why the Bible is such a Powerful Book?

The bible, as well as most religion based books, are very powerful because each are deeply encoded in ancient metaphysical knowledge that has been hidden from the majority of humanity awareness by those who rule. Based entirely upon your level of understanding when reading the bible for yourself, instead of simply following along as scriptures and interpretations are being read to you by a priest or pastor, determines greatly the message your subjective mind receives about the real esoteric or metaphysical value inherent within. You see, the ancients were far more advanced than we are, and they also knew much more than modern science is willing to acknowledge.

Withholding real meanings and interpretations of all ancient religious materials has been helped along with the acceptance of Aristotle's dichotomy of dualism of which fear and greed, the dominance of materialism has delayed humankind's evolution and growth into spiritualism. The concept of dualism shaped the mental faculties of society into seeing God as a physical being overlooking human affairs from a mythical place called heaven, which was in sharp contrast to the philosophies inspired by Yeshua. And for these activities, Yeshua bin hur was murdered and turned into the world's most misquoted martyr and misunderstood prophet of all time.

By way of repetitiveness by the world's dominant religions, dualism and all its components have been imprinted into the subjective mind of humankind. This line of thinking over the years is chiefly responsible for the creation of demonic thought-forms such as the one we call Satan (aka devil) and his demons, which gained worldwide momentum with the creative writing and imagination of Italian poet Dante Alighieri's Divine Comedy, and was covertly endorsed by Pope Boniface. Not only did Dante create the image of Satan, he also depicted what hell looks like. The overwhelming success of Divine Comedy changed dramatically the way ordinary people perceive religion and esoteric matters to this day.

Now here's something else to think about! The image of Jesus was also sanctioned by the Vatican when Pope Alexander Vi hired Leonardo da Vinci to paint a portrait of his son, Cesar Borgia (1475 - 1507), to represent the image of Jesus. Inquiring minds must ask this question: in a land of dark skinned people (Northeast Africa), how is it that Jesus was born with blond hair and blue eyes? The only way to make this story stick is to insinuate that Mary was a virgin, who was miraculously impregnated by God! But the truth behind the images of Jesus which has been hypnotically pushed into the subjective-mind level of consciousness of most, if not all religious conservatives the world over. Stranger still is why almost no one of authority from countries that host other religions other than Christianity ever dispute these images of Jesus.

Now, does this suggest that Jesus did not exist? No it doesn't, because intuitively I believe he did. Nor, does my opinion imply that Jesus was black, either. But it does bring into focus a myriad of lies and inconsistencies which are at the very foundation of the church's main argument about the life and times of the man known as Jesus in Christendom. For inquiring minds, the image of Christianity's version of Jesus fits right in line with the beliefs and hidden knowledge of the power elite.

You see, unbeknownst to most academically trained historians, who are deeply programmed to never challenge acceptable ideas of the establishment, the image of a blond-haired, blue-eyed Jesus is really a generalized description of a Nordic sun-god.

Sun-gods is the least mentioned topic within all religions the world over, even though secretly they are worshiped by them. What better way to continue a hidden tradition by utilizing an image of a sun-god as that of Jesus. Furthermore, mummified remains of giant sun-gods with blond-hair and blue-eyes have been unearth on almost every region of the earth, especially among the white Pyramids of China, where nearly 500 mummies of sun-gods have been found. But the public at large will never be told of these findings simply because it invites people to ask: what else is being purposefully withheld?

Jesus never read the Bible, but he did recite quotes from the Book of Enoch.

Rodh de Sailor

Ancient Metaphysical Knowledge
(That shaped Religion)

Nearly 90% of the world's population has ever heard of such things as the "Epic of Creation (evolution)" nor the Rosetta stone, so they don't have any idea how these ancient relics are somewhat responsible for shaping what they believe about religion. The Epic of creation is considered by many to be the world's first and oldest bible. Arguably the Epic of Creation, which was written in cuneiform, is at least 14 million years old. Many stories of the bible are very similar to those told within the Epic's cosmic narrative of planetary, creation of humans and cultural evolution. The Rosetta stone is essentially an Egyptian decree presumably passed by priests, which inscribes in stone the same phrases in various ancient languages. As with the Epic of Creation no one really knows how old it is or how it was made. The mysteriousness concerning these two ancient relics is not known by the public, but anyone would be amazed to learn that both of these ancient relics are indestructible by any means available to modern man. Furthermore the full scope of information these relics posses is kept in total secrecy.

We do know this, that there are a number of scientists, for instance, who have researched and documented the existence of psychic phenomena and its various associated skills such as telepathy, or mind to mind talk at a distance without the means of any technology or drug enhancement. So it is safe to say, skeptics aside, that PSI has been proven to exist in laboratory testing under very restricted conditions for at least the past 80-plus years or so within the United States alone.

The Original Prince of Peace

Many countries outside the US readily accept the existence of psychic phenomena, their acceptance dates as far back as 2600 – 6,000 years BC, back to the era of ancient Egyptian philosopher and mystic known as Imhotep. Ironically, Imhotep is also a long lost name to most historians whether on purpose or design.

It is widely believed that Imhotep lived for more than 3,000 years as a physical human being. It is also believed that Imhotep taught secrets of magic to Greek philosophers such as Themistoclea, who in turn taught Pythagoras, whom many speculate was his only known sister. And, it was Pythagoras who would later coined the word: 'philosophy,' which, at the time meant one who wants to know things. Pythagoras passed his wealth of knowledge on to others, started a movement and later founded a school that specialized in teaching students about mysteries of the kingdom (aka: tapping into the source) and, how to make use of the forces from within themselves to create or manifest things into physical reality.

The oracles of Delphi--as they were known, were widely recognized for their knowledge of the *Universal Source*. These oracles, and Greek prophets were mostly women, all carried the same name of Sybil. Lessor known among these women due to history's injustice were Themistoclea, Pythia, and later Hypatia, each were sought-out by Greek, Roman, and Asian politicians alike for their powers of foresight abilities, which, as a source of non-traditional information was extremely reliable and accurate.

Fast forward into today's modern era, there is very little references, or information made available to the public at-large about one of the world's greatest prophet, miracle worker and philosopher of ancient times. The name Imhotep (mentioned earlier) of Egypt is known only to a very select group of scholars, researchers, high-priests and mystics. It is a growing belief within the modern reintroduction of new-age and spiritually enlightened communities that Jesus (Yeshua, in his native language) was a reincarnation of Imhotep. Imhotep was often referred to by earlier Egyptian scholars and high priests alike as the original 'Prince of Peace,' simply because Imhotep routinely performed medical miracles while healing the poor, and produced real magic before thousands of witnesses more than 2,600 years before the birth of Jesus.

It is also a historical belief and speculation that a young Jesus was reintroduced to the mysteries of the kingdom from within and without (black magic in those days), while living and growing up abroad in Egypt--studying under the auspices of Egypt's mystics, taught by high priests and priestesses.

Open-minded people should find it very strange and peculiar that modern historians, researchers and scholars alike, know next to nothing about the whereabouts of the most famous man in world history from the ages of 3 to 29 years old. Based solely upon the time-line provided in the Bible, we learned about the birth of Jesus and, then virtually nothing else at all is mentioned about him until he was nearly 30 years old.

Anyway you look at it (or spin it) the missing years of Jesus' earlier life provides for much speculation among biblical scholars, conspiracy theorists and skeptics alike---and yet it is no secret that almost all prophets of the biblical era received their knowledge base and training about the mysteries of the Kingdom, directly or indirectly from the high priests and sorcerers of Egypt. Which, subsequently, survived the downfall of Sumeria and the destruction of Atlantis. Atlantis and Lemuria; two very advanced civilizations that once existed on earth, suddenly vanished without a trace---as they say, that's another subject in and of itself. I'll conclude this paragraph simply by saying, "intuitively, I know that they did exist."

Hidden Knowledge

It began in ancient Egypt, and Sumer; based upon recorded data; where efforts to hide the keys of knowledge were launched, forbidding ordinary people from knowing the truth. Jesus spoke about this event in the Gospels of Mary (an apocryphal book). Jesus said: "The Pharisees have taken the keys of knowledge and hidden them." For those of the kingship and upper echelons within their respective societies. I believe that this is when and why the priesthood was formed; and, later a cast system which openly discriminated against the poor and uninformed. These priests basically served as gatekeepers of the *Source*.

In other areas of the lower African continent, shamans rose to prominence among the many tribes that were spread far and wide across the land. The shamans and priests had one thing in common, which was to control the minds (soul) of their people, and to keep them working on behalf of the elites, building structures for the storage of raw goods and mining for precious minerals such as gold, silver and copper. In order to maintain control of the people they had to create a fictitious idol or image of the *Source* for them to worship in hopes of someday receiving salvation and a better life when they returned to innocence. While the lower continent Africans labored to their deaths in the mine fields for the glory of the Gods, those in Egypt were charged with constructing cities.

Early Egyptians witnessed first hand the awesome powers and abilities of those in knowledge of the *Source* because virtually all the pyramids were built by supernatural means. And since only the elite people of Egypt occupied these structures, many of them also possessed supernatural powers of godly origins. So, ordinary people were taught over time to worship those living high above the ground, as royalties, or direct stewards of the Source. To the rank and file of Egypt, the elites were lords, or better known today as gods.

Priests and mystics of Egypt eventually formed mystery schools to teach up and coming priests born within the ranks the ways of the *Source*, or, how to become sorcerers. These schools were open to other priesthoods beyond Egypt; as far away as Asia, Europe and the lower African continent.

Overtime, early Egyptians were influenced into believing in only one god, who was almighty, eternal and invisible, but watched over their activities constantly from atop certain skyward structures (pyramids). This all and powerful human deity was said to be the source of all things in existence. The Egyptians credited this human deity with uttering the first words ever spoken, the words from which creation became, a reality. Also, Egyptians would later assign a name to this awesome and powerful deity; the name became known as, "Thot."

Throughout time other names of human deities, or Source would emerge around the world within different cultures similar to that of the African continent. In the Americas, very similar occurrences to that of Egypt were taking place among its' original people. Structures that were too technically advanced for the people of the time to build were constructed by supernatural means. The rulers of the land withheld knowledge from those of its' commoners, thereby insuring that only those initiated by priests were taught how to access the *Source*.

There are obviously a lot of questions that comes to mind than I have answers for, so, what we are left with are hypothesis from scholars whose interpretations are somewhat politicized into conforming with that of an established paradigm. Our world has become accustomed to routinely accepting or misjudging newly discovered ideas that are deemed as unrealistic if it bucks the established trend, or simply does not fit in with the status quo. In the case of any religious findings that would shed a new light on the entire belief spectrum as to a true nature of god, or world history in general, or one that hints at the inner powers within the minds of all human beings, were easily pushed-off as mumblings of an unlearned society from much earlier times. Such are the impressions a formal history has placed on images of earlier societies as that of Egypt, South Africa, Australia's aborigines, and American natives. According to the status quo, these people simply did not exist, historically, that is. And likewise, as conventional thought goes, almost all of the world's knowledge originated from Europe.

Ancient Egyptians gave birth not only to the pharaohs, cause they were home to the original prophets of the old Bible testaments as well. In fact, it is common belief among many new age and spiritually based communities that the earliest instances of psychic phenomena, most likely came about as a result of some Egyptian priest's ability to access this source of power, and, were then able to demonstrate such abnormal abilities in the presence of others. These priests became known as sorcerers. The answer to any questions you may have can always be found, if you know where and how to look for them. For instance, human history, the story of creation and the life of Jesus as depicted by religion is absolutely wrong. There are enough holes in the theory of evolution and creation to write a second addition of the bible more voluminous than the one printed by Johannes Gutenberg and the Origin of Species written by Charles Darwin, combined.

Anyone with common sense and intelligence can see through the inconsistencies of creation depicted in the bible and the theory of evolution still being offered by Darwin, which is taught in schools and churches respectively to people at every level. And yet, each time a new finding or discovery that contradicts the established doctrine of both church and state becomes quickly quelled by special interest groups.

Religious Indoctrination
(Programming)

Religious indoctrination fulfills an innate primal need, a sort of code that is deeply rooted at the core belief of the inner consciousness of all human beings, which seems to verify one way or another that there is something out there much greater than ourselves, that is over looking all human affairs. It is because of this reason alone that religious indoctrination at such an early age has become the unwritten law of the land and is such a powerful tool for the church. Religious indoctrination is just another way of saying a person has been brainwashed overtime into a certain belief system. Harsh as this may sound, it is however an unspoken truth. A truly spiritually awakened person simply will not buy into any religious indoctrination programming, for he or she knows and accept the notion that whether good or bad, each individual is solely responsible for their own life's experiences as a result of the way they think. And yes, this means that there is no grand plan, your life is not predetermined. This doesn't mean that others can't construct your way of thinking, because they can, but only if you are unaware of it, which means subliminally you allow it to happen.

When my daughter was a little girl, growing up in the south, she wasn't exposed to religion by my wife and I. We had decided early on as parents that we would allow our daughter to choose for her self, whether or not, to accept or reject religion based on its own merits once she became of age. However, we did encourage her to believe in the existence of God and Jesus, for my wife often read bible stories to her. My daughter believes in God, not as a lone male figure overlooking all human affairs but, as a presence of uncreated energy existing everywhere, all at once in both space and time. She also understands that the real God is willing and capable of helping everyone good or bad, if it were called upon.

The decision not to program our daughter before she was old enough and intelligent enough to discern for herself whether or not to accept or reject religion was a sharp departure from the way many young people are raised by their parents, especially those living in religious sects, occults, or the the bible belt.

As for the false history that is continuously being taught in all schools, we didn't have much of a choice in the matter when it came time for our daughter to study this subject. But you can be sure that as a young adult, who was eager to find meaning in life, we often discussed history along with other topics in the comfort of our home.

When it comes to religion alone, most people, regardless of where they were born and raised, were preconditioned into the acceptance of certain religious denominations. At first, children are introduced to religion by their parents and/or guardians. Additionally, they all become programmed into culture and, to some extent, tradition by what I've termed as systemic programming. Basically, most people born into this world do not have the option of choosing from among themselves whether to accept or reject religion using their own intellect. In my view, preconditioning a child into a religious belief system is akin to mind-control and there's just no other way to describe this kind of ritual which has become so widespread and accepted as a normal human behavior for mainstream society.

So, out of concern and a deep love of freedom and free-will of mind, my wife and I made sure that this sort of early behavioral programming into the acceptance of religion one way or another just wouldn't apply to the one we love more than anything else in this world, our precious daughter.

My daughter was very fortunate to be born to parents with such understanding and open mindedness, but others are not so lucky. I know what many of them are faced with on the day in which they become inquisitive, and begin asking intelligent questions pertaining to the bible and religion. Some are encouraged to accept what they are told as truth, while others may simply trust what they hear from church pastors as a given. Nevertheless, at some point in life many of these unfortunate souls will just stop inquiring about the inconsistencies of events outlined in the bible because the answers they seek simply do not sound right.

Authoring the Bible

Here's the thing... If you receive all your information from a single source, and if that source is controlled by those who rule the world, how can you, in all honesty, trust that information?

Arguably the most read edition of the Christian bible is the King James I version. Its not that King James I actually wrote the version that bares his initials himself, but he did use the power of the thrown in an act of plagiarism. The KJV is simply a copy of the Geneva version with King James' name printed on its cover. I often wonder just how many devout Christians actually take the necessary time and effort to read their version of the bible from the beginning? For if they do they'd likely come across these words: TO THE MOST HIGH AND MIGHTY PRINCE, JAMES, BY THE THE GRACE OF GOD, KING OF GREAT BRITIAN, FRANCE, AND IRELAND. DEFENDER OF THE FAITH. Great and manifold were the blessings, most dread Sovereign, which Almighty God, the father of all mercies, bestowed upon us the people of England, when first he sent Your majesty's Royal Person to rule and reign over us. For whereas it was the expectation of many, who wished not well unto our Sion, that upon the settling of that bright Occidental Star, Queen Elizabeth... Virtually, this is a written decree by the royal family which states that they are the most high rulers of this world, and everyone else, by law, are their subjects. After all, we are living in the year of our lords, of which A.D. (Anno Domini) means in Latin. Most people seem to think that A.D. means after the death of Jesus, it does not. But it does imply that we are under the rule of kings, and queens.

The Bible

Even though the physical book itself didn't take shape; at least in the form of a printed book, especially in volume for centuries after the crucifixion of Yeshua. The very last book canonized in the bible, Revelations, still bares a fearful presence on the minds of strict Christian fundamentalists. An anonymous survey by researchers once revealed that the most educated members of society, along with those sufficient in fundamental literacy skills of communications; such as reading, writing, comprehension and math, if not already, are most likely to become victims of undetectable mind-control methods.

There are two topics of conversation people tend to shy away from and disagree with most: religion and politics. Could this be the X factor that is causing people to believe so mindlessly in a book, such as the bible or other religious based works, even when it is quite obvious, even common sense, that historical evidence suggests that the bible was sanctioned and authored by both politicians and bishops at the council of Nicea between the years 325 – 328 AD?

To those of us with an open mind-set, on the outside looking in, who view religion as the chief cause promoting all human suffering, both historically and in the present, realize that religion is the most powerful form of mind-control ever to be unleashed unto humankind, Period. Religious books, the bible in particular separates people from the truth of knowing that each are an aspect of God. There is no need in pointing fingers at any particular religion, especially when one considers that a countless number of people were mass murdered historically in the name of almost every religion on the planet at one time or another. For this reason, all are guilty as charged.

Sample Listings of lessor known Massacres (US) in the name of Religion:

1.   inquisition of Europe: total unknown,
2.   River Vale, New Jersey: September 28, 1778,
3.   Boston, Mass: May 1770,
4.   Lancaster, South Carolina: May 29, 1780,
5.   Gandenhutten, Ohio: March 8, 1782,
6.   Mountain Meadow, Colorado: September 11, 1857,
7.   Indian Territory, Washita, Massacre: November 27, 1868,
8.   Ludlow, Colorado: April 20, 1914,

People have been massacred everywhere in the world, in both communist and capitalist societies alike throughout history because of religious ideology. The Catholic church alone was responsible for killing more than 10 million people during the inquisition period, combined with the estimated 6 million Jewish people killed during the Holocaust, and the 70 million Chinese people that were annihilated by the regime of PRC chairman Mao Zedong, nearly 90 million people have been killed in the name of religion.

If God really is just a man after-all, then he should be fired for allowing such harm to be committed in his name. Now, this is not to imply that religions' impact on human behavior has been totally a very bad thing, nor, is it to conclude that religious minded people are not intelligent, easily manipulated, unethical and somewhat unsuspecting of their respective doctrines... This is just not the case at all. There is, however, no doubt in my mind that for all the massive killings committed during the inquisition that was perpetrated in the name of religion throughout the world, society has also benefited tremendously in many ways from it too.

What I am saying is that underneath it all, people are just as fallible as they ever were. As inherit in nature itself, people of all stripes and color seemingly harbor a deeply rooted, conscious emotional feeling, which can easily and willfully become attached to the idea of belonging to something much higher than themselves.

Such innate emotions gives those who buy into it eternal hope and salvation in the afterlife; mainly because, religious doctrine teaches that beneath it all, everybody is a transgressor.

Debunking History's Inconclusive Theories

Footprints of early humans, alongside dinosaur tracks were unearthed near a riverbed in nearby Glen Rose Texas, this indicates that modern humans first appeared on this planet much earlier than archeologists theorize, possibly around 140 millions years ago during the Jurassic period. The site where human footprints were found in 1984 is known as the Taylor Site.

Mere Acknowledgment of such findings discovered at the Taylor Site should have debunked Darwin's Origin of Species theory; which was accepted by scientists under the auspices that the actual missing link between humans and apes will be discovered at a future date. But this has not occurred, and history books based on Darwin's flawed hypothesis should be re-written to reflect the truth. However, the powers that be do not give up too easily; as history has proven time and time again; mainly because admission of such revelations will encourage people to question everything, including religion.

So, even if you take into account the bible's version of the earliest humans who walked the earth literally, which is the event told in the book of Genesis about the life of Adam and Eve, then this time line only dates back to nearly 10,000 to 7,500 years BC..

Hardcore Christian fundamentalists are okay with such hypothesis, even-though there is no proof. Some are even quick to point out that carbon dating; a technology used by scientists as a means of establishing a time period; is not that much better than guess work.

So, how can one go about explaining such ingrained disregard for scientific methods among religious fundamentalists, especially when considering the fact that most believers of the bible fail to realize that science as a discipline owes it's founding, more or less, to the blessings of the church. Which recognized Roger Bacon

(1214 – 1294?); a British born monk (Franciscan), as being the world's first scientist. You must conclude to some extent, covertly or otherwise, that science was not only sanctioned by the church, it is governed by it.

The end result is that almost no one professing to being a Christian; regardless of their denomination, actually do the reading and interpretations of biblical scriptures for themselves. They have always been read to and interpreted by someone else. In terms of history, there is a different approach. Many institutions of higher learning rely on the mind of a child's innate self induction state; which becomes a direct memory during the second stage of a growing mind. Once that happens it is essentially up to the individual to awaken, and this could take several life-times to manifest.

Religion and history collectively remain the world's oldest means of massive mind control, second only to forcible labor and the fear of war. History, as it turns out, is used to paint a glorious picture of those in power while hiding the true nature of human origin. You see, the ones who control history, also has the mental power of perception over the rest of society (about 80%) and, are able to project their mind-control efforts into future generations with very little effort, thanks in part to systemic programming, which is so pervasive in modern culture.

Those who rule this world control virtually every aspects of our daily lives, be it educational, healthcare and economic systems in which we have come to rely on for overall well being, extending into political and civil rights organizations, elections, and all levels of law and local governance.

Basically, if someone has that much control and dictates nearly 95% of the information we receive, which begins at the time a person is born, until the very moment they die, they can say and do almost anything they want. Keep in mind, though, not all information put forth is necessarily correct.

Incest Among Elites

Before reading this article it's only fair and out of respect for those ingrained to certain levels of control that a warning is cautioned. This article contains subjects that are contrary to those you have been preconditioned for as a person. We're not out to turn your world upside down, but we must speak the Truth where-ever it may lead. To that end we seek to do just that.

As you might already know by now, the off-springs of the nephilim-human hybrids, in addition to being the world's first healers also became the kings, queens and ancient political leaders of the world. Their survival as a unique species among humans has been built around secrecy and inbreeding. This is why the pharaohs of Egypt, as well as other dynasties, all practiced incest. This is also why the people who rule the world today all have per-arranged marriages, even when it doesn't appear to be that way. If one were to dig deep enough into the backgrounds and relationships of the world's most powerful people, they'll know this to be true.

Even the beloved Princess Diana was a distant relative of Prince Charles. In this day and time we consider such behavior among family members as incest. But for members of the world's elite families such practices, even though they are conducted under the table as much as possible, and is frowned upon by modern society, still goes on as business as usual.

People who rule the world didn't earn the right to do so by way of virtue. They rule the world simply because they are blood relatives of alien intelligence and look out for each other. Regardless of where they live, or the color of their skin, they maintain purity of their hybrid based DNA bloodline from one generation to the next by practicing that which is taboo to mainstream society, incest.

In no manner, shape or fashion am I advocating the practice of incest. But, its so difficult for some people to believe that these so called Kings, queens, princes, princess, presidents, and prime

150

ministers of the world, just to name a few, from the ancient past to the present are all blood relatives.

A former US president once openly admitted to the press that he's a distant relative of the royal family of London. An eleven year old girl discovered via research that all U.S. Presidents, except two are related. This includes America's first black president in the modern era as being among those related to the royal family, even though he is of a different race. So from the information mentioned earlier one could easily connect all the dots of the power elites of the world. And from what you'll eventually realize is that their network is both wide and deep.

Bloodline Tracking....

Some countries have made it easy to track their bloodlines in openness. In Korea, it is customary and standard practice for all members of the same bloodline to hold onto the family name, even in marriage, this makes it easy to identify members of the same clan throughout generations.

For instance, every Korean, man or woman, with the same last name of Wei are related. Those with the name of Chung, Li, Kang, are related to each person living or dead with their same name. It's the same name tracking system used openly for 50,000 years in tracking bloodline linage for all of Asia. But in Europe, Canada, South American countries, and the United States, the practice of holding onto the original bloodline namesake through generations has been discontinued. In in place of open tracking only a few old line families still practice this form of tracking. The practice in place today has gone underground, which makes it harder for people to know who's who among the power elite.

Such cloak and dagger practice by the elite power structure of the new world has allowed them to divide, conquer and control the whole of society in the most technically advanced nations on earth. By encouraging generations of people to voluntarily drop their family namesake upon marriage has allowed the elite to conduct their rituals undetected. In a sense this is what gave rise to secret societies all over the world.

151

But not all members of the ruling bloodlines are bad people. Some of them really want to do good things to advance human life. It just seems as if the ones who want to good are out numbered by those in favor of exacting violence and fear as a means of controlling the minds of those lacking truth about their existence, and of god.

Briefly...

The power elite has dominated reality of this realm by staging wars, conflicts amongst villagers, famine, plaques and disasters to maintain control of the human race. They won't stop at anything, even to the point of killing a member of their own blood relative to ensure that their rule over humanity remains intact.

Case in point, in the year 1917, King George V refused to grant asylum to his cousin, Tsar Nicholas II and family of Russia. Instead leaving them to the fate of the Bolshevik revolution, which meant a certainty of death.

The fact that King George ascended to the throne of England upon an untimely death of his brother, Prince Edwards, was no fluke either. Edwards' death went largely unnoticed because doctors of the royal family stated that Edward died of natural causes. The women that Edwards was due to wed, a cousin, princess Mary of Teck, became the bride of King George V, Now, how convenient was that?

All but two presidents of the United States, to leaders of the Nazi movement, including Adolf Hitler, are all related to the royal family via bloodline. For instance, Laura was George's cousin prior to their marriage.

Keep in mind, incest is against the law and is frowned upon by most civilized countries around the world, but when it happens at the elite, royal levels, people seem to think it's no big deal. Then again, it all falls back to the golden rule: he who makes the rules, rule!

You didn't know This!...

In the last presidential elections in America, 2000 and 2004; it made no difference who the winner would be. The fact that George W. Bush won both times should make you wonder, though. First off, all the candidates who ran for the nation's highest office new well in advance what the outcome would be. Most Americans would think you're nuts if you believe that George W. Bush, Al Gore and John Kerry are all blood relatives of Queen Elizabeth. And also blood relatives of the late Princess Diana and King James I who's chiefly responsible for commissioning the current translation of the Bible. Remember, he who rule, sets all the rules. In fact, George Bush, John Kerry, and Al Gore are related to the following former US presidents: Thomas Jefferson, Teddy and Franklin Roosevelt, George Washington, Ronald Reagan, and yours Truly, Bill Clinton.

Hum mm!

Case in point...

In 1997, Princess Diana was killed in Paris shortly after the press mentioned her intentions of marrying someone outside the bloodline, presumably Jody Fahed, an Arab. To this day there are those who insists that Diana's death was not accidental. History is littered with strange and unexplainable deaths of members of the royal family and power elites leads to only one conclusion: if anyone mixes the bloodline with that of outsiders: death soon follows. Now look at Prince Charles' plight; he had nothing to do with Diana's death but he does have some idea of those responsible for ending her life. Charles took advantage of Diana's death to finally break loose of the inbreed/incest relationship that is practiced by the royal family and the power elites. Charles decided to marry outside the bloodline.

I am the breath of life, and life is my religion. I am forever connected to my soul and spirit. I am, that I am.

Rodh de Sailor

Mental Induction

In 1908, author and new-age philosopher William Walker Atkinson, of Chicago, formally blew the lid-off mental induction technologies that were being systematically deployed by governments and powerful individuals by publishing a book on the subject titled: Mental Induction. Over the next ten decades his insights would prove prophetic since virtually all world governments and clandestine agencies are now using mind-control technologies in much the way as the methods described by the late author.

Atkinson's revelations has since been forgotten, as it occurred more than a century ago, which means the likely hood of there being anyone alive to bear witness to it is remote. Most people today are unaware of the fact that each time they become a member of a religious doctrine, attend a movie or watch TV, regardless of the content or programming, there is a 90% chance of becoming a mind-controlled victim by way of subjective (subliminal) means. It should also be obvious by now that the media in this country, and for that matter the world, is no longer independent of corporate influences. Freedom of the press is now non-existent. This means that almost every bit of information is censored before it reaches public consumption.

What is mental induction? Most people have never heard of this term. Mental induction is an insidious, inconspicuous means of deploying mind-control methods and technologies in a seemingly harmless manner for the sole purpose of being able to control, influence, or condition a society to act or think a certain way in response to authority, by unknowingly allowing information to become impressed upon each individual's subconscious mind, as if

155

it were put there by themselves. In other words mental-induction is a technique that allows for the application of massive mind-control.

You don't think mind-control of a crowd is possible? Well it is...

Mind-control as a technology is older than most modern religions combined. The technology itself has been among humanity for a very, very long time. In my opinion, mental induction is just like religion, which means it is a very powerful, and yet subtle mind-control method, and to a certain degree, it has been used by the following industries almost since their respective creation: education, corporations, government, military, sports, health and science. In fact the only areas in life absent of some sort of mental-induction technique or methods are the arts. Even though mental induction is a subtle mind-control technology, it is still very, very effective when applied and programmed by a trained professional. You know, due to the the true nature of being human, people really can be made to do almost anything without ever realizing the effects of mental induction.

In a sense, it is somewhat difficult for anyone to honestly assign a value to the number of years mind-control technologies have existed, but we can safely estimate that it is slightly younger than the advent of modern humans entrance onto the earth's landscape. With that being said, most folks who are somewhat familiar with such things are under the false impression that the mere act of controlling the mind of others from a distance is only something doable in science fiction movies. And you know what? That's just the way mind-control advocates want you to think! Keep in mind, some people still believe hypnosis is a joke. But, for the millions of people who've been under hypnotic influence, induced by a psychiatrist or trained hypnotist will attest, it is very much real.

Government Agencies

The central intelligence agency (CIA) once called their top secretive mind-control program of the early 1940s to 1980s *MK Ultra*. MK Ultra was involved in more mischief than mind-control technologies alone, according to whistle-blowers. The MK Ultra program played a key role in the cover-up of UFOs, alien visitations from other dimensions and time travel experiments conducted by other US government agencies.

With mental-induction technologies and methods, highly covert government agencies are able to control the amount of information of their own insiders from being leaked to the public, even though such numbers range well into hundreds of thousands of people.

US government and various agencies within it regular deployed mind-control methods unto unsuspecting citizens. It is a known truth that every governmental body in the world, whether they're large or small, has (unleashed) a version of mind-control technologies of some sort in which they use against their very own citizens time and time again, in an effort to control their overall thoughts and actions.

Note:

For the use of this book I have selected the name 'mental induction' to refer to mind-control methods that are used on a massive scale.

Subtle Effects of Mind-Control

Take a look around: what do you see? Most likely you see people you do not know, and some you do know, simply going about their daily routines: consisting of work, traveling back and forth to church, dropping their kids off at school, the day care, grocery shopping, running errands and so on. At night and on most weekends, some routines you observe become somewhat of a ritual, as people begin to unwind the burdens of a ho-hum, treadmill work-week with some sort of relief in sight as they exchange it all for form of entertainment, including watching or participating in sports or attending other worth while events.

What you will soon realize from such observation; if you haven't already; is that people are basically the same where ever you look.

Activities being carried out everyday by ordinary people is the result of mental induction programming methods, or societal mind-control technologies as it relates to a cultural setting. You see, no one is ever born into this world with the idea of reporting to work five days a week, giving roughly 40 hours of their personal time to someone else, and spending only two days a week with their family and/or friends. However, this work-related ritual has become their routine activities for at least 40 – 50 years of their lives. So then, beyond raising a family and making some corporation richer, what have they done to contribute to the advancement of their overall being other than having and raising children? The answer is quite obvious, not that much at all...This is not an accident!!!

Mental-induction helps Governments control Society

Mental Induction has provided the powers that be the ability to control almost all of humanity without ever acknowledging that such technologies and/or methods even exist. To this very day there is still no acknowledgment by any government official or agencies that mental-induction exist, and were put to use during both World War I and II. If such acknowledgment were to ever see the light of day, there would have to be an explanation for using this technology against its own people, especially in the US. If mental induction was in use during the Jim Crow era, which eventually led to the civil rights and equal rights movements. Mental induction was used to help solicit public sentiment for the wars in Vietnam and Iraq.

The fact remains, mental-induction in one way or another has been in constant use by the US government on a number of instances to control the eventual outcome of certain situations, for both good and nefarious reasons more than once. In a sense, you might think that a civilized society can not exist without some kind of means to ensure civil order, and the laws and rules to help govern the overall actions and behavior of people. Such arrangements and agreements are supposed to represent the good side of mental induction technologies, but, as with all things in existence, there are always two sides to consider.

Essentially, the existence of mental induction illustrates the inherent inter-connectedness between of all the world's people at their core level of being. If this level of inter-connectedness did not exist at all, then things like energy healing, psychic phenomena, telepathy, and even prophecy would not exist, either. What I'm basically saying is that the same energies that allow us to heal, can also be used to kill. Why? Because at the core level of our very existence is the tie that binds us all together, and that tie is consciousness, which I believe is the causation of all things, even space.

Make no mistake about it, mind-control technologies and methods are very real, and it happens to more people than you think on a regular basis everyday, it even happens to the most intelligent minded people in the world, too. The greatest myth and difficulty in the world today lies in act of explaining, or trying to help awaken those living among us in total darkness of truth, who have so much invested in programmed logic, and are impulsively dependent upon materialistic things just to make themselves feel worthy. In realizing that they have been subjected to a constant stream of ritualistic mind-control technologies most of their lives, specifically during their first seven years.

In some cases, the higher the level of education an individual has attained within the system, the more unrealistic the chance of their understanding that their mind has been methodically tapped into by someone else, and that they are a mind-control victim. In fact, you may even argue that the reality itself is only an illusion which depends upon the ability of a few to control the collective minds of many by way of mental induction or some other form of subtle mind-control methods. If this is somewhat your belief, then you just don't know how close you are to truth?

The world we have created is a product of our thinking. It cannot be changed without changing the way we think.

Albert Einstein

Mental Induction
(in Action)

E ven though mental induction has been around and in use by all rulers of the world historically to insight wars and to enslave certain people, it wasn't deployed successfully on such a large scale by the powers that be until the advent of the wars known as WWI and WWII. Until that time mental-induction technologies were somewhat limited to local and regional events, or wars being fought on the same continent. The African slave trade and the revolutionary war for independence between the continental states (which later became the United States) and England showed that mental-induction technology was possible and could indeed be used on a wider scale.

In 1934 Hitler and his infamous Nazi party became the right pawns to begin experimentation techniques aimed at the general population, which eventually culminated in the death of at least 6 million Jewish people, 4.5 million Poles, Ukrainians, Russians, 250,000 Gypsies and 200,000 Freemasons and other European citizens and soldiers on all sides of the war. The total number of deaths that occurred at the hands of the Nazis and both world wars will never be written down or fully accounted for anywhere. For if the truth were ever known, people would begin to realize the total destructive nature caused by those who wage wars and mentally induce others to fight it for them.

With both aid and guidance from certain well known European psychics, astrologers, Tarot-card readers, and mystics of the time, such as Erik Jan Hanussen, a Viennese-Jewish born psychic who became known throughout Europe as the prophet of the Third

Reich and Hitler's personal psychic. He freely traded his inner knowledge of the inner workings of the human mind, black magic and other esoteric phenomena for pay and status. With Hanussen's help the Nazis were able to deploy mental induction against their own people, and other societies across the oceans in an effort to breed a superior race of human beings, who would have (in theory) been able to rule the world. Many people would be surprised to learn that Hitler himself was a mystic. He was taught by Dietrich Echart of the infamous Thule Society which practiced occult rituals and openly worshiped Satan.

The untold truth about the war in Europe is that Hitler and the Nazis nearly succeeded in their efforts to rule the planet. That was until other world leaders realized that they themselves were also in grave danger of being subjugated by the Nazis thirst for world dominance, and begin consulting in private with well known and documented psychics of within their own countries for advice. While the official historical version of the two world wars speaks volumes about a conventional confrontation on the battlefield, it was in reality, nevertheless, a war fought on all fronts, which included the rapid deployment of psychics and other mystics in response.

The only difference between what's happening now in America, and what occurred when the Third Reich unleashed mental induction methods and techniques on to an unsuspecting and at the time a very reliable and trusting German people. Who were comprised mostly of low information types and ignorance, that the advancement in mental-induction technology has been perfected and upgraded with modern improvements in mass communication systems, that are by far more superior, stronger, enhanced and infinitely more powerful than the radio signals that were used by the talk show formats and print media of that era. Technology today has come a very long way since the the late 1930s through the present, which means that mental induction is now an exact science.

Healthcare Reform Battle

The battle over reforming healthcare (2009, 2010) in the US, was mostly a partisan effort by congress and senate controlled by the democrats, even though a few republicans signed-on. The healthcare reform effort tested the extreme limits of mental induction as both parties of house and senate began unleashing their version of this technology via signals of fear and intimidation. Which were seemingly accepted subjectively and most easily by those who stood to gain the most from a nationalized health plan that covered all of America's people. If you were to take a closer, more unbiased look at the healthcare reform debate (civil unrest, is more descriptive) as it unfolded, and how such key players in certain positions of power were able to yield undue response and influence on the minds of so many people, simultaneously, you have to clearly conclude without a doubt that mental-induction was at play. Here's the thing, when you become awakened to what is actually occurring in the world, and to what has already taken place. You tend to become truly unaffected and somewhat immune from all mental-induction vibrations originating from within the earth's inner atmosphere and those of human generated noise.

Racism, an effect of Mental-induction

First and foremost most Americans of every culture are unwilling to admit that a disease called racism still exist, and it is the core cause of their emotions about whether or not all Americans should have universal healthcare coverage, one where everybody participates in the system. Racism itself, is an aspect of mental-induction. Racism as a virus has managed to survive the test of time among those of intelligence and ignorance, alike. And from time to time, when Americans can't seem to agree or compromise, racism rears its ugly head. A second argument against providing healthcare for everyone is really an argument about money, or the capital system it represents. Almost everyone, except a paid lobbyist for the healthcare industry, admittedly agree that a vast majority of insurance companies are out of control, by continuously raising premiums, dropping patients for what is known as: *'policies at will,'* and simply flat-out refusing to accept new patients with preconditioned illnesses and so forth. They argue that patients with precondition illnesses simply burdens the entire medical insurance network system and the country, as a whole.

Note:

Although all agree that the healthcare system in America needs to be fixed, opponents against a true healthcare reform has always favored profits over the well-fare of people. In America, no one is willing to openly admit to the fact that their true and undying religion is: Money...

It is stated that the most single cause of death in America is not having some type of health coverage, but the fact is that many sick people often put their illnesses on hold until it is far too late, for preventive care measures to make a difference. This sort of thing could end if everyone is required to participate in the costs of a universal program. The only way to prevent those who are healthy from gaming the system by waiting until the are in need of health services before getting involved.

With so much to gain and virtually nothing to lose healthcare reform should have been a no-brainier...But, for those of the opposition party, power just didn't give up so easily.

Now, lets take a look at how and by whom, the technique of mental induction was last deployed successfully unto an unsuspecting population, and what were the results. For the Nazis' Fuehrer, Adolf Hitler, who authored a best selling book while serving time in prison titled: 'Mien Kemp,' provide details of the basic blueprint and framework needed, in accordance to the law of attraction using mass hypnosis. To help those wanting to unleash hate, murder and bigotry at the onset of the deepest economic downturn and political instability in the US since the great depression. Aided by radio commentators posing as commentary talk shows, newspaper editorials, with opinionated TV news and reporters, collectively provide the most negative vibrations aimed at the minds of Americans that had not been seen before.

Does this ring a bell at all? How is it that nearly half of the population of the U.S. were convinced into acting out against self interests, toward something that everybody stands to benefit from? Look at it this way, just about everyone agrees that healthcare needs reforming, and that costs are too high. So instead of cheering the accomplishment of the Obama administration for successfully getting the healthcare law passed, just the opposite has occurred: hatred. And on top of that, many have been convinced into hating immigrants, who are in this country (some illegally) working mostly unwanted and low waged jobs that many U.S. citizens simply refuse to do at a time when many people are out of work in this country.

The so-called Tea party solution: deport all dark-skinned immigrants, and hire only white Anglo-Saxon Americans in their place. Of course they don't come out and say these things openly for fear of being labeled a racist, but such sentiments have been echoed in coded form in one way or another, time and time again on all conservative radio talk-shows and news programs.

Thus, creating a frequency of mental suggestions in the minds of a vastly uneducated American people who do not see, nor care to take notice of like similarities to what has happened, and how it closely mirrors methods used against the German people which contributed greatly to their treatment of Jewish citizens.

American neighbors are now turning against neighbors, children are turning against parents. People are marching in the streets, many holding signs proclaiming that the newly elected president is a monkey, a Nazi, a communist, a racist, and is not a U.S. born citizen.

The people of Germany overwhelmingly, without questioning bought into the Nazis' propaganda disinformation network about national patriotism fueled by hatred, massive unemployment numbers and fear mongering. This ideology became the country's goal, which was made possible with the use of mental induction methods available to them at the time.

Comparing what actually transpired in Germany during WWI and WWII, and to what happened in America during the healthcare debate, the means to deliver a vibration of fear, giving rise to disorderly actions across the country at town hall meetings, have proven to be much more effective using modern technologies of mass communications than what the Nazi's had available. So-called conservative radio talk shows (republicans of a different name), control a huge chunk of the broadcast airwaves of almost every major city and small to mid size town in the country. They have accomplished this feat as the result of networks which are owned by a total of six conglomerates with a particular political ideology (very similar to the Nazi's).

As it turns out, to control the views of each radio or TV host personality is a fairly simple and straight forward process. In addition to mental induction or hypnosis techniques, all a company has to do for favoritism is to simply increase the amount of advertising spending for each conservative radio, or TV news program supporting their positions, or that of political action group that holds a similar view, and you guessed it, the country ends up in one very big, and at times uncivilized healthcare debate.

Now, to be honest, most conservative talk show hosts have had plenty of practice leading up to the healthcare debates, which falsely led them into believing that they would be able to persuade enough democrats in congress to vote it down. While hoping the Obama administration would simply give up, as Bill Clinton did, and simply walk away from it altogether. Such political posturing by congress had killed efforts for healthcare reform over the previous 70 years.

After successfully using mental induction methods to convince Americans of the need to invade Iraq. Certain members of TV news broadcasters, reporters and commentators were unaffected, as a result they were highly convinced that the benefactors fearing change in the nation's healthcare system the most were the health insurers themselves. And that healthcare insurers were putting so much money into the propaganda network of disinformation that many talk show commentators made millions of dollars more than their usual income provided.

Healthcare insurers channeled an enormous amount of capital into radio and TV advertisements, political action groups, and to make matters worse, they indirectly funded a group of people and deployed towards local democratic offices and town hall meetings with specific instructions to appear disorderly, loud, and irate at the prospect of a rumored government take-over of healthcare. They also made sure that certain news networks were in attendance to record such reactions for TV.

Anti-healthcare rebuttal plans went off like clockwork, as if they were generic reactions of a few concerned citizens, that quickly morphed into the national spotlight with help of the media. Such antics seemingly from ordinary folks provided a boost to the far-right wing and fledgling groups of aging and angry white males, calling themselves the 'Tea Party. Inquiring minds would ask Tea party members one question: where were you when George Bush and the industrial military complex convinced Americans of the need to go to war in Iraq?

During the spring and summer of 2009, the attempt to overhaul healthcare seemed as if it would fail once again, as a member of the republican party appearing on national TV and was bold enough to describe the situation this way: "it will break him, this will be his Waterloo," echoed Jim Demint, a South Carolina senator who believed the outcome of healthcare reform was certain to meet with failure as all previous attempts did. The phrase: "it will break him," by Demint, was reminiscence of America's slavery past. The comment was replayed on the shows of talk radio hosts more than it should have been, because, their main intent was to reawakened a sleeping ignorance held deep within the minds of angry whites, especially those of the south, of a time long ago. There were numerous and repeated references in code form, just to remind people of the president's skin tone. And that's just what the effect of the "it will break him" comment was designed to do.

Needless to say the passing of the country's first national healthcare reform act since the advent of medicaid and medicare finally became the law of the land. Within a year of its existence, the fears of those benefiting the most have realized that all the talk about death panels and such was just that, propaganda.

How Mental Induction Works
(The Mechanics)

Now that you are somewhat familiar with the terminology of **Mental Induction** (forerunner to what is now called the '*Laws of Attraction.*'). It is now time to explain how it works, and why it will always be a weapon of choice in the greatest race of all, the race for mind-space. Mental induction basically works along the same principles as that of electromagnetism. Mental induction is the ability to remotely influence others with the projection of your mind to act a certain way, or to do something that you want them to do, unknowingly of course, on their behalf.

Mental induction can be applied directly by mechanical means as well, such as:

1. frequencies via open airwaves
2. drugs, food and vaccines
3. microchips
4. torture
5. hypnosis
6. propaganda

Anyone adept at telepathy can deploy mental induction technology on an unsuspecting person from any location in the world in just a matter of minutes. In a sense mental induction techniques allows for the making of an excellent Manchurian candidate.

Developing Your Spiritual Powers

The underlying force of all creation, manifestations, dimensions and parallel dimensions, the universe and everything in between has to be the mind. The mind creates vibrations via thoughts, it is the engine that drives the universe on all planes of existence. Nothing can exist, or does exist, without the mind as the origin. It is pure speculation as to what comes first, the mind or vibration. Also, it is highly possible that mind and consciousness are one and the same thing. It is also possible that this is one gigantic mystery that may never be solved to the satisfaction of everyone.

Psychic powers consist of both consciousness and vibration in the form of energy waves, or undetected charged particles generated by the mind. Within the mind also lies other forces which play a crucial role in both creation and manifestation. These forces are known as imagination, visualization, and intentional will.

The mind communicates with all of nature via thought-waves, simultaneously, which travels by vibration. Without thought-wave energy generation, the intentional will of the mind would not manifest matter into physical reality. Psychic powers (mental forces), therefore, exist across all planes of existence because the mind is omniscient, omnipotent in power and abilities. In essence the mind is causation, and the spirit of the mind is consciousness expressed within and without infinity.

Those of us who are interested, is chiefly concerned about ways of developing individual psychic powers to better our life. And this is what this chapter will address. But first I must say this, you cannot develop that which does not already exist. In this case each of us are lucky because deep within the unused levels of our conscious and subconscious mind, all the abilities of psychic powers. You see, we were born this way from the start. So before venturing off into the land of psychics of all types, it is best that we take a look at the lives of those who came before us as to how did we forget about these hidden abilities in the first place.

Life in the Beginning

In the beginning, the earliest of humans lived a fairly simple and straight forward existence. Basically, all that mattered to anyone at the time was that which was needed most on a continual basis to sustain life. Food, water, shelter and clothing all comes to mind, which means most lived as hunters and gatherers, a nomad's style of living. In a sense early societies were held hostage by their environment; and this is what caused many of them to wander the lands in search of more necessities and friendlier environs.

None of today's modern conveniences, brought to the fore-front by advanced technologies that many of us are accustomed to using were available to early humans. Just think about it for a moment! There was no televisions to watch, movies to attend, radios to listen to, sports events to excite them, schools to educate their kids, businesses to drive commerce, nor were there any debts to pay. In fact money hadn't been invented.

Looking into the past at how our ancestors must have lived one could easily imagine that life was harsh, sterile and quite frankly, boring, when compared to the way we now live. In fact, those born into this world during the mid 1980s – 2000 could think something similar about those of us born before their generation. My daughter, now in her early twenties, can't imagine living without the use of a computer, the internet, a smart-phone, Ipod, and cable TV. While many of my generation couldn't fathom being without the use of a car, color TV, a job, and a date. Such inventions of our modern lives have become the underlying forces---driving all technological advancements, and passing them on from one generation to the next. Inventions have become our legacy, a gift to those who follow in our foot steps.

Long Physical Lives

But there were certain advantages to early life that were widespread and fairly common to folks a long time ago. For instance, contrary to popular myths, early humans lived much longer on average than modern day people, even when considering 21st century technological achievements and advances in medical knowledge. If you take the writings of the Bible literally, then you must agree that the average life span of a healthy person from that era, was extraordinarily long and productive well into the mid to upper hundreds. And I'm not talking about living to the age of 105, and dying a short time later, either.

Enoch, as it is stated in the Bible, lived more than 365 years and did not know death, because it is said that God came and took him away. It is written in other religious and ancient texts, about many people who lived to be more than 800 years old, and among the oldest person mentioned in antiquity is said to have lived for nearly 3,000 years.

If these sayings about people who lived very long and healthy lives are true, then the question is, why and how? And another question should be, why do we live far less than they did, especially considering how much more advanced we are in comparison? Don't we have more technologies than they had use of? Think about it for a moment! In today's world when we see someone who has lived beyond the century mark we tend to think of it as a great accomplishment, and that this event is nothing short of a miracle. By comparison to those of biblical and ancient times, the length of our average life-span has to be considered a joke.

Early societies had a much greater demand of their overall health, and also their environment than scientists and scholars are willing to acknowledge. For one thing, there were no self imposed mental limits on how long life should be. For the most part no one really kept track of time; at least not in the manner that we now do. Ancient people used in greater detail other senses that were available to them, especially powers of the mind, such as imagination, visualization and spiritual will. Distant healing; or what is sometimes known as telepathic healing was fairly common; as were most other aspects of mental forces that we now recognize as psychic phenomena. The methods used in their development of ESP are essentially identical to that which has allowed numerous societies that succeeded them to discover unknown regions of the universe without aide of a telescope or space travel.

We, as a society, due to one reason or another, have been systemically programmed for a much shorter physical life. This systemic programming is something that occurs during the first seven years of life as acceptable conditions of raising a child. Nothing during the early developmental years of a child's life ever mentions the inherent spirituality, the forces of the mind, and individual will. When the properties of one's true existence are not expressed or touched upon early in life, there is but one option available for the mind to latch onto, and that is the ideal of a very short and limited physical life span. Even then, there is no mention of the mind as a very distinct and separate aspect of the physical body.

Essentially each of us, with help from parents, culture, the educational and information industries, undergo subliminal programming of the mind into accepting the notion of a limited physical life. This initial programming becomes very deeply rooted and placed within our spiritual will; which is the chief-in command of our being; that it then manifests such ideology into reality.

We now know that we are spirits, and as spirit we do not know death. With new instruments now available to record on film and measure actual spiritual energy surrounding the body, this is no longer a concept, the evidence is overwhelming and indisputable. Even though this does not provide a complete answer as to why the ancients had on average very long and healthy lives; it is a beginning towards understanding and learning more about them, and about ourselves as we continue the journey of discovering truth.

What you will soon discover from reading this chapter is that the

172

same methods used by ancient psychics and prophets are to some extent the same methods in use today by those knowledgeable about such matters. You can obviously spend a ton of money for means of learning how to unleash these spiritual powers within yourself from a number of sources that specialize in teaching others how to do it. You could also learn how to do it in the same way it was done in the past; by trial and error.

Whatever path you decide to take the underlying principles are the same. It is simply limiting your mind's exposure to light and sound wave frequencies for a period of time. This allows you to sense the scope of and vastness of the mind, this is also where meditation can become most helpful.

Little about me

Initially this book was going to be about the experiences I had as a top-tier stockbroker with a New York Stock Exchange member firm. At first glance, it would have been an excellent real-life account of what goes on behind the scenes of deal making and winning big in terms of personal success as a result of making other people rich, and some even richer. But, before page one would ever see the light of day, my entire view of the world, and sense of reality began to shift, profoundly.

Even though I have witnessed numerous miracles and unexplainable circumstances and events throughout most of my life, the thought of having psychic abilities, and of being among a select minority of people in the world with such powers was the furthest thing from my mind. To say that I took this newly found insight and ran with it is quite a stretch – because it simply didn't happen that way. In a sense, I was more worried about being considered a nut case, than elated about being psychic. Our ability to replay things in our minds is a beautiful thing. We have reached a point in our lives to where reviewing the past in its complete details allows us to understand how we got to where we are – we attribute this ability to remember things with such richness as hindsight. The saying goes – hindsight is always 20/20 vision. With that said, it is best to begin at a time in life that I believe was key towards awakening the psychic senses within me to a point that I began to take notice of it, and soon discovered other ways in which these powers could be useful to me on a daily basis.

In my opinion, everybody has the potential to develop the psychic powers that lie within them. You can't develop psychic powers if you don't already have them, but fortunately for you, you do. My research has shown that this particular belief; that everybody is psychic is highly debated among many within the psychic community. The fact is that these abilities only standout, because most people don't realize how common psychic powers really are. So, this is why I say that all psychics are gifted naturally, then they go about improving their abilities even more, mostly by experimenting with them. The path each one takes towards improvement of these abilities varies. There were several options available when I began looking into the best course of action that I should take.

The choices before me were as follows:

Plan A.

Since there are plenty of reading materials available, including books written by number of researchers and former members of the government's own funded research and development programs, which lasted for more than eight decades; there should be enough detailed data about PSI and ways to develop these skills on my own. The cost of doing it this way would be minimal compared to other options.

Plan B.

This choice calls for hiring and working with someone that is knowledgeable and capable of teaching you how to develop your PSI skills. Cost of this plan varies from one guru to the next. But, if you have the money it could cut in half the amount of time it would take to do it on your own.

Plan C.

This plan was the most expensive option of the choices available. It requires enrolling in one of the many schools around the country that offer psychic training. This route is most likely the best option of all. If you have the money and time to travel, I recommend that you at least look into this option. There are numerous schools located out west in the San Francisco and surrounding area that have the most schools that specialize in training others to develop psychic skills.

Final Analysis

In the end, plan A was the choice that I chose to learn more about PSI and develop the skills on my own since there was so much information available. I read as much material as I could possibly ascertain for free. And then I purchased enough books over the course of ten years to start a psychic book store. The way things work in the universe, is that like attracts like, so without really knowing much about the Laws of Attraction, I had actually invoked its power in the pursuit of truth. Combined with a meditation technique that I developed, and a continual flow of information that the universe was sending me, I finally realized that I had been using PSI powers for most, if not all of my life. It was as if someone had suddenly turned on a light in a darkened room, I finally could see the real world.

As more and more of my past experiences indicated that the use of psychic powers were present, unknowingly at the time, I soon realized that there are essentially two forms of psychic powers that come from one source for us to use while in the physical. The first form of PSI is a more natural response or basic defensive mechanism that occurs spontaneously – everybody has had use of it at one time or another in their lives, and it is always on alert, constantly communicating with us all the time. It usually takes form as an inner voice out of nowhere that whispers to you, mentally. Sometimes it may actually flash a mental image of an upcoming event. This is what is sometimes called premonition.

The second form of PSI is what I call intentional – everybody has it, but some people don't realize that this is available to them.

Mostly, we are lead into thinking that only a very select group of people throughout world history has ever been blessed with such gifts. These people are known as prophets.

If I was teaching you how to develop your psychic skills, the very first thing I would have you do is to read about it. After you have consumed enough data to where you've become familiar with the terminology involved, then I would encourage you to adopt a daily routine of meditation.

Once you've establish a daily ritual of meditation, I would then instruct you to practice the following mental exercises at least three times a week:

1. Visualization

2. Imagination

3. Telepathic Communication

Visualization- happens to be the language of choice for the mind. Everyone has the ability to visualize.

Imagination- allows one to practice the art of creating, using the mind, and then visualizing what you've created.

Telepathic Communication- is much easier than you imagine. Once you learn how to visualize properly from a psychic point of view, and imagine with your mental faculties, telepathic communication is the next logical step. It will also boost your confidence.

Everyone alive today has at their disposal a small and subtle voice that speaks to them, at least every now and then. You also hear this inner voice in your mind each moment of your life. I call this inner voice: "Genie." Others may call it (the inner voice) the "Giant Within." Together with improved techniques to meditation, visualization, imagination and access to the small, subtle inner voice, you are now in possession of what it takes to develop your psychic skills.

Of course, there are more advanced methods developed by researchers, that if practiced would enhance your skills even further. But the methods mentioned beforehand are very effective. The other thing to remember about this is that there are many ways to develop PSI skills, and that not everyone will respond favorably to the same techniques. There is no magic bullet (at least not yet) that will suddenly penetrate your mind and develop PSI for you, mainly because the tools are already inside of you.

Basically, I developed my PSI skills in the same manner in which I have taught others to develop their own. I have always been a strong believer in ascertaining as much information as possible about any interests that I pursue, psychic phenomena is no exception, even though it hit me like a freight train.

If you have decided to develop your psychic skills, do so with fore knowledge that it will happen, in time. Keep in mind that it's slightly different for each of us, although we all have every attribute of PSI abilities within, we seem to be more skilled in certain areas than others are. In a sense, this could be a big reason for our apparent feelings of separateness, even though we are entangled as one.

You are encouraged to work at each PSI skill. Keep practicing the basic fundamentals of all skills which are: meditation, visualization, imagination and telepathy. In due time one or all of these attributes will surface within you. When it does, life will never be the same.

I have come to know thyself, and thus understand that I am the event horizon of creation, and that within me emanates the powers of Source.

Rodh de Sailor

Tapping Into the Source
(Your Subjective-Mind)

If you have even a little bit of faith, you can say to a mountain "move," and it will move. Nothing will be impossible for you to do.

Matt 17:20

There is a smorgasbord selection of books to choose from regarding how you can use the laws of attraction to make a difference in your quality of life. But the most popular book available has to be the one titled 'The Secret' by author Rhonda Byrne. The Secret had been the topic of discussion and appearance on Oprah, CNN, Larry King, and a host of radio shows across America and the world. Having purportedly grossed in excess of 500 million, US dollars in sales.

The Secret DVD version had been available on the market for newly two years before I knew the book existed. Even then, I thought it was such a great and simplified way of explaining to my wife and daughter about hidden powers within them, a system that I had used successfully while working as a stockbroker to amass more money in just a few short years than most of my relatives had ever accumulated in their entire working life. So I bought two copies for them.

What Rhonda Byrne called the Secret, is known by many as the law of Attraction. The law of attraction is based upon the hypothesis that your thoughts, whether positive or negative, precedes physical form when combined with the visualization and imagination powers of your mind. Of course, each frequency or vibration is matched with like signals. And of course, this all happens in the mind.

Skeptics are quick to rebut such claims publicly, but they always fail to mention that the principles of LOA are relied upon in both the medical and pharmaceutical industries when testing the efficacy of new treatment procedures, or experimental drugs. In these industries LOA is known as the placebo effect.

Use of the phrase 'law of attraction,' when referring to the mysteries of how the mind works is not a modern day discovery, it just seems that way. The phrase itself was coined as early as 1915 by William Quan Judge, a theosophical author and new-age practitioner. But, the earliest books encouraging the use of the law of attraction as a means for getting rich was written by Wallace D. Wattles in 1910, titled: The Science of Getting Rich, and again in 1937 with the release of the following books, Think & Grow Rich, by Napoleon Hill, and The Art of True Healing by Israel Regordiell.

The most compelling authoritarian book in my humble opinion ever published about the mysteries of the mind was written by, author Thomson Jay Hudson in 1893, titled: The Law of Psychic Phenomena. It makes me feel very confident and inspired with my own hypothesis about the workings of the mind to learn that well over a hundred years ago, someone else was able to reach similar findings as the ones I have attained.

For the record, let it to be known that not everyone who wishes to harness the power of the subconscious-mind (source) do so with intent of becoming rich. We all know that living in the west to a large degree, money determines your quality of life. But, as many will attest: money doesn't always equate to a happy and healthy life.

So then with that being said, whatever you decide on doing with your new found abilities. Once you discover that this infinite power is both real and to a certain degree demonstrable and acknowledged by the law of physics, when properly brought into reality both intentional and unintentional.

Exceptions to Every Rule

There are always exceptions to the rules, for instance it is a known fact that God, (subconscious-mind) is speaking to each of us all the time, constantly from within and on rare occasions will speak to us with an external voice. In rare situations where God chooses to speak externally, knowing and following any protocols become obsolete, for the source within knows every language ever spoken.

Why and when this happens no one knows for sure. In some cases such an event occurs as the result of difficult situations that some may face at a given time; or it may just be an elevated display of love and caring; or a simple act of giving to someone in need without any expectations that causes the normal stillness and silence of God's voice to become verbally noticeable. The point I am making is this, God speaks to us in so many ways that it is hard to list them all. For example, instead of hearing an actual voice speaking to you in a moment of need, the response from God may manifest in the form of mental images or even from the presence of a total stranger.

Note:

Keep in mind that not even Moses had the experience of hearing an external response from God. Moses; according to the Bible, stated that God had spoken to him through his mind.

Most of you reading this book are probably wondering: What does all of this, if any, have to do with creating or manifesting the things you want or need into physical reality? The answer should be obvious: EVERYTHING! Besides, it is best to be prepared to hear God's response before your requests are ever made....

With all of that being said, I am compelled to share this brief but true story with you at this time. As an example of how mysteriously God (subconscious-mind) acts on your behalf, MANIPULATING reality to manifest your sustained, focused thoughts.

181

Late one night after showing several people (four) how to remote view events of the past, future and present at a local bookstore in central Florida. I decided to go home a bit earlier than usual only to discover that my car wouldn't start. From past experience I knew the problem of the car not starting had something to do with the battery. Immediately, I walked back into the bookstore and asked a total stranger; who was in attendance on this night; if he could help me charge the battery. However, after several attempts of trying to administer a charge to the battery, the car still wouldn't start. Intuitively, I began to examine the car with my mind and within a short time later knew exactly what the problem was. A battery that I had purchased new from WALMART just a couple months earlier, suddenly developed a few dead cells and wouldn't hold a charge.

There I was, smack in the middle of nowhere and my usually dependable car wouldn't start; worst of all it was now past midnight. Upon becoming aware of my problem; a young man; whose name was George, was willing to help me out of a bad situation even though he didn't know me that well. He volunteered to drive me to the nearest WALMART so that I could exchange the battery, or get a new one. Getting another battery was not a problem, I thought, since the battery was purchased from this store. Also, WALMART is the type of company that stands behind the products sold at its stores. I didn't have proof of purchase, but they were still able to accommodate my request by using a scanner on the bar codes to determine that it was there product.

The young technician on hand stated that she had to run a test on the battery to see if it was in good working order. A short while later she emerged from the shop and informed me that test results showed no problems with the battery. And, at that moment my subconscious-mind spoke to me, saying: "Ask her to retest the battery," of which I did. The young lady said to me that she'll ask another mechanic to use a more stringent testing device to see if one or more of the battery cells were failing. True enough that was the case.

Now the time came to calculating how much it would cost to

replace the battery, and this cost was extrapolated from time of use from the previous purchase date, verses the price of a new battery to replace the old. In other words, WALMART would stand behind its product, but I would have to make up the difference in cost of the trade in value of the old battery, verses that of a new one. Only one small problem with this solution at the time, I had no money on hand. Without saying a word, George offered to pay for the cost difference of a new battery, and he then took me back to the now empty parking lot where my car lay idled. He waited until I completed the task at hand to make sure that it worked. As soon as the car started up, George left the scene without once asking me to pay him back. Needless to say, even though George and I exchanged emails, my efforts to remain in touch with him has failed.

Analysis: God worked through a total stranger who knew very little about me at the time, and also God spoke to me in a still, silent voice within my mind, asking me to have the technician retest the battery.

Bible Verses

The following Bible verses refer to hearing the voice of God: John 8:47, King I 19:12, and Revelation 3:20.

Tapping into the source is akin to having a private conversation with God, the ability to do this has been the most well kept secret of all mysteries. You see, the ability to tap into and talk to the source go hand-in-hand in order of importance because you can't tap into the *Universal Mind* without knowing, or at least having faith in a higher power other than that of your earth bound physical body. I have a saying that goes like this; *"You don't need faith in something if you know it to be true. Faith is for those who are unsure if*

183

something like a higher power exist." But when god speaks to you for the very first time via your subconscious-mind, and the information received checks out, there is nothing in this world that could convince you otherwise, that such a thing is the work of your imagination.

Contrary to popular belief, it doesn't matter one iota if you are religious or not, nor if you do or do not attend church, because the moment you decide within yourself to use any of the skill-sets mentioned herein to tap into the source, means that you have at least for the moment, acknowledged the existence of God.

Knowing that God exists within you, all the time, and that you can establish your very own personal relationship at any time, any where, is what some religious denominations work so hard at preventing. You see in a world where everyone speaks to god, there is no need for a middleman.

Basically, most religious doctrines have accomplished the task of separating you from the true source, at first by misrepresentation, and secondly, by misinterpreting the words of religious scriptures. At the same time discouraging people from ever learning and practicing particular techniques and arts that has been known to enhance one's ability to communicate with source in a meaningful way. This is also why some (quite a few) very powerful people have managed to remain in control of the planet we call home for such a very long, long time without ever being seriously challenged.

Historically, the forbidden arts that will be discussed in this chapter were at first taught only to a select group of human hybrids (children of fallen angels and earthly women), by the watchers so prominently mentioned in Genesis 6:1-4, whom later would become known as witches. The arts they practiced became known as witchcraft. It was the watchers (witches) who gave rise to the high priests of Egypt and a few other select group of initiates. Among the most well known students of Egypt's Mystery Schools (even though it is not written in the Bible) were Abraham, Joseph, Moses, Enoch, Noah and Jesus. Centuries later the forbidden arts and skills were acquired by a latter generation of human-hybrids such as Pythagoras, Socrates, Plato, Joan of Arc, Nostradamus, Sir Isaac Newton, Nikola Tesla, Albert Einstein, Edgar Cayce, Jose Silva, and many more enlightened human-hybrids throughout modern history. To many of you the name Einstein and Sir Isaac Newton are not known for having displayed any special abilities, a side from being smart, but they should be known for what they really were because, even though history does not recognize alchemy as being a legitimate science, it should be known that Newton and Einstein each practiced the art of alchemy, among other so-called forbidden things. Also adept at tapping into the universal mind were Galileo, Christopher Columbus, and all disciples of Jesus.

No One Has a Monopoly on God

Hearing the voice of God; and for that matter; having a conversation with God has never been reserved for the church, its clergymen, ministers, pastors, nor, is it reserved strictly for the use of prophets and psychics. Because everyone posses the gift and inner ability within themselves, to have a personal relationship with God, directly without help from anybody, or without having possession of any specialized skills or training to do so. History has proven time and time again, that the source universally identified as God, will speak to anyone who's prepared and willing to listen. Basically it all boils down to free will from within yourself.

The problem faced by most when trying to speak to God for the very first time in their life seems to be a matter of perception and reception. You see, while it is true that everyone has the potential gift of prophecy in all respect, not all are familiar with how the art of prophecy works; which in and of itself, is key to understanding all mysteries, manifestations, and miracles that has ever occurred in this reality. In other words, what it all comes down to is having an in-depth knowledge of how to go about fulfilling the task of communicating with God, and then having the ability to receive information that is certainly forthcoming.

Consciousness, mind, spirit and thoughts, are one and the same. Collectively they are the essence of all things, the forces of nature.

Note: The following stories, incredible as they may sound at first, are totally based in truth upon their source of origin.

Ted's Story

What you and everyone else reading this chapter would really like to know, is how can you tap into the universal mind for your very own purpose? And as promised, everything that I know about this subject will be revealed to you in this section. But, first it is best that I describe for you ways in which some in history, and modern society have used this unlimited power for themselves.

In the process of completing this chapter, I was influenced by the laws of synchronicity to pay particular attention to a modern day story of a miracle event, one involving a homeless man who proclaimed before all on live TV, that God had given him a golden voice. While many of those familiar with this story are quickly dismissive of the "God" claim, nevertheless the results of Ted Williams' overnight transformation of life and reality was nothing less than the results so often experienced first-hand by those who have learned the art of tapping into the universal mind for their needs.

Ted Williams had prayed numerous times, asking God to intervene in his life for the better. First off, Ted had a drug addiction to overcome, secondly, he had many years of homelessness, and at the time of this manifested miracle, Ted was living on the cold winter streets of Columbus, Ohio. Once he became inspired by the still, silent inner voice of his mind, Ted had suddenly developed a willingness to ask God for help in the only direct manner known to him, prayer. In the silence and stillness that accompany many of those who find themselves alone, sleeping in the streets as they struggle to navigate each day for a place of shelter, safety and solitude. Ted somehow managed to hear the voice of god within himself, and followed the advice that was given. Ted Williams created a sign made from a cardboard box, written in black ink, that spelled-out a phrase that any motorist who happened to drive by him would easily see. It read: "God has given me a golden voice."

Believe what you will about this story, but from the very first moment people heard the voice of Ted Williams, there was no doubt in their mind, nor that of others, who'd listen to his pitch, about the origins of his voice. In response to Ted's plea for help the universal spirit sprang into action, providing him with many offers of well paying jobs that Ted became so overwhelmed by the sudden attention he received from well meaning people from all walks of life familiar with his plight. The NBA sports franchise, the Cleveland Cavaliers offered Ted a house and a job, NFL Films put an offer on the table. Ted's story has since appeared on national news and talk shows alike, such as NBC, CBS and ABC. And the offers for Ted's golden voice keeps pouring in. The queen of daytime TV, Oprah Winfrey, offered to hire him. After spending time at a facility for substance abuse Ted has quite a few options to build a quality style of his choosing. All he needs to do now is pay attention to the inner voice of wisdom within himself known as the universal mind for guidance...

The Story of Joseph
(And his Still, Silent Voice)

The story of Joseph (Genesis: 39 - 50) impresses me a lot because, if it was factual and true of how the Genie within us sometimes works, it indicates a clear case of someone in biblical antiquity other than Abraham, Moses and Jesus, who had a clear understanding of how to access the mind of God. Joseph was known throughout the land of Egypt as a dream interpreter, historically. However, it was made clear in the Bible that Joseph did not interpret dreams, God did!

As stated elsewhere within this book, the power of God manifests in mysterious ways. I have asked on a number of occasions for an example, for a way that would easily demonstrate or explain to people what it is like when talking directly to God, which is something that most people are programmed and discouraged from doing by religion, science and politics. Well, I was directed (encouraged) to the story of Joseph within the Old Testament of the Christian and Hebrew Bible, sub-consciously. Keep in mind that I am not a Bible toting type of guy, but time after time while working on this book, which is about the Secret Mysteries of the Kingdom, I found myself wanting to read the Bible a lot. As weird as it may seem, many hidden or overlooked secrets began to manifest themselves the more I read the book. Basically, the story of Joseph is about the still, silent voice that so many have spoken about over the years as being the voice of God.

Life of a Dream Interpreter

Joseph, son of Jacob, was sold into slavery by his brothers, who were all jealous of him. As a slave he worked at the estate of

Potiphera, the Pharaohs captain of the guards, where he soon became overseer of all prisoners and the most trusted among all servants. Being of a bright mind and well conditioned physique, Joseph's appearance did not escape the wandering eyes of his master's wife. One day while the master was away on business, he had left Joseph (his most trusted servant) in charge of his estate until his eventual return. The master's wife saw this as an opportunity to have her way with Joseph sexually. In rejecting her advances, the master's wife felt scorned and sought revenge against Joseph upon the return of her husband. She proclaimed that Joseph had tried to have his way with her while he was away, and so the Lord of the house had Joseph imprisoned.

Most Trusted Prisoner

Instead of rotting away in prison, Joseph quickly became the most trust worthy of all inmates. And once again he was elevated above all other prisoners to that of overseer, as he was shown favoritism. After time had past, the king of Egypt had committed two of his servants to prison, and Joseph was given authority over them. One was the King's cup bearer, the other his chief baker.

Rise of the Dream Interpreter

One day the king's imprisoned servants approached Joseph about a dream that each of them had. They wanted to have them interpreted and asked Joseph if he could do it. Joseph's reply was: "Only God can do that." So the cup-bearer told Joseph about his dream. "In my dream there was a vine, and on it there were three branches. As soon as the vine budded, its blossoms came forth and the clusters ripened into grapes. The Pharaoh's cup was in my hand, and I pressed grapes into his cup." the cup bearer proclaimed.

And Joseph's interpretation: "The three branches are three days. In three days the Pharaoh will release you and bring you back into his home as his cup-bearer." "Remember me" Joseph said, "And speak kindly of me to the Pharaoh, for I was sold into slavery by my brothers out of jealousy. I had committed no wrongs." Seeing that Joseph's interpretation of the cup-bearer's dream was favorable, the baker asked that his dream be interpreted. As soon as the baker told Joseph of his dream, Joseph said: "In three days the Pharaoh will cut off your head." and what Joseph said about both dreams came to pass.

Several years later, the Pharaoh had a dream of which he wanted interpreted. He called for all of Egypt's magicians, priests, and wise-men to interpret his dreams, but none could do it. The cup-bearer then told the king about Joseph, and how right he was about his dreams, and that of the baker. He told Pharaoh that Joseph said the baker's head would be cut-off in three days, and it was.

Then the Pharaoh sent for Joseph, and immediately asked him if he could interpret his dreams. Joseph said, "No, but God could." So the Pharaoh began to tell Joseph about his dreams. When the Pharaoh finished, Joseph began interpreting his dreams; he said: "The dreams are one, God has revealed to you what is about to occur. The seven good cows and seven ears, means seven years; and the seven sick cows and seven empty ears are also seven years. There will come seven years of plenty for Egypt, followed by seven years of lack and famine. A shortage of food will result if you do not act accordingly."

With the information the Pharaoh received from Joseph's interpretations, he sought advice from his wise-men. Based upon their recommendations the King ordered that food be stored away during the seven years of plenty, so that when the seven lean years lack of and famine occurred there would be enough provisions for the kingdom to survive. And so, just as predicted it all came to pass.

The Pharaoh was so impressed by Joseph's ability to communicate with God, so he appointed Joseph the governor over all of Egypt's land and interests. Joseph was second in command only to the Pharaoh. It was then that Joseph's name was changed by the Pharaoh to: Zephenath-Paneah. And he was then given the daughter of Potiphera, as his wife. For those of you wondering why there is very little mentioned of his wife in the Bible it could be because she was not a Hebrew. She was Egyptian. And, after reuniting with his father, Jacob and his brothers, lived a life of prosperity until he died at the age of one hundred and ten years.

Comments on Dreams and Interpretations

Everybody dreams whether they realize it or not. Dreaming occurs at various stages of sleep as the your physical brain receives brainwave frequencies from alpha to delta range, but only a very small percentage of people have the ability to recall their dreams at the delta state.

The ability to read dreams is a prophetic gift that everyone has if they are willing to accept the notion that such a thing is possible. Dream interpretations are mentioned in various places throughout the Bible for one reason, and I believe that reason is because there are still people in the world today who are very good at decoding dreams. Known as the interpreter of dreams in the Bible, Joseph's story gives some of the most classic examples of how the mental forces within works. Please keep in mind that this ability is far from being unique. Accessing the mental powers within you allows for correct meaning and/or definition of your dreams. And sometimes dreams offers the only solutions available.

Known as the sleeping prophet, Edgar Cayce recorded more than 45,000 dream interpretations which provided everything from medical and illness diagnosis to stock market and business advice. I've mentioned Edgar's name simply because some folks would have you believe prophets only existed during biblical and ancient times, and that there are none with this ability living among us today. The point I am making is that life is far more than what it seems, and that everyone dreams a dream that becomes a part of their reality.

Truth about Healing Powers

What if I told you that all disease and sickness in this world are curable. Would you believe me? Better yet, what if you could routinely cure anyone in need of medical help? What if you had the same powers to heal people as Jesus did? If all of the above were true, what would your life be like today, or tomorrow? What would you give in order to have this kind of power?

In this current lifetime, I have seen miracles happen to people from all walks of life. Miracles can and will happen to you—when you begin using the forces of your subconscious mind in a conscious manner. These things are possible because the powers to heal yourself and others are within you, they have always been there for you to use. The power to heal lies in uncovering the true nature and abilities within every human being. You see, we are all spirits having a physical experience in a reality we call life. Our minds are totally non-physical, and it lives-on even when the body ceases to exist. In fact, a body can't live without the mind.

At first, when I realized the ability to tap into the healing powers of nature are within me, and that I can heal myself and, also help others to heal too, my entire outlook on life became clearer. Suddenly I became very knowledgeable about how to apply these special powers at will.

What is about to be revealed to you in this chapter might be somewhat difficult for you to believe at first. As a matter fact, there are a certain number of people living amongst us in the world today, for whatever reason, will do anything to keep you from knowing the truth about this subject. Logically speaking, healing miracles performed by ordinary people could not exist, according to many theologians and professional skeptics. Most religions would still have you believe that such events only occurred during the biblical era by a certain chosen few. Some scientists have stated that all purported claims of miraculous and/or instantaneous healing events in today's society are anomalies, fabrication, or, are the work of charlatans. Speaking of charlatans, no professional community on earth is immune from them. Even modern medicine and medical practitioners have them among their ranks, too.

Trained medical practitioners and energy healers alike should form a coalition and really begin working together. It is time for all healers regardless of their methods to put aside any differences and opinions about which side of the debate is right, and start focusing on making life better for those in need of treatment. Only when working together as one will society finally be able to stamp-out all diseases plaguing humanity. For far too long both communities have waged open war against each other with no end in sight, if these selfish motives were to continue, everyone stand to lose in the end.

Please keep in mind as you mentally consume the information available in this chapter, that from a historical perspective, events of miraculous healing didn't just occur during the life and times of Jesus. There have been and continues to be in fact, a smorgasbord of manifestations that were unexplained medical miracles that have occurred in every human era throughout earth's existence. And to anyone who has really studied the life and times of Jesus on a scholarly level will duly attest that Jesus himself never stated that only he, and he alone had powers to heal people. In fact it was just the opposite---because in Matthews version of the Bible, which was first published in 1537 by John Rogers, states that Jesus said: "That these things that I do, and have done, you can do also, even greater than I." Furthermore, according to various passages written within ancient biblical texts about Jesus, it is stated that he taught his disciples how they could perform healing services and then encouraged them to go out among the people and perform healing miracles for those in need. And as such, many of them did just that. Secondly, little is ever mentioned about the healing powers displayed by Abraham, Moses, Enoch, Noah and others who lived thousands of years before Jesus. Today's modern society seem to conveniently forget Joan of Arc, Nostradamus, Edgar Cayce and the young Canadian healer who simply goes by the name Adam, who all came thousands of years after Jesus.

Basically what I'm trying to impress upon you or anyone else willing to read this chapter and take it to heart, is that we all have it within us, the ability to heal both ourselves and others. But, we must first be totally willing and accepting of this wonderful aspect of being human. For it is only by way of accepting this gift where it counts most that we can begin to unleash its awesome capabilities.

Just think about it for a moment! Wouldn't it be nice to live in a world where everybody has the ability to heal themselves and others of any known or unknown condition? Better still, wouldn't be nice if no one ever becomes sick?

Mind is the master. What hasn't been created by thought does not exist.

Ayya Khema

Telepathic Healing

I have chosen a form of energy healing that I've termed as 'telepathic healing' in all of the healing services I partake. First, lets clear-up some misconceptions that anyone might have before things get out of hand.

Unlike some members of the energy healing community, I don't claim to know all there is to know about the energy healing process. But, for what I do know, the method and form I choose to use is very effective, and I am willing to share my system of energy healing with anyone wanting to know how to do it. Secondly, the term telepathic healing; although the phrase simply came to the forefront of my imagination one day; is not a terminology that I created.

Such words, in one phrase or another has been in use a very long time by many practitioners throughout time. Thirdly, by using this chosen method of energy healing provides me with a built-in protection mechanism for defending myself against any possible charges of practicing medicine without a license that some legal-eagle might want to bring forth.

Another built-in shield that protects me legally from such a claim is that I prefer never to meet with a prospective client prior to performing a healing service. In a sense, I don't want to know what the nature of their illness is before hand or afterward simply because it really doesn't matter.

There is a philosophical purpose behind the insistence of not communicating with a potential client about the nature of their illness. I'm a strong believer in the adage: there are no sicknesses nor conditions that makes the body ill, there are only those who imagine themselves to be sick or ill. In other words, illness is simply a condition of a bad imagination. Heal the mind, end the condition.

With all of that said, I do find it helpful to have the most recent image, or something that belongs to them, or someone close (relative) of the person I am trying to heal. It also helps a whole lot if the patient is willing to be healed. And lastly, I never charge a single dime to anyone for healing services.

Before discussing further any actual healing procedures and cases with you, I want to share a story about the first time that I performed an intentional healing service of a total stranger. Prior to this event I had only performed healing services on kids and those close to me.

You know, kids really are the easiest people in the world to heal. The reason for this is simply because most kids spend a lot of time in the alpha brainwaves frequency mode, this allows their imaginative energies of healing to take effect that much easier and faster than an adult.

By comparisons, adults spend most of there waking-state in beta mode; which takes far longer for healing energies to manifest. What I'm saying, is nothing new at all. Shamans, mystics, theologians, and some scientists have known about these natural healing properties in younger people for centuries.

Healing yourself and others is easier than driving a car once you know what to do!

Instantaneous Healing
(Telepathically)

The stories you are about to read are all based in truth. With that said, I had never tried to heal someone without their acknowledgment before, but a whispering voice resonating deep from within me kept saying: "You can do it." Although I could hearthis voice in my mind, it sounded as if it came from outside of me. I know that I'm not crazy, and I know what I heard, and I know what I hear. Overtime I have learned to tell the difference between the voice, and the inner workings of my imagination.

The voice from within is always helpful, and never destructive. I say this for those of you reading this, you should know if the information you hear from within your mind is ever detrimental to you or anyone else, then the source of what you are receiving is coming from somewhere else and should not be trusted.

Now, this is about my first adult cold case. It involves someone who didn't even know me, or what I was capable of doing for her, nor did she ask for help. She was a beautiful young woman and a total stranger.

It was obvious to me and others on this night that this young lady was experiencing a great deal of excruciating pain when she entered the emergency room of a local hospital in central Florida, screaming at the top of her lungs.

There was no doubting the level of pain she harbored as her screams for some sort of relief could be heard well beyond the walls of the ER room, and into an adjacent parking lot. And the only help that medical staffers could administer to her for the moment came in the offering of a wheelchair, of which she immediately slumped down into the chair. I listened to her screams for help intently as they became louder moment by moment, as did everyone else in the room and within range. It seemed as if her body was somehow being violently tortured by a cadre of unseen forces. At one point her screams for help and relief grew so loud I begin to feel the beat of her heart. After what seemed like a final plea to members of the medical staff to intervene, her voice became grossly harsh, and she then called upon God to quell the pain. "Oh GOD! She screamed, PLEASE… HELP MEEE!"

She yelled out at the top range of her lungs until there was no air left in them, again and again, repeating the same phrase for help. Until finally, I could stand it no more and remain on the sideline, I was compelled to intervene and take action by the voice from

199

within me to do something that I'd never done or tried before. Instinctively, I knew that something of an unconventional nature had to be done to help her. So without much hesitation and thought into the matter, I sprang into action!

Without making a scene, I gently closed my eyes – and entered into the Alpha mode (basic psychic level one). Telepathically, I visualized and then imagined sending out white streaming energy light beams to her (the woman) higher consciousness. I imagined that this light of positive energy entered into her body from the top of her head, and then worked its way downward towards her feet. As I did this, it pushed and removed all negative energies from her head to her toes, and replaced it with a loving and positive white energy light. I then imagined that this renewed energy from source encircled her entire physical body. And then, I imagined sending another message to her higher consciousness telepathically that said: You are now healed!

The moment I completed this task, she instantly became quiet, settled down in the wheelchair, and at that moment the young woman looked directly into my eyes as if she somehow knew what had just transpired. As if she had awakened in that moment to powers of spirit, she thanked me with direct contact from her eyes, and a slight smile of approval. To me, my first case of instantly healing a total stranger without prior knowledge was a great indication of synchronicity and the law of attraction at play – the universe's way of not only helping this young lady get rid of the pain, it also helped me to understand more about the energy healing process in ways I never did before, as a result I've learned a lot from that first chance encounter.

Since that event, I've gone on to heal a number of people with issues of bad health and/or sicknesses ranging from pancreatic pain, intestinal cancer, throat cancer, migraine headaches, knee injuries, and a single case of someone who just wanted to quit smoking. Once I helped a patient that was bleeding so profusely from a head injury that it left a one inch gaping hole in her. The healing manifested instantaneously cause my mind was cleared of light and sound. This all came from within me to help.

Of all the miraculous healing successes that I have witnessed from myself and others, I have never physically laid a hand on anyone. In fact, I've never asked any of my clients beforehand about the nature or condition of their problem. I prefer it that way—so that no one could ever accuse me of practicing medicine without a license. And, since I conduct all healing services free of charge to everyone it would be hard-pressed for anyone to call me a charlatan or a fraud. The simple matter is that all miracle healing of people starts in the mind, and is then manifested into reality by the heart.

Over the years, I've performed telepathic healing services over both the internet and telephone successfully. Once you have an idea of who the patient is, it really doesn't matter one iota if they are with you, across town, another city, or somewhere in another part of the world. Once you build confidence in your energy healing powers, the results are the same whenever and where ever such services are in need.

Bare in mind, each healer is different, as well as each person needing to be healed. Its all a matter of preference. Sometimes it may take several sessions before healing takes effect, while other cases may become instantaneously effective. Why this happens, I don't know for certain but I do have an opinion. I believe it all comes down to the spiritual will of both the healer and the patient at the time of service. A strong spiritual will can be produce stronger healing energies than a weaker one.

A Chance to Heal

At this time I would like to share with you another story of a healing event that occurred instantly. The names of the people involved in this story has been changed for reasons of privacy. This story begins with a bit of synchronicity involved. Robert and I have met only once in person, but we've communicated numerous times via telephone since our chance encounter. Robert stood about 6 feet in height, slender build, and medium brown skin.

As Robert and I continued talking, I learned that he holds a degree in business administration. By chance (synchronicity) we bumped into each other at a Barnes and Noble bookstore in Winter Garden, Florida. He was there in search of a good book on metaphysics. As it turned out, Robert was in the process of writing a book about his theories of how the universe is made. At the time, I was there seeking a good book along the same topic.

Immediately I sensed that this guy was somewhat puzzled about which book to purchase, and I offered my help, since I knew first-hand the subject matter of each book. From that moment on we began to share information about ourselves to each other and that is when we realized that we had something in common. We were both in the process of writing a book in the subject area of psychic phenomena and metaphysics. While I lived only about 20 miles from that particular bookstore, Robert was just visiting the from Pensacola, Florida with his fiance – Monica.

As synchronicity goes, we began to openly discuss various aspects of psychic phenomena when Robert suddenly realized – based upon my experiences, there might be a chance for his fiance to received psychic healing for pancreatic pain. According to Robert she'd been taking numerous pills prescribed by doctors and none seemed to help her condition. So, right then and there, he asked if I could help her. I then proceeded to explain the procedures involved in the healing process when all of a sudden, his fiance, Monica emerged from a nearby restroom. Robert introduced us but did not mention the nature of conversation, especially the part that I may be able to help her heal.

When I finally met Monica, my first reaction was to pay very close attention to her facial features and details of her body so that it would be easy for me to imagine her into my mind later that same night.

For some unknown reason my healing method seems to work faster and better during the night for most patients. This could be because most physical changes to the body occurs during the states of low brainwave activities, or altered states of mind which happens automatically every time we close our eyes and fall asleep.

For instance, we grow taller, lose or gain weight during sleep.

Basically, the best time for the body to heal is during the stages of sleep. So, for that reason alone I prefer to perform all energy healing services late at night when most people are sound asleep and there is less ambient atmospheric interference from other signals.

Just as I had promised earlier to Robert , I performed my brand of energy healing to his fiance, Monica later that night. Within a few days I received a call from Robert, he wanted to know more about psychic healing because he had noticed a major improvement in Monica's condition.

As usual all questions asked by Robert pertaining to the process of healing were answered to the best of my knowledge as much as possible. I did received a few more calls from Robert about energy healing insights – and in particular, Robert wanted to know how he too, could learn to become a healer. Since departing the information Robert requested, I have yet to hear from him again. To me, that is a sign of success.

The Holyfield Miracle

This was a story that manifested with national media attached all over it, but for one reason or another has since been long forgotten. It was also high profile and it reverberated around the world. It is now being told from a certain point of view, and it is very possible that others who were somehow involved in this story to hold an entirely different perspective about what actually transpired. Some, if not all of this information may even be searchable; or as they say nowadays--Google via the Internet. Incredulous as it may sound this story is based entirely on truth insofar as it can be retold.

It all occurred sometime during the month of May 1994. It involved the reigning heavy weight boxing champion of the world, Evander Holyfield. The champ had recently lost a match, and the world heavy weight title that goes along with it to a challenger named Michael Moorer; yes, he's the same boxer that was later floored in a losing effort to George Foreman (oldest boxer to win a heavyweight title). Anyway, the night Evander lost his match to Michael Moorer, the doctors who examined the the ex-champ discovered something unusual about his heart. An MRI would later confirm their findings. Evander was told that he had an enlarged heart, and that his life was at risk if he continued fighting. It was not good news for the ex-champ because it seemed like the end of the road for what had been a very successful and rewarding sports career, for it meant that the champ was at the top of boxing chain.

As you might imagine, such a revelation was sports biggest news at the time. By all accounts it seemed as though the boxing industry had seen the last of Evander (real deal) Holyfield, an undersized heavyweight ex-boxing champion who defied logic and moved up in weight class from the light-heavy division to the heavyweight division and became champion of world of boxing. At the time that all of this hoopla, I had just managed to open an investment account for Ron Bell, who was Evander's close friend and personal manager. Later, the champ himself opened an investment account with me. It was also a good thing that the champ's limo driver was a distant cousin of mine. From these connections I had became privy to a lot of information that many of those in the media would have died for. But as a man of my word, I didn't give out any insider's information, not even to my wife.

Yes, the former world heavyweight boxing champion was briefly a client, and I had visited him at his home in south Atlanta on several occasions. While this news became international headlines, and most everyone had included the ex-champ to be among the newly retired, somehow they forgot to mention this to Evander.

Evander's Miracle Healing

Apparently Evander decided to have a second opinion about his heart condition after receiving a healing-prayer from an evangelical pastor named Benny Hinn. This healing event was shown live on

TV, as Hinn performed a healing service expressly for Evander. The press was wildly crazed over this story. About a week later, after the healing service was performed, Evander announced to the media that his heart had been healed, and that he would soon fight again.

One could only imagine the national ruckus this announcement caused among those within the medical community and the press. Later tests conducted and released to the public by medical doctors would later confirm that Evander's heart was normal. You be the judge!

Attachment to matter gives rise to passions against nature. Thus trouble arises in the whole body; Be in harmony... If you are out of balance, take inspiration from the manifestations of your true nature.

Yeshua

Everybody is a Potential Healer
(If they Chose to be)

The ability to psychically heal someone is only one aspect of psychic phenomena. Reason for this assumption is because we are all spiritual beings, who are experiencing a physical manifestation in the realm of earth. The gift of being born into the physical realm does have a minor set-back, and that we temporarily forget our spiritual core origins. As for why this happens is a mystery, but if this was not part of the overall grand plan of things, your physical world would be tremendously different than it is now. Since we are all spiritual beings at the core level of existence, we have at our disposal the power to summon energy into existence out of pure thought. Energy by its very nature must obey the will of spirit. Another metaphor of understanding this phenomenon is to realize that energy follows thought, always.

Energy can be manifested for good or negative purposes. If the cause of creating it is healing, you can assume its use is for a positive effect to change the condition of another spirits' physical property (body) in an effort to correct any problems there may be. This is all possible because there is only one of us here in existence.

We are all interconnected to everything there is, from sub-atomic particles so small in size that their existence can only be theorized at this moment in time, to the more commonly known exotic subatomic particles all the way up the chain to atoms, microbes, molecules, cells, organs, and finally human beings. Our interconnectedness extends to further to every planet in the solar system, the galaxy, the stars, and the universe and all its exotic elements, dark matter and dark energy. If you were to look at this from a purely metaphysical perspective, you'll discover that this interconnectedness extends to both seen and unseen forces of nature, which includes forces of the mind and to all who lives, and to all who have died.

The force that connects us all is known by many names around the world and throughout the course of human history. What I am saying to you is this: the name used is not that important, it is only important that you know that there is something which exists outside conventional knowledge and beyond physicality, and that we each have access to it. Basically what it all comes down to is that each individual is responsible for and is in control of their own thought process. Everyone is born with the ability to be an energy healer whether they except this notion or not. Unconsciously, everyone has healed someone – somewhere in time and space many times before. It is consciously that many of us seem to forget our innate powers of being uniquely human on the third rock from the sun.

By reading this chapter it is my hope that I'll be able to convince you that healing yourself or another is not only a given aspect of reality, it is also the way nature is designed...

Things You should know

Before you start practicing the various techniques of energy healing outlined in this book, it would be remiss of me not to point out to you that there are other ways to perform energy healing, and that no one way works best for everyone. You are encouraged to seek other methods of energy healing just to see what works best for you. Because, knowledge is only powerful when you know how to apply it, at the same time you should realize that there are common tenets present within all styles of healing methods from which you can learn about. Psychic healing (or energy healing), involves the mind of a healer and of a patient. I say this because no matter who you are or what you do, if the mind is not willing, no healing will take effect. This statement applies to all healers, even Jesus. And last, but not least, the patient's permission must always be granted in order for the healing to manifest within them, no matter what. There are many healers who would challenge that previous statement, but the laws of the universe governs every aspect of our abilities. It's quite simple really, for if a patient is unconscious, or simply unable to speak to you for whatever reason, you may still obtain permission to perform a energy healing services on them by making contact with them on the spiritual plane.

Techniques of Healing

The techniques of psychic or energy healers are all performed in the realm of the mind. Your mind has a unique universal language and nature of communicating with other minds that defies all logic, time, dimensions and space. This is known as telepathy (see chapter on telepathy). Telepathy can be both auditory and/or visualized imaging, but in every situation telepathy involves your mind's ability to transmit. In the case of energy healings in which I've been personally involved with, both forms of telepathy have been applied with equal results. Whatever approach a healer chooses to use is obviously the best option for them. If it works, use it.

Additionally, the following types of energy delivering methods must also be accompanied with the use of telepathy (each covered in telepathy chapter):

1. intention (thoughts),
2. use of hands,
3. prayer,
4. imagination,
5. visualization,
6. distant healing.

When the methods mentioned above are performed within the environment of an altered state of mind they are very powerful, as a result a healing will manifest into reality according to God's promise, which is also known as the law of attraction.

Healers of the world

There are many energy healers in the world. They come from various backgrounds and walks of life. Healers can be found in every country, statehood, community, culture and household.

One things for sure, contrary to some religious tenets no one has a monopoly on energy healing, mainly because everyone can do it if they understand the processes involved.

Many energy healers have no idea of what they are truly capable of doing; while others are aware of their abilities. Some people believe that there are restrictions to certain types of conditions whereby a healing can manifest, while other healers are of the belief that there are no known limitations. The term energy healing, as defined by the nature and aspect of the word energy, generally implies that there are no limits or conditions that energy healing cannot correct. There is a good reason for this belief, because the very nature energy itself cannot be limited, created nor destroyed. However, it can be used, and used again ad-infinitum, because the universe itself wastes nothing.

Those who've become familiar with their innate healing powers either learned about such abilities accidentally, or were taught how to invoke these powers by some formal or informal school of metaphysics or mystics. There are some who have managed to develop healing powers entirely on their own as a result of spiritual will and/or psychic intuition. In the end we must realize that healing powers are developed within us, and are not created, for creation has already occurred.

Energy Healing & Hollywood

There is a bit of truth, good and bad about all movies and fictional-books, alike that includes in some manor feats performed by miracles works or energy healers. When I first became aware of Rasputin, it was from watching a two hour made for TV movie. The way Rasputin was portrayed easily brought forth thoughts of evilness. Years later when I finally researched his life and times it was discovered that Hollywood had this man all wrong. I am often reminded of impact from assumptions based in part are in whole, as a result of stereo-types portrayed by the Hollywood entertainment complex when it comes down to showing scenes that involves healing people. There is a lot to be learned from ancient healer archetypes who lived before modern times. For instance, the greatest story ever told is inspiring, it makes people believe that there is something out there other than themselves that has the power to perform miracles at will.

Unlike the portrayals of Rasputin, not many people alive today ever bring into question the exploits of Yeshua's medical mysteries, but when it comes to someone of this era displaying like abilities as Yeshua did nearly 3000-5000 years ago, it seems to always be accompanied by fodder. Why do films producers almost always include evil when showing what many have come to know is possible?

Pushing Hollywood and the entertainment complex aside, even just for a moment, as we look beyond entertainment values and skepticism and realize that there is a field of knowledge existing independent of traditional means and information pertaining to an ever growing profession of reliable energy healers. In a society where giant pharmaceutical companies are allowed to virtually create new diseases by way of TV advertising and marketing. It is quite obvious, or should be, that such bombardment of the subjective mind with detrimental information is at the root of most ailments. What these giant, legalized drug-dealers won't tell you is what you need to know. Here's something for you to think about! All new drugs must be tested against the placebo effect before being allowed to sell their new drugs to the public. In other words, new drugs must perform better than your own ability to heal yourself with just your mind. So now, you should wonder, why do they still insist on saying that energy healing doesn't work when they must test all new drugs against it?

As for Hollywood, you can't blame movie producers for wanting to make money. Let's face it, secondly only to sex...evil sells!

Witches, Sorcerers and Witchcraft?

You may be wondering, just what does witches, sorcerers and witchcraft have to do with energy healing? Short answer; Everything! So, for that reason, and that reason only, this subject

211

may be highly controversial in some social circles, it has the potential to even upset a lot of folks who may consider themselves open minded. Based upon research and intuitive knowledge, among the oldest energy healing methods, or means of psychic healing and medical procedures performed in human history; which occurred eons before the healing miracles of Jesus; were performed by what we now know as witches. And here is the evidence behind this assumption: the initial healers were women who bore children of the fallen angels. This is stated in Genesis 6, verse 4. It states that the Nephilim were on the earth in those days--and also afterward, when the sons of God went to the daughters of men and had children by them. They were heroes of old, men of renown.

Now, here me out on this. In common English this means that the children of God (fallen angels), chose to mate with women who born here on earth. And that these women were the daughters of human beings, and that these women bore children of mixed blood, and these children became some of histories greatest characters. They were the best fighters, hunters and thinkers of most groups. Also, these women were taught mysteries of the kingdom, enchantments, roots, spells and drugs. They were shown how to make fire and mix metals to form swords, shields and weapons of war. Most of all they were shown the art of energy healing.

Overtime and throughout history, because of their in depth skills that were shrouded in mystery and hidden from ordinary humans, many of these women became known as witches, and the men born of such unions became known as sorcerers. And their mysterious methods for healing, and their abilities to cast spells and engage in strange rituals became known as witchcraft. For the rest of society we have benefited and learned quite a lot about how to help an injured person heal. You might even credit historical witches and sorcerers as the true founders of modern medicine and medical procedures. But one has to wonder why they chose to leave-out information pertaining to energy healing among such disclosures?

The Field
(Space)

The field, as it has come to be known, is where everything originates, including psychic powers, astral projections, miracles, and energy healing vibrations, need I say more here? This is why it doesn't matter which method a healer chooses. If a healer looks into a bowl of water for signs or symbols, or use what is called the mental video technique approach to diagnose an illness, the end result is all that really counts. Meta physicists believe that there is an electromagnetic field which permeates all of space and time. In my view, I believe that there is nothing other than space (the void), which connects everything, and that consciousness fills this space, which also allow for thought-waves to emanate, which basically vibrates (telepathic signals), traveling vast distances much faster than the speed of light. And since consciousness is mind-vibrations, which takes on the properties and characteristics of electromagnetism within the void. In short, whichever theory may be correct the world may never know. But most importantly, we do know that whatever it is out or in there, it is also within each and everyone of us, and that it is very interactive, it is responsive to our inner most feelings, intentions and thoughts.

Each healer has a preferred method for obtaining information about their prospective client, and/or unleashing energy healing powers from within. Chief among any method or technique is a core belief. Without a core belief, nothing happens at all. As for as the field is concerned, in my view it is just another way of expressing the powers of God that is present and available to anyone who unlocks and taps into the powers within themselves.

Belief in Your ability is Key

Belief in your ability is the key to unlocking the gates of the temple (your body) to manifest a healing. In other words, according to the Bible; "A sickness is not unto death, rather it is for the glory of God, that the son (light) of man may be glorified through it."

It doesn't stop there; John 14:17 states: "For the spirit of truth, whom the world cannot conceive, for it neither sees nor knows, for it dwells within you, as you."

What I get from reading like passages from the Gospels is that it is not you or your body that is sick, it is just your imagination. And if you were to imagine that you are healthy instead of being sick, a healthy body will manifest irregardless of any ill-conceived conditions to have attracted to it with bad thoughts, this is in accordance with universal law.

There is a well known healer-author in Canada known only as Adam. Adam states in his book that he heals people in a dream. I for one am a believer. Prior to knowing about the existence of Adam I had long suspected that healing is most effective during the stages of sleep, and especially when performed at theta or delta mind-wave levels. Adam calls his brand of energy healing, dream healing. I prefer to use the term telepathy-healing for what I do. Both methods are similar in that a recent image of the patient is preferred, but not totally necessary, the mental forces of imagination and visualization of light rays entering a holographic image of a client's body. It also helps to have a detailed knowledge of the human anatomy.

Personally, I have been successful on several occasions where a healing took effect without an image of the client. In one instance only a name of the client was known. This is why I prefer to call my particular version of energy healing: telepathic healing; simply because there are times when an image of a person in need may not be available for whatever reason, even so a healing is still a possibility.

Energy Healing Procedures

1. You must have permission from the patient to heal them, for without their will to heal, no healing can take place according to the law of free will. So begin by asking: do you want to be healed?

214

2. Belief. You must believe and expect a healing to take effect on your client within your mind and heart.

3. Imagination and visualization. Take 5 deep breaths and exhale normally. Then imagine & visualize facial features of the person in question within your mind. Imagine surrounding their body with white or yellow healing rays of light. See them in a healthy state.

4. Healing can take place at great distances (unlimited) using telepathy to deliver healing energies to a client.

Make it a habit to end all energy healing sessions by saying these words (believe it in your heart): YOU ARE HEALED!

Final Note:
In conclusion the methods, technology, and the educational background of a healer has no bearings on the eventual outcome or why the healing process takes effect. It does matter if the belief of both healer and patient are positive towards the outcome. I believe that if a patient does not believe that a healing will occur, then the healing will not manifest. In cases such as these, I would make contact with the patient on a subconscious level for permission to heal. If the answer is still not allowing you to heal them, then there is nothing that can be done about it.

PS.
Meditation is a great way to increase your personal force-field, it builds strength in the energy healing process and allows direct communications with the infinite source.

I have come to know thyself and thus understand that I am a sun of God, and that within me emanates all the powers of Source.

Meditation

There are many forms of meditation techniques, complete with a number of postures from which to choose. Since learning how to meditate by way of trial and error as a teenager, I'm of the opinion that there is no one way suitable for everyone. And, there's certainly no one style of meditation more beneficial than others; simply put, when all is said and done about the benefits one can attain from meditation. After all, we are essentially dealing with the mental powers of the subconscious-mind; in a natural state; which is the most powerful state of being within the entire universe.

Meditation is a practice that has the distinction of being much older than Christianity, Judaism, and Islamism combined. In fact, all ancient spiritual gurus and prophets meditated.

However, it's important to note that meditation is not a religion, it is simply a means of reconnecting with cosmic energies between the individual self, and the universe. When you are just being, as when meditating, you are much closer to the UN-created source than at any other moment in your life; aside from the act of dreaming and death.

Meditating is not the only way to calm your conscious-mind when trying to experience total mental relaxation and bliss. But, it has become the most widely used technique second only to sleeping and the use of drugs; of which I am totally against. The mere act of meditating simply allows anyone to reach an alternate state of mental being, safely.

Besides, alcohol and drug use tears a molecular hole in the flow of vital energy (spiritual-energy) that surrounds, animates and protects the physical body, which weakens the body's defense mechanism making it susceptible to the flow of negative energies, which causes all known sicknesses and disease. One of the easiest ways to achieve the benefits of meditation is to allow a few more minutes of time before falling asleep each night, or about 15 minutes before getting out of bed in the morning.

Just let your mind wonder as it may. After spending some time doing this (it varies with everyone), you should be able to hold your mind on a single thought (mental video) for at least a few seconds at a time. Overtime and with consistent practice your ability to perform this task will become noticeably enhanced and you'll be able to focus your mind a great deal longer on a single thought, image or event. When you reach this stage of meditation you'll be able to accomplish some amazing things in your life; such as healing your body of any illnesses or disease. In fact; as many who meditate will attest; you may never become sick again!

Meditating will help to keep you looking much younger than your years would indicate. One might even be lead into believing that the fountain of youth can be found in the art of meditation. And you know what? They just might be right!

All prophets of the Biblical era and throughout antiquity had some unique way of altering their mental state of being for various reasons while tapping into the universal source. In other words; the main techniques that were being used by renowned prophets; seers; mystics; alchemists and so on; although not mentioned or recognized by scholars, nor historians as fact, clearly indicates that the art of meditation in some form or another was chiefly practiced.

"There is no doubt in my mind that Jesus once lived amongst us, and he too, meditated. From my point of view Jesus was the most gifted psychic to ever walked the planet...."

Why I Started Meditating?

When I first began meditating as a teenager, I would simply close my eyes--remaining still and quiet for as long as possible, while sitting in a lotus position. I meditated a lot back then, mainly because it was a cool thing to do after watching several martial arts movies that always seemed to have someone engaged in meditation. Back then, not once did I ever concern myself with breathing in any particular way. For starters, breathing is a natural activity for everybody. We don't have to think about it because it just happens; it's a part of nature. As an adult with half a century of wisdom behind me, I have learned quite a bit more techniques to use when I meditate. Pretty much, everything I do now when I practice is the same as before, except that I have added mind scanning and mental projection skills to my meditation technique.

Since there is no one right way of meditating for everybody; my advice to you is to experiment with a number techniques and methods until you have discovered what works best for you. Remember: the fundamentals of meditation; as its original definition; is to do nothing; while practicing the art of being.

Practice as often as possible and eventually you'll discover a system, or invent a new way of doing things that may become helpful not only for yourself, but for others as well. The thing about meditation is that its residual effects are all beneficial.

Also, as you have most likely figured out by now, meditating allows you to access a part of yourself that has long since been forgotten; your psychic abilities. Sooner or later you'll realize as I have, that when you learn to reactivate your psychic powers you'll gain invaluable insight into many of life's mysteries; and maybe, just maybe you'll be able to save the life of someone you love in the process of rediscovering your higher self.

Note: The secret to meditation is to do nothing except normal breathing, for a while. All that is required of you other than doing nothing is to close your eyes and breathe normally until you are done.

Why Should You Meditate?

Meditation in one form or another; is used by most psychics and remote viewers to slow down brainwave frequencies (activities of the mind). By doing this simple form of mental relaxation; it allows them to enter into an altered state of mind; that I call borderland. While in this altered state of mind (borderland), psychics are able to gain access to their subconscious mind while maintaining a full state of awareness at the same time. Once anyone has successfully gained access to their subconscious mind, things of a supernatural nature can be done.

As mentioned before, there are benefits to be gained from meditating; such as unleashing your psychic senses; increased memory ability and enhanced intelligence beyond your wildest belief's; and the skills necessary to completely heal yourself and others of any illnesses that may manifest in the body. And when I say any illness that may exist; I literally mean just that. In a sense, it is never our bodies that need to be healed of illness, for it is only that of our imagination that is sick; every single time..

With time, effort and patients anyone can learn this time proven and tested art of meditation that is slowly, but surely, becoming more widely accepted and used by many traditional medical practitioners in the west as an added course of treatment.

So far to date there is only one problem with meditation, and that it is so easy; cheap; and virtually cost free; anyone can learn to do it.

Do you believe that drug companies will ever encourage people to meditate to get rid of pain as a course of treatment first; instead of being medicated with drugs? Why do you think they call it medicated in the first place?

How to Meditate?

Find a quiet place where you can relax without being disturbed for at least 15 minutes. You can sit in a chair; on the floor; or lie flat on your back on the bed, or on the ground (if outside). I would prefer that you not lay down on the bed for this exercise because the bed is very conducive towards helping you to fall asleep. You may cross your legs or extend them, it's really a matter of individualized preference for whatever makes you feel relaxed. If you are using a chair for this exercise, please keep your back and spine as straight and relaxed as humanly possible. The main objective is for you to become as relaxed and comfortable as you can for this exercise without the act of falling asleep.

Breathing

Many practitioners of meditation will tell you that breathing is the bridge between altered states of the mind. In other words, they strongly believe that the simple act of breathing holds the secrets to entering the spiritual realm. Breathing is a physical and non-physical phenomenon--controlled by spiritual means. Once you are settled into a position that is right for you, gently close your eyes and begin focusing on breathing, normally. Keep your eyes closed for the duration of this exercise.

Chakra-Energy Scanning
(Instant Healing)

In your mind only, begin counting backwards from 10 to 1 in a slow pace. After you have reached the number "1" in the countdown process, move your mind (thought) to that of your "crown chakra." Imagine that you can see this energy around your head. While focusing on this area of your head surrounded by this energy--you should soon began feeling this energy's presence; using your mind's imagination and visualization powers. Another way to accomplish this task is to mentally visualize this energy around your head using your third eye.

When you begin to feel the actual energy itself, slowly shift the focus of your mind onto each energy-chakra area of your body until you reach the root chakra. Now move your mind upwards in reverse, spending time at each chakra area. When you reach the top of your head (crown chakra); say (mentally): I am are now completely healthy.

Third-Eye Activation (Pineal Gland)

The next meditation exercise is a repeat of the first, with a slight addition. It involves activation of your pineal gland (psychic eye). When you close your eyes, point them inward gently and slightly

221

toward the center of your nose, aiming them slightly above and between your eyebrows. This movement might feel a bit uncomfortable at first, but in time the discomfort will dissipate.

The purpose of turning your eyes inward towards the top center of your nose, between the eyebrows, is that this position allows more control over the movement of your mind; and this positioning also activates your pineal gland; which is positioned about one inch inside your frontal brain at this point. Your ability to focus on the moment and receive non-traditional information is greatly enhanced by this simple action.

"Many people in the new age community call the pineal gland: the third eye."

Now that you've learned how to scan your energy chakras using imagination and visualization powers of your mind, allow your mind to become quiet do absolutely nothing (standing-still) for a moment. After a period of time, you may now notice, from the stillness and silence of your mind, that flashes of colors began appearing and disappearing out of nowhere--moving as waves and sometimes as particles. These colors may even explode into other more vivid and exotic colors as they move from left to right across the mental video screen of your mind. These colors; as they appear; are actually scalar waves. Although many in the science community won't say so, but scalar waves are at the very beginning of creation. It is how the Mind (spirit) conjures up energy into becoming visible matter. In my opinion this is how we; as human beings create our reality every single split-split seconds of a second, every moment.

Note: Most are taught to visualize their mind as scanning the body during meditation. I have discovered, or re-discovered that by focusing on the energy chakras instead of the body, is more beneficial, instantly.

I am certain that my meditation knowledge and technique was used at some point in time during antiquity by students of the mystery schools.

Creating Your Daily Activities

The Judea-Christian Bible speaks of several miraculous events by prophets of old who somehow engaged in direct conversations with God, as if this activity alone is reserved for a privileged few. When in fact these types of events (talking directly to God) occurs all the time among so-called ordinary people, and that this sort of thing has been going on ever since the very beginning of humankind.

If you put into perspective the story of Adam and Eve, it illustrates an incredible event of a three-way conversation between Adam, Eve and God. The story of Adam and his second wife, Eve, (Lilith was Adam's first wife) is strictly from a Christian's point of view as being something out of the ordinary. When, in fact, there are numerous examples of such events occurring throughout the world with a growing acceptance and less skepticism within religions that are much older than Christianity, whose followers are openly encouraged among the rank and file to talk to their deity on a regular basis. Whatever your religious persuasion may or may not be, it should be noted that no one (religion) has a monopoly on God's ability to respond and manifest miracles on behalf of regular people, and even those who may not even be religious. God is God to everyone or source without exception. If this weren't the case then none of us would ever have reason for hope, redemption, and forgiveness.

Deep down inside everyone of us lies an undeniable belief in something, a source much higher than that of ourselves---we may not know exactly what that source is, or even care to know, but we all feel that something is there. Even people of science often find this to be very confusing within their ranks. At the behest of their profession and peers, many in the world of science are taking a leap of faith in going public with such personal revelations. Personally, I have always known within me that there is something, other than plain luck that has helped me to overcome many obstacles that were placed in my path. That's not to say that never again will such challenges occur, however, it does mean that I am better prepared to face any challenge in light of what I now know to be true.

There are Exceptions to the Rules

There are always exceptions to the rules; for instance; it is a known fact that God is speaking to each of us all the time, constantly from within, and on rare occasion God will speak to us with an external voice. In rare situations where God has chosen to speak externally, knowing any of the protocols outlined in this article becomes obsolete. When and why this happens no one knows for sure except to say that God makes the rules. In some cases, such an event occurs as a result of difficult situations that some maybe facing at any given time; or it may just be an elevated display of love and caring; or a simple act of giving to someone in need without any expectations that causes this normally stillness and silence of God's voice; only perceptible to the mind; to become physically audible.

The point I am making is this, God speaks to us in so many ways that it is hard to list them all. For example, instead of hearing an actual voice speaking to you in moments of need, the response from God may be in the form of mental images, or even the presence of a total stranger.

Note:

Keep in mind that not even Moses had the experience of hearing an external response from God. Moses; according to the Bible, stated that God had spoken to him through his mind. Now, many of you reading this article are probably wondering: What does all of this, if anything, what does it has to do with creating or manifesting the things you want or need into physical reality? The answer should be very obvious: "EVERYTHING!" Besides, it is best to be prepared to hear God's response before the your requests are ever made....

Note:

The paragraph above is a repeat from one mentioned earlier. As with any thing worth doing in life, repetition is needed. I don't know of any other way to put it. What we are trying to accomplish in this quest is to establish a personal line of communications with the source, intentionally.

I highly recommend to anyone pursuing this matter to begin by altering their state of mind while maintaining a grip on reality. In other words, it won't do much good to speak with God and not remember the conversation. As a first step you should become familiar with ways to relax your mind of all worry, and then relax your physical body afterward.

Preparation:
Before entering into a meditative state of mind completely I suggest that you make a statement (mentally) to yourself as follows:

1. There is comfort in knowing that "I AM" constantly enveloped in the presence of my true self and creator.
2. "I AM" SPIRIT, WHOLE AND CONNECTED TO ALL THAT EXIST. ALL IS FORGIVEN AND RELEASED.
3. "I AM" well deserving and fully capable of CREATING and MANIFESTING all that I desire and need, into physical reality, WITH GOD'S LOVE, for me to enjoy.
4. "I AM... THAT I AM."

You should learn this statement and make it your own. Change the wording to suit your personality, and recite it without reading. You must be able to convince your inner and deep feelings that this is your WILL. After learning to put forth a statement as that mentioned above it is best that you begin meditation. For those of you unfamiliar about how to meditate, I recommend that you read the chapter on meditation first.

How to create or manifest events in your life

The ability to create or manifest things into your reality is all about learning how to access the source from which all originate. And the best way to do that is to develop your psychic skills. Teaching others how to develop their psychic skills is something that I really enjoy doing. The very first thing I would have you do is to read about it.

Once you have consumed enough information to where it becomes familiar, and that you somewhat understand all terminology involved, then I would encourage you to adopt a daily routine of meditation.

But this is A.M.E.R.I.C.A....and Americans are accustomed to receiving or achieving the things they want or need, rather quickly. Basically what I am saying in a round-about way is that unlike people living in other countries, we lack PATIENCE!!!

Being PATIENT IS A VIRTUE...

When you've establish a daily ritual of meditation, I would then instruct you to practice the following mental exercises at least four times a week until you get the hang of it; visualization, imagination and telepathy.

Visualization

Visualization allows you to add an extra dimension to imagination known as animation. Animation brings images to life in your mind. In layman's term without visualization images of the mind is like watching a portrait hanging on a wall. Portraits don't move, but they are visually appealing. To become mentally efficient in this area you should spend a lot of time practicing the art of meditation.

Imagery
Allows you to practice the art of creating, by using the pineal gland and your mind's ability to visualize actually seeing events of what

you want to play out. From time to time I may refer to this as "Mental Video, Mind Movies," or a variation of the two.

Telepathy

Telepathy is easier than you'd ever imagine once you learn how to visualize properly from a psychic's point of view, and imagine things clearly with your mental faculties, telepathy is the next logical step. Without telepathy psychic powers will not work.

"Whom ever shall adhere to these words will not taste death."
----Yeshua

Learning to Hear the Source Within
Everyone alive today has at their disposal, a small and subtle voice that speaks to them, at least every now and then from within their own mind. You can hear this inner voice in your mind each and every moment of your life. I call this inner voice: "Source." Others may call it (the inner voice in their head) the "Giant Within."

Together with improved techniques in meditation, visualization, imagination and access to the small, subtle inner voice within you, you are now in possession of what it takes to develop your psychic skills, which in my opinion, is a necessity for anyone seriously wanting to create or manifest things into reality.

Meditation is so crucial.
Of course, there are more advanced methods developed by researchers that when applied it would enhance your psychic skills much faster and even further. But the methods mentioned beforehand are very effective. The other thing to remember about this is that there are many ways to develop PSI skills, and that not everyone will respond favorably to the same techniques. There is no magic bullet (at least not yet) that will suddenly penetrate your mind

and develop PSI for you without you trying, mainly because the tools are already inside of you.

Basically, I developed my PSI skills in the same manner in which I have taught others to develop their own. I have always been a strong believer in ascertaining as much information as possible about any interests that I pursue, psychic phenomena is no exception, even though it hit me like a freight train when I finally realized that I have psychic abilities.

If you have decided to develop your psychic skills, do so with foreknowledge that it will happen, in time. Keep in mind that it's slightly different for each of us, although we all have every attribute of PSI abilities within us already, we seem to be more skilled in certain areas than others, at first. In a sense, this could be a big reason for our apparent feelings of separateness, even though we are entangled as one MIND.

You are encouraged to work at each PSI skill as you would at achieving a level of efficiency in sports. Keep practicing the basic fundamentals of all skills which are necessary, such as: meditation, visualization, imagination and telepathy. In due time one or all of these attributes will surface within you in a substantial way. When it does, life will never be the same.

This article comes with a complete plan on how to develop your psychic skills. I suggest that you read through this entire article more than once before using any of the techniques and or methods within to become better familiar with each step on a second- hand nature.

Note:
When images within your mind become visible to people, the light that is within (their own mind) becomes invisible. It is then that your visions shall become manifested into reality.

Silencing Your Mind

Silencing your mind, or keeping it still is theoretically impossible to do. I know how this sounds, and that it is a contradictory statement and a sharp departure from what many mind experts in the art of meditation claim is possible. So before you write me off, let me explain what is meant by the phrase, you must silence the mind: your mind is infinite in every way imaginable and unimaginable. It cannot, nor will it ever die. Granted, a time will come when the sun shall rise and set for the last time for all humans in this reality; but your mind is a non-physical entity, an aspect of yourself that is not bound by time or space. In fact, your mind and spirit are one and the same, an expression of the one Mind responsible for all.

Think about it for a moment! Even as you are reading this article, which means you are mentally focused at the time, your mind is still picking up flashes of images---subtle as they may be, that has nothing to do with this topic. You'll notice that you are constantly refocusing your mind on the task at hand. The reason for this is that even though you are reading this article your mind is still open to vibrations from the universe and receiving ambient signals everywhere. This is why you sometimes pick up ideas, events or images in your mind and don't even know why such things have entered into your train of thought. This is simply the nature of your miraculous, wonderful mind. In other words the nature of mind is that of an ambiguous activity brought forth by vibrations; of which everything else in existence also vibrates. This also why we know that there is only one mind that exist. But that is another topic.

Since there is no way for you to technically silence and keep your mind still, we can still learn how to focus it on the present (moment). It is in the moment whereby your mind becomes fully opened to all signal inputs (frequencies from your super-conscious, your subconscious and conscious mind simultaneously. When this happens, great things are not only possible, but are certain to occur, if it is within your inner will.

Exercise for your mind

The following exercise will help you to focus your mind in the present (moment). Along with visualization and imagination techniques we will discuss later, you'll have all the tools necessary to begin manifesting or creating your reality. But you must know that it can be done, not believe that it can.

"Knowing how to do something is greater than believing you can.."

Telepathic Mind Scanning

While relaxing in a chair with your eyes closed, direct your mind to focus on the scalp area of your head. Make your scalp itch in several places by thinking about. Mentally say to your scalp, "itch!"

Once this has been achieved continue to move your mind downward into each external part of your body, making it itch until you reach your feet. Then reverse scanning directions by moving your mental awareness back towards the scalp area. Making each area itch along the trip back shows that your mind is beginning to focus and obey your commands.

Note:
This is what I call, "Telepathic Mind Scanning."

Visualization/Imagination

Past- event:
Now that you are completely relaxed, please direct your mind to recall the events of yesterday. Start at the very moment that you opened your eyes from a well deserved good-night's sleep. What did you do next? Did you simply lay there for a brief moment in order to collect your thoughts? If so, see yourself doing just that at this time. What did you do next? Did you stretch or make your way

to the restroom? What did you do after that? Did you freshen up in the shower, then brushed your teeth and goggled with mouthwash? What did you do next? Did you began preparing your wardrobe for the day? Did you have breakfast? Whatever you did on that day you should relive it all in your mind. Take your time with this and do not rush. See yourself, sense what you smelled and tasted at breakfast while you were getting ready for your day. Relive this entire day in your mind by visualizing and using your imagination, and when you finally find yourself back in bed, move your mind to…

Future - event:

Now that you are relaxed, please direct your mind toward the events of **Next Monday**. Start at the very moment that you open your eyes from a well deserved good-night's sleep. What are you doing? Are you simply laying in bed for a brief moment trying to collect your thoughts? If so, see yourself doing just that at this time. What are you doing now? Are you stretching, or walking towards the restroom? What are you doing now? Are you freshening up, or taking a shower? What are you doing now? Are you brushing your teeth? What are you doing now? Are you goggling with mouthwash? Use your imagination and see everything you are doing.

Next Monday. Whatever you are doing on this day you should see it all in your mind. Take your time with this and do not rush. See yourself, sense what you will smelled and tasted at breakfast while you are getting ready for this day. See this entire day in your mind by visualizing and using your imagination, and when you finally find yourself back in bed, move your mind to…

Now- Moment:

Now focus your mind and thoughts on the moment,

Open your eyes and begin focusing on the things you'll do today…Say mentally, show me what is in store for this day. Wait for an answer to come, do not force it, it will come to you. Write down only what you see, hear or feel. Do not speculate.

You must choose your own life's adventures and destiny, or others will select them for you....

Instantaneous Manifestation

Behold, I show you a mystery, we shall not sleep, but we shall all change in a moment, in the twinkling of an eye, at the last trumpet; for the trumpet shall sound, and the dead shall rise incorruptible, and we shall be changed.

1 Cor 15:51-52

Depending on whom you ask the word manifestation and its applicable use, or rather its realization means different things to most people who practice tapping into the universal source. For the purpose of this article when the word manifestation or a version of it will apply to the actualization of recognizing your imagination from the subtle realm of the invisible to that of both the physical and visible. In other words, manifestation occurs when you imagine creating something in your mental vision and it then becomes real. Manifesting something that is already created in the physical realm is essentially manipulating circumstances to favor your ideal.

As in all instances we have become an impatient species over the course of history. We expect things to happen instantaneously at the snap of a finger, very similar to what is seen on TV when a magician pulls a rabbit out of a small hat. But that is the lure of Hollywood and entertainment, and we've come to expect nothing less. Even though it may not have been seen or noticeable by the senses; in all situations of instantaneous manifestations into reality creation occurred beforehand.

Note: There are two types of manifestations:
1. Spontaneous, and 2. Intentional

My First Intentional Manifestation

What you are about to read is an actual event and experience that I incurred in the hot summer of 2009 while I was living in central Florida. I am describing this in the best way that I am able to write about it, but keep in mind that there are some things that happened to me during this event which are indescribable from a language point of view. The only witness to what happened is myself and God.

On a hot summer night while working on my book, I had become physically and mentally tired, so I decided to suspend writing for the remainder of the night. This sort of thing happens a lot when you are working on a book, in fact, many writers can attest to it. Shortly after retiring for the day, I fell into a deep level of sleep – and for what seemed like a 15 minute nap, turned out to be at least ten hours in duration. Hastily, I arose from bed the next morning and quickly showered, got dressed, and headed outdoors to a favorite spot of mine at a nearby park.

Upon arriving at the park, it suddenly dawned on me that my car had expended its' fuel, and this meant that I would have to travel the caveman way 25-blocks to the nearest filling station to purchase gasoline, then tread back another 25-blocks to where the car was parked and put in the fuel. And suddenly I realized another problem was facing me at the moment; although I had my wallet with me, there was no money in it. The only thing in my wallet at the time was a pre-paid Visa card that I carry most of the time. So I did a quick balance check with my smart phone only to discover that I was overdrawn. Which in this case was just as good as being broke. Immediately I called my wife on her mobile phone to let her know about the situation. I knew somehow luck would have to play a role here because my wife was somewhere on Hilton Head Island, she and my brother in-law would go sailing almost everyday morning until late in the day, so I needed to get a hold of her before they departed Spanish Wells.

I got lucky, or God intervened, I reached my wife minutes before they were set to leave. After braving a few of her silly attempts to tell a few jokes about my predicament, she made sure that money was available for me on my Visa card. With that out of the way, I then preceded to my favorite spot in the park and resumed writing. About seven hours later, it was time that I began walking to get some fuel for the car. But before I began step one, it dawned on me that I needed a container to hold and bring back the fuel. The problem was that I had no fuel container in the car and would have to buy one.

This meant that I would have to walk an additional 15 miles to the nearest WALMART, and then tread back the same way. When the thought of all the walking I would have to do just to get some gas for the car had finally entered my mind, a quiet day at the park working on my book and meditating in the forest had suddenly become a nightmare. To make matters worse, it was a very hot and humid day, and people all across the city were falling victim to the heat. Needless to say, I didn't want that to happen to me.

With all that had to be done in mind, I summoned into action the full creative powers of my mind, using my imagination and visualization energies from within to tap into the source and manifest what I needed and wanted to happen. I had done this many times before accidentally, as many have. But this time would be very different, because it was the first time that I would intentionally set out to manipulate reality to fill a need.

Using a technique known as mental video, I imagined in my mind seeing a gas container in my hand. I then went on to imagine and visualize how I wanted the entire trip of getting fuel should happen. I didn't want to walk there and back, it would take far too long. In fact it would have taken all day to walk there and back. And to make matters more challenging for me, I had a publishers' meeting to keep that evening. So, along with everything else, I imagined and then visualized on my mental video screen being driven by total strangers there and back to accomplish the entire task.

Procedures

Note:
"The scenario that I envisioned while in the comfort of alpha was a ride to and from the gas station in a vehicle. I also imagined having a gas container, too."

After settling down into a comfortable position on a bench seat in the park, I gently closed my eyes and soon entered into a state of mind known as Alpha, or level one. Scholar waves of bluish, green and yellow tones appeared on my mental screen shortly afterward. I then released my intentions unto the universe by asking God to help me.

The Manifestation

A few short minutes later, I began walking along the joggers trail that led back to my car. After a brief moment of rest I began walking towards the park's entrance when all of a sudden, from the deepest levels of my mind, a small, subtle voice spoke to me. It said: " look to the left". And when I did as instructed to do, I saw a vacant and abandoned house on a corner that I had seen many times and never noticed that a house was there before.

I thought about it and spoke to myself: "as often as I've driven to this location to write, practice golf and sometimes walk along the joggers trail, how could it be that I've never seen this vacant house?" I looked at the house again, and immediately its' two-car garage caught my attention. Just then, a flash of insight caught my attention as I could see that the garage door was ajar about 12 inches above the ground.

Suddenly, an image of a red gas-container quickly flashed onto my mental screen. I decided to follow-up on this insight to see if there could be a red gas container inside. Upon approaching the garage, the silent and subtle voice at the back regions of my mind said: "enter the house through its' front door, for it is not locked."

Once inside the house the voice guided me into the garage.

When I reached the garage, I noticed several large containers on the floor that could possibly hold gasoline, but these containers were yellow and full of fluids. Suddenly the voice inside of me spoke again: "look up, to your right." I couldn't believe my eyes when I saw atop a metal shelf, slightly to the back and right, rested a red gas container. At this very moment I quickly became one happy guy, but this story continues. A block and a half up the road, two complete strangers in a pickup truck volunteered to take me to and from the gas station, and back to my parked car.

The only limitations in this reality is a lack of imagination...

Imagine Greater....

Remote Viewing

In the final section of the "B.O.A.T. " I decided to include a chapter on "Remote Viewing" after having a series of successful group experiments which consisted novices; people with no previous experience into what is known as remote viewing. Many had no idea of what it was about.

Like many of you, when I first heard of the term "remote viewing" I had no clue as to what it entailed. It was some time later after reading various books on the subject that I came to realize what the claim was all about, and how anyone possessed with the right information can learn how to do this technique beneficially. So, before I describe to you what I know remote viewing, it is simply my nature and desire to talk it a little bit more.

A first cousin of mine so eloquently commented once that I am the type of person who likes to know the history of whatever topic he becomes interested in. This cousin of mine, whom I have not seen in years, was absolutely right on the mark. Even to this day I tend to do a lot of research on topics of interests to me, sometimes to the point of exhaustion. I believe that there is no limits to the mind other than those that we self-imposed on it based upon our finite sense of logic.

Remote Viewing
Although I'd had a wide range of self induced remote viewing sessions that began in the year 1997, I had never heard of the term remote viewing nor provided instructions to others into this area before these this technology became publicly known. Nevertheless in the year 2009 I would find myself conducting independent research into this matter.

Unlike the researchers at SRI, my experiments didn't cost tax payers any money. So, in this chapter I will provide selected details about my own adventures into the ether as a solo remote viewer, and also an instructor to others. The results and testimony of these first time viewers are unique in and of itself. The remote viewing experiments began on 12 September 2009 at approximately 6 pm at a local bookstore in Altamonte Springs, Florida. Perhaps it is best to explain the reasons behind these extraordinary people's decision in allowing me to conduct a daily remote viewing experiment on them without compensation of any kind, after all, this is America, the land where capital means everything.

Ever since I began working with an editor on formatting the B.O.A.T. for submission to a select group of publishers, I'd become a creature of habit, hanging out at local bookstores, mainly in the very back of the store where the majority of books on metaphysics and other paranormal topics are shelved. Every now and then I'd strike up a conversation with someone who was in search of spiritual answers among the numerous titles from psychic phenomena to astrology and mysticism. You see, most of these people find it difficult when confessing their thirst for spiritual knowledge among family, friends and colleagues out of fear of being called a lunatic. After all, most of the people I met, of which I will only identify with a first name only, are considered professionals with careers ranging from managerial, digital-graphic designers, psychiatry, entrepreneurs and lay persons. And as such, I have decided that protecting their identities is very important even though some had chosen to partake in a group photograph session.

While there are many people within the remote viewing community who've managed to make a substantial living, charging hefty fees for instructions, traveling the world and appearing before rock-concert type audiences. There are also others who have chosen to make this skill readily affordable to the masses by writing books, free online blogs and releasing well produced documentaries at reasonable prices.

I first became aware of the term remote viewing sometime in the year 1996, when I glanced at the cover of a book while at the library titled: *Psychic Warrior*. Didn't know what it was about at the time but I quickly learned from reading that it was about something that I already done for many years. To me, remote viewing is similar to a conscious state of dreaming. The difference know is that finally someone other than myself has reached a like understanding that we can see and do things while in a certain state of mind.

I still believe that there is more to this story of remote viewing than what has been told by those who were part of a government and academic sponsored program. I'm also inclined to believe with good intuitive instincts that the U.S. Army may have been involved in psychic phenomena experiments as early as the late 1920's, with certainty the Soviet Union. Now Russia, has been involved in remote viewing research and deployment activities for at least 150 years.

Discovering Telepathic Remote Viewing

After twelve years of practicing remote viewing on my own (this is where a new twist was added to the process of remote viewing), I accidentally discovered a unique method and technique that allows almost anyone to experience remote viewing for the first time. You see, what I did was add telepathy techniques to each remote viewing student I would teach, without their knowledge, from within my own mind.

That's right, unlike the scientists at SRI, all remote viewing targets used in my classes existed only in my mind and were referenced on paper with randomly selected numbers. The date and time of each target were never known by the students before hand. What I'm saying is that each telepathic remote viewer (TRV) had to ascertain information about each target that existed only in my mind, using numbers written on an envelope as the only source provided to them before each TRV session.

Why did I use Telepathy?

Ever since I began reading publicly available articles about the results of remote viewing studies and experiments conducted at certain universities and scientific laboratories in America which were funded directly and indirectly by the US government, about how they attempted to shield, or exclude the possibility of telepathic transference between human minds, it just seemed like the next course of action to take as for as experimenting goes.

So I took this information to heart as validation about the infinite powers of the human mind. In particular, where it involves telepathy. I had long suspected that even-though researchers had tried to eliminate this effect, they were never successful at doing so, the reasons for this is quite simple, there is no way possible to block the transference of mental communications, or telepathy, regardless of what measures are taken to insure that it does not occur. Telepathy cannot be shielded by any means divisible by science. As it turns out, telepathy vibrations (energy) cannot be detected, only the results of telepathy can be examined.

As an example, I will highlight for you an experiment conducted by members of the original researchers of Russell Targ and Hal Putoff, in which a submarine was used to test whether a telepathic signal (which remote viewing clearly is) could be successfully transmitted under deep oceanic waters from a submarine. Since it is a known fact that radio transmissions are difficult under such conditions, it was only human curiosity to know if the same applied to mind transmissions.

In the book *Mind Race*, authored by Russell Targ and Keith Harary it states: in 1959 the American government carried out telepathy experiments on the submarine Nautilus. This experiment showed – and herein resides its principal value – that telepathic information can be transmitted without loss through a thickness of seawater and through the sealed metal covering of a submarine. Retired astronaut Edgar Mitchell went much further when he tested telepathy from the vastness of space to a receiver stationed on earth. The successful conclusion of these little known experiments should put to rest several questions pertaining to telepathy that is that telepathic signals do not consist of electromagnetic low frequency as once theorized, and also such signals cannot be shielded (For more in telepathy read that chapter in this book).

About The TRV's

For the record, I don't expect you to believe everything you are about to learn from this chapter. But you should know that these events did occur. And now, in no particular order, I will describe for you the amount of experience each viewer had in regards to psychic phenomena and all skills associated with it, such as remote viewing, clairvoyance, medium-ship, etc. at the time these tests were conducted. You see, for them if was all about curiosity, for me it was about furthering my own understanding. Keep in mind though, no one was ever asked to submit a formal detailed application before being allowed to participate in this experiment. It is possible, but not highly likely that some of these people were it fact, psychic, knowingly or unknowingly.

First among TR viewers to participate in this daily program was George, an aspiring singer and lead guitarist, who has created his own unique brand of music of which he has high hopes of someday succeeding in the near future. He became the first of the group to participate, and has shown a tremendous amount of potential for becoming a very good remote viewer of any style used, if he decides to further hone his skills ability in this arena.

Jason, was the second TRV student to join the program. His talents were also quite impressive. Jason has a twin brother who plays drums for George as a member of his band.

Besides George and Jason, there were several others who would drop in and participated in the program from time to time out of curiosity. George and Jason both became very good at remote viewing as they began to show signs that other psychic abilities within their senses such as precognition became evident.

Targets

We usually began each session with a general discussion about spirituality and the role it plays on the individual minds and activities throughout each day. There's a lot you can learn from open discussions about people and their daily lives, for each has some valuable lessons pertinent to the continued growth of humanity. For me, such openness only served to confirm and deepen my love for all people and nature. Often the topic of conversation was centered on the Mayan Prophecy of 2012 and the spiritual awakening of humanity. It is because of these topics that the focus target of remote viewing also included events, locations and time lines for the year 2012 and 2013. Other targets chosen were Atlantis, Egypt, Planet X, Jesus, God, and the next day's newspaper headlines.

Terminology

As with any unique method, event, topic or profession, I've added a new term and component to the remote viewing process. The new term added is TRV: it was coined by me and is short for telepathic remote viewing.

Alone with its own delineations, the following abbreviations may come into use:

RV = remote Viewer
CRV = controlled remote viewing
TRV = telepathic remote viewing
V = viewer
M = monitor
MC = mental chatter / mind noise

Telepathic Remote Viewing

Telepathic Remote Viewing (TRV) involves the ability of a viewer to attain target data that exists only in the mind of the coordinator. In other words, there are no images of the target available for the TRV to focus upon before hand. TRV viewers must use telepathy to ascertain target information independent of the instructions received.

Procedures

Most books about remote viewing tend to be written with little regards to information on how to achieve, or experience the phenomenon for yourself. While in some cases the authors appear purposeful in a lack of procedural information, this is not an end result for some. Over the years I have read numerous books and online articles on remote viewing. From my point of view and opinion there are insider details about RV that is insightful. The problem noted with most RV books are not in a lack of details, but instead, it is how the books were written. In other words, most RV books are clinical and some seem to have been scholarly fashioned. Basically what it all amounts to is that such works have limited appeal outside certain circles. For common folks it is not worth the time in trying to understand these books. I find by way of trial and error that it is best to keep things as simple as possible as long as it accomplishes the goal.

Mind Scanning

Mind scanning is something uniquely added to TRV. I don't know if anyone else does this before remote viewing events, but it makes things a lot easier.

Direct your mind to focus on your scalp. Make your scalp itch. Do this by mentally saying to your scalp, "itch." Once this has been achieved, continue to move your mind downward into each external part of your body until the feet are reached, then reverse directions and move upwards back towards your scalp. Make it itch again.

Note: I call this "Mind Scanning."

Meditation

Past- event:
Now, direct your mind to recall the events of last Sunday. Start at the very moment of opening your eyes and getting dressed, eating, events of your day, etc... when you reached the end of that day, move your mind to...

Future – event:
Next Sunday. Begin at the moment of opening your eyes and end when you retire for that day.

Now- Event:
1. Now focus your mind /thoughts on this moment.
2. Open your eyes and begin focusing on the set of numbers written on the envelope before you... Say mentally, what do these numbers represent?
3. Wait for a response from your subjective mind; do not force it; it will answer you according to law.

245

4. Write down only what you see, hear or feel. Do not allow your conscious mind to speculate. If this happens, begin anew...

Focus...

Note: For best results, it is best that you have someone else read these procedures to you at first. Once you are confidant in your own abilities, then you may go at it alone.

Master Data Targets

Random Numbers:	Destination	Date / Time
0742	Planet Pluto	Now
1976	Planet Uranus	Now
1874	Joan of Ark	???
7562	Washington D.C	Now
1566	Lotto Numbers (FLA)	Now
4673	Planet X	Now
2364	Planet Mercury	Now
4126	Star-Sum	Now
09280901	Jebel Barkal, Egypt	10,000 BC
09280902	Heliopolis, Egypt	10,000 BC
09280903	Kush, Egypt	10,000 BC
09280904	Elimite City, Iran	(3000 BC)
09280905	Persepolis, Iran	10k - 7000
	People: of Egypt / Iran	
09280906	Zoroastrianism Zoroaster	6000BC /
200BC		
09280907	Atlantis	8,000 BC
09280908	Atlantis	7,5000 BC
09280909	Atlantis	3,000 BC
09280910	Manila Philippines	Now
09300901	Samoa, American	29 Sept.

Master Data Target Numbers

Target Number & Destination	Period / Time	
Target no. # 291101 World Trade Center New York, NY	Time: 12:00 Noon,	Date: Sept 11, 2001
Target no. # 37149 GOD	Time: 	Date: Now
Target no. # 49469 Planet X	Time: 	Date: Now
Target no. # 56702 Inside Georgia Dome Atlanta Ga.	Time: 3pm	Date: Sept. 20, 2009
Target no. # 71786 Headline News Events Anywhere, Earth	Time: 10 am,	Date: Sept 22, 2009
Target no. # 262595 Atlantis	Time: 7am	Date: 10,000 BC

TRV – Procedures

The system used for TRV is similar to those that may be practiced in one form or another by anyone trying to access nontraditional means of information.

Procedures

1. Sit or lie down. Relax your body muscles.
2. Meditate for 5-10 minutes.
3. Formulate task in your mind.
4. Creative visualization of task.
5. Focus on target (mentally).
6. Draw as best you can, any shapes or forms, pictures

(impressions) that enters your mind.
7. Do not analyze what you see. Just write it.
8. Focus your mind for no more than 15 minutes on a target.

Procedures Simplified

In the beginning…

I want you to stand-up, tighten all your muscles at once, as hard as you can. You can do this by extending your arms clinch both fists as hard as possible. Tighten-up the stomach muscles, leg muscles, and even your jaw-bone and muscles. However, do not grit your teeth. Hold this forced tightness of the muscles for at least one minute, then relax all at once.

Secondly…
Sit or lie down, remaining as relaxed as possible.

Breathing

Concentrate on breathing slowly and with depth, deep into your lungs with as much air as possible. Exhale slowly.

Mind Scanning

Close your eyes, slightly turn both eyes toward top-center of nose. This action will help you to visualize.

Astral Projection

Allows you to leave your body - walk through walls - fly around your neighborhood or the planet, leave the solar system and visit a distant galaxy - meet your deceased loved ones and astral spirits - communicate with your guides and teachers - experience other dimensions - and even travel through time to witness past or future events!

Astral Projection is the process of temporarily separating your mental awareness or spiritual self from your earth-bound physical body. It is an extraordinary experience, and the thing is, that it is more widespread than you think... All who have experienced it can testify to its lucidity and magical quality.

Astral Travel is very different from normal dreaming. In fact it seems much clearer than your normal daily life; your senses seem much sharper and the environment somehow more real. It is often believed that astral projection (out-of-body experience) is only experienced by people that have had a near death experience after an accident, or on the operating table. But, astral projection is and can be attained easily by anyone with the right information.

Even you can quickly learn the secrets of how to start or expand your existing astral travel techniques and become an experienced user of this ability, simply because it is possible to do so. Based on the most authoritative scientific discovery revealed by the late Robert Monroe, whose methods has been shown to induce astral projection effects in almost anyone who attends his courses. Now for those who are financially incapable of enrolling in the top-notch course recognized by many the world over, there is still a cheaper way for you to do this yourself. And basically that is what this chapter is all about? Accessing astral projection on your own.

Why should You Astral Project?

In the Astral realm the sky is not the limit. One can fly way beyond the blue skies, into deeper regions of space while exploring planets not yet discovered by astronomers. One can consciously project his or her mental awareness to any part of the world simply by concentrating on it... You can even fly through the air without wings, having a bird's eye view of the world below, while traveling across the surface of the planet... Just imagine being able to glide over the oceans like seagulls, or being able to penetrate the waters and breathe beneath the surface the way oceanic life does.

You can meet enlightened beings, even of distant or ancient traditions, which can help guide you to a spiritual path toward enlightenment. Or you can attend the esoteric schools and temples of ancient Egypt to learn more about the mysteries of life and death. You can even discover who or what built the pyramids...

There are all sorts of hidden knowledge you can acquire from astral projecting, the kind of knowledge that cannot be attained in every day life, or from other people and books.

Is Astral Projecting really possible?

A group of scientists who were conducting research into certain paranormal abilities at Stanford Research Institute (SRI), with the assistance of a well known psychic named Ingo Swan, discovered some very startling facts about what Ingo later coined as remote viewing. Which was used to describe the mind's ability to travel anywhere in space and time while retrieving information to use for intelligence. Over 50 million dollars later, give or take a few spent researching and actually using remote viewing to a certain successful degree proved one thing, that the mind is a non-local entity whose powers are ungoverned by the laws of physics. One things for sure is that we may never know nor understand the full extent of humanity's ability without first knowing what the mind can do. Astral projection and remote viewing are very similar. In fact they are essentially one and the same.

How does Astral Projection work?

Special brainwave detection equipment was used to produce acoustic audio patterns that when played through headphones are slightly different in each ear. This effect is capable of shifting the brain waves into a desired frequency range. This finding was a discovery of the late Robert Monroe of the Monroe Institute, bearing his name. During repeated experimentation through an entire range of brainwave frequencies known to man, it was realized that alpha and theta brainwaves (from 5 - 12 Hz), showed the most promise for the purpose of astral projecting while maintaining consciousness. It's been discovered that a combination of specific brainwave frequencies consistently caused a complete shift in consciousness to occur.

While your brain is locked into these specific frequencies it triggers an altered state of awareness. This feeling is like all of your awareness suddenly being focused into the center of your head through your pineal gland (third-eye) believed to be the seat of the soul. As you read deeper into this chapter there is a very good chance that you'll agree with some, if not all of my assumptions on this topic as well as that of the other topics. Most psychic-based phenomena are rather easily explained if those giving the explanations would simplify the language and terminology. For some authors it is quite understandable they write in the manner that they have chosen.

Many of these authors have advanced degrees in science, or a medical related field; so I believe that they unknowingly write their book manuals to impress their peers first, and the general reading audience comes second. At least, that is the feeling I get when reading many of their works. A great number of the reading public do not possess a science degree, or read on a scholarly level. We often find such books a bit choppy, or even difficult to conceptualize. So this book it written from a layman's perspective in hopes of being very reader friendly.

I was around 11 or 12 years of age when I first experienced what is commonly known today as astral projection, and sometimes called an out-of-body experience (O.B.E.). This phenomena, when observed or reported by patients during a medical procedure has been dubbed a near death experience, or NDE for short.

Now, it is quite certain that if you are not familiar with this topic and your reading this book for the first time, that you are bound to question whether or not an individual (such as I) could have experienced all of these known PSI phenomena in such a short life. And rightly or wrongly due to religious doctrine many assume that only certain people, anointed by some holier than thou form of life has these abilities. My quick reply is this, all PSI phenomena mentioned in this book are born of a single source, and that source is consciousness. And consciousness permeates all fabric of space and time, infinitely. Even skeptics would be hard pressed to argue with that assertion. As for as astral projection is concerned, it is simply a natural occurrence of all living beings who have attained self awareness, whether such beings are dead or alive.

Maiden Astral Projection Voyage

My first recalled episode into the astral realm, via astral projection, took place at the home of my grandparents, which just happened to be a few doors north from a home occupied by the late Dr. Martin Luther King's family in northwest Atlanta, Georgia. Recalling the details of my first astral projection is akin to remembering indiscretions of your first sexual experience. We all astral project on the very first day of life until we depart our physical body.

You see, astral projection is the sole reason that we must all sleep. And it is during the stages of sleep, which happens everyday for everybody; that the body is somewhat rejuvenated by the subconscious mind, or the spirit that dwells within.

It is a known fact that the human body comes equipped with the ability to repair itself (healing), this mostly occurs during moments of sleep. It is because of this particular activity or event (body rejuvenation) that scientists wrongly suggests or theorize that we have become so fatigued or tired during the day, and is in need of resting our bodies at least once a day for at least 6-8 hours. What happens to someone who is unable to sleep, and yet, suffers none of the known symptoms associated with that of a sleeping disorder? There are people in this world who simply have no need of sleep, at least in the conventional sense.

Could it be that somehow certain people have transcended the need to physically sleep because they are able to astral project at will? I believe such people do exist. Also I have come to the realization that I need less and less hours of sleep due to actively practicing astral projection and meditation on a daily basis.

The Astral Event

Memories about my first known astral projection episode, like most people, I had no idea as to what was happening to me. To be totally honest, for a moment I thought that I had died in my sleep. Efforts to move any part of my body seemed useless at the time, but somehow I came to realize ultimately the choice of whether to live or die was mine, and mine alone to make. So, for what seemed like it took an eternity to find myself and spring life back into every inch of my body, was in all actuality only about thirty seconds to one minute in duration.

As I layed there, I kept thinking within my mind, demanding my body to move. Then suddenly, as mysteriously as the symptoms of helplessness arrived, my once motionless body began to re-animate itself, a region at a time, as I kept trying to regain full movement and control. It all begin very slowly with the opening of my eyelids – revealing nothing but total darkness. Slowly, as light begin to filter into the lens of my eyes, other parts of my external body began to function as I began to regain total movement, as willed.

At the time of this event I had no idea at all as to what had just happened to me. I constantly questioned myself over and over again, if indeed, did I die briefly during my sleep and had I somehow miraculously managed to revive life into my body. The following morning I briefly mentioned this experience to my uncle, who reasoned that maybe the soft pillows of the sofa that I had fallen asleep upon, could have played a key role in what happened. His line of thought was: "maybe the couch was way too soft, and allowed my muscles to relax a bit too much." For awhile, I bought into this line of reasoning until many years and many astral projections later, that I began to understand – little by little, more of what was actually going on with me. It had suddenly become abundantly clear that what was happening to me during the night, was also happening to everyone else at various times during sleep. Sometime later, as I regained more insight into this matter, it also became known to me why it seemed as though I had died in my sleep during that first experience of astral projection.

What I'm about to disclose herein might help everyone who reads this chapter to understand the nature of astral projection and how each of us can control the destination and purpose of every projection, on a conscious level. The things mentioned here are my personal opinions based upon years of observation into the phenomenon known as astral projection.

Before going further into this topic it is necessary that you become familiar with a few words defined herein, so that when they are used, their exact meaning would be well understood. Most terminologies listed herein where actually coined by myself. At the time, I needed a way to properly describe a given thought – process at the time of its reference.

Quick trip into Astral Land

I wrote this chapter in a reverse fashion when compared to what some writers do---what can I say other than the fact that I don't consider myself as being a writer even though I wrote this material. I simply kept thinking about what is it that I'd wanted to know while reading a book that catches my interest? I would simply want good information, and not necessarily all the stuff that comes with it.

Now that you've seen the information, it is time to fill you in on the details about some of my astral land adventures. I picked up this phrase sometime ago while serving in the military, " kiss, or keep it simple stupid!" and that is exactly my objective. On one particular night I recall experimenting with the idea of entering astral land on purpose. At the time I had read and researched several books on the subject and there was one book that impressed me most. It was a book written by Robert Monroe. Since I had been actively using my psychic abilities to help guide my daily activities I thought that it was now time to move beyond my comfort zone and venture into other areas of what the mind can do.

Late one afternoon I decided to astral project myself into the skies between Orlando, Florida and New York. I wanted to know if it was worth renting a van for the evening and provide shuttle services for incoming tourists back and forth to the airport and Disney World. It was 2008 and the economy was really slowing down. So renting a van without direct knowledge of incoming flights could be a financial disaster if I was on the losing end. So I entered astral land on purpose to scan the friendly skies between NY and Orlando to see how many flights were on their way that particular night into OIA. I was simply hovering around 3,000 – 4,000 feet in the air when all of a sudden I could sense, and then see that the skies were full of jets all flying into Orlando that night. Needless to say I rented a van and made quite a bit of money on that day.

Somehow without fully understanding the full process involved, I intuitively knew that on this particular night it would become very, very busy even though earlier flight forecasts by the airport flight information boards had stated otherwise.

Astral Projection
Terminology

Astral Projection

Refers to a phenomenon experienced during a state of sleep by everyone, including animals. The essence of our being, or spirit, disconnects from the physical body and is then free to roam about in space and time, into any dimension or parallel universe it chooses at will. I have determined that there are two types of Astral Projection experiences: conscious and unconscious.

Astral Cord (connection)

This refers to a connection maintained between the projectile (astral body) and physical body after extrapolation has been achieved.

Astral – body

This term refers: to your subtle body upon separation from the physical. Some insists that the astral – body looks exactly like the physical. However, this has not been the experience realized of my exteriorized activities. This doesn't mean that I am right, and that others are wrong – or that they I have no clue as to what an astral – body looks like. I don't think it really matters at all what it looks like. But what I am saying is that this aspect of astral projecting from my physical body hasn't been an experience of mine. While such claims my help to sell books, it also serves to confuse those genuinely interested in truth.

When we become used to the idea of controlling the destination of the projection by way of consciousness, we soon realize that there is a lot that we can attain in the form of information that could become very useful on the physical plane. On one particular night in the spring of 2008, I was in a conscious astral projectile when suddenly I found myself hovering above a nearby Texaco convenience store. While in this astral state we become knowledgeable of things. I soon realized at the moment that a lottery ticket that I had purchased just days before was a winning ticket. Upon waking the next morning I went to the Texaco station where I acquired the lottery ticket and it was confirmed that I had won quite a bit of money.

So, at this time you are probably wondering how you can consciously direct your astral projectile so that you can benefit from it in a material way? I have two words for you about this: "its easy!" And I mean every word of what I just stated. It's easy for me to do, it's also easy for you, too! Now, here's all that needs to be done prior to falling asleep to help you astral project? Simply remember this one statement: You can consciously will your subconscious mind into astral projecting simply by focusing on it and asking it to do so before going to sleep. You might be wondering that if it it that easy to do, how come everybody can't do it?

The answer to that question all boils down to belief! You must believe that it can be done, and it will be. "Ask and it shall be received."

Astral Vision

This refers to the ability to see while exteriorized into the astral plane sometimes referred to as true sight.

Astral Plane (realm)

Sometimes referred to as astral world or dreamland, etc., it is where the astral projectile ends up.

Alpha/Theta/Delta

Brainwave frequencies.

Borderland

Refers to a state reached before deep unconscious sleep where consciousness is maintained.

Cosmic Energy

Sometimes used interchangeably or referred to as universal energy. It means the ability of the astral projectile; or phantom to draw upon powers of the cosmos or God in order to revitalized the physical body. The phantom is able to heal the body of any bad conditions that exists. Manifestation of any material desires are also possible while in this state.

Directed Dream

Refers to an ability to consciously direct the events of one's own dream.

Dream State

The activity of/or state of dreaming.

Exteriorized

Refers to actual separation of the phantom from the physical body.

The Field

It is sometimes referred to as the force, the universal field, the cosmos. But I have come to call it space. Space is the one thing that connects everything in existence as one. What many quantum scientists call the field is simply an attempt to explain a hidden and mysterious phenomenon about the unknown origins that permeates all things of existence; anywhere.

There are those who describe the "Field" as an energy capable of performing miracles and can manifest things into existence at the command of thought. And there are others who describe the "Field" as consciousness. It is my belief that consciousness exists simultaneously in the fabric of space itself. Think about for a minute! Space is everywhere at the same moment and time. Nothing exists without space, not even the universe. So whatever you decide to call the mysterious force connecting us all, is up to you. I, for one, don't think it really matters.

Interiorized

Refers to the act of the phantom when fully returned to body.

Phantom

Referred to as the astral body, subtle body, and projectile.

Projectile

See phantom

Projection

The ability to separate from the physical body.

Will

There are basically three levels of what we call will; they are conscious – will, subconscious – will, and super conscious – will. At each level the will is your dominant thought of focus.

Dreaming

Dreaming is a form of unconscious meditation, and meditation is a form of conscious dreaming, which means that everyone has them. I'm of the opinion that whatever occupies your mind the most (focus) will affect your dreams at some point in time. If it affects your dream state, then it also determines what activities and/or events will be created by the forces of your mind. This usually means a conference of your abilities to visualize and imagine things, during what is actually an altered-state (sleep), that your mind uses as a means to return back the astral realm. So, from this point forward you should be mindful of the things that you focus on during the day, because it really does have a subconscious affect upon what appears/happens in your unconscious dreaming, which in turn also manifests eventually into physical reality.

For instance; if you were focused on a certain task relating to the type of work you do during the day this may become the basis of your dream later that night. Now, we have all dreamed about what we do at work. So it goes to show that in spite of all the expert advice out there, which make the claim that in order for you to learn how to direct your dreams, requires many months, or even years of meditative practice and solitude in a cave. Keep in mind, all dreams involves astral projections of the astral projectile from the physical body. And all that you are trying to accomplish is an event known as self directed – dreaming.

Everybody dreams, therefore everybody astral projects while they are sleeping. This is a fact of our reality...

Purpose of Sleep

What is the purpose of sleep? Do we really make-up all the

things appearing in our sleep, as many would have you believe? Why do we have nightmares? Sleep is necessary simply because it allows your astral body to recharge itself with energies received directly from the cosmos; or if you prefer – God. Scientists know that sleep also helps the physical body to heal. Now with this knowledge and understanding you now know why there will always be certain aspects of dreaming that are not remembered by an individual, and that this all occurs during the states of receiving Delta brainwaves. The Delta level of the sleep stage is where all commands received from the subconscious mind become reality.

Astral Projection Technique & Exercise

By now you have already realized the wonderfully, miraculous benefits of meditation, so please keep in mind that it helps in this situation, too. To begin programming your mind to consciously remain somewhat actively aware of who you are, and what you are doing during the time of your nightly planned adventures into the astral plane. I highly recommend adopting the following techniques until such a time that you are able to develop procedures you feel will work best for you. Keep in mind, no one knows it all except God. So, in due time and with a focused will on both the conscious and subconscious aspects of astral projecting, you will eventually be able to perform this task when you desire to do so..

Preparing to Astral Project

Wait until you are ready for bed before trying this exercise. Lie down as straight as possible on your back. When you lie on your back it allows all of your internal organs to remain in their proper place, as nature intended. When you sleep on your side, this causes your internal organs to shift towards the lower side---basically gravity takes over. In any case, sleeping properly has tremendous overall health benefits.

1. Close your eyes and breathe as you normally do.
2. Say (mentally) to yourself, "remember my dreams."
3. Relax your entire body as best you can.

Visualization and Imagination

Now, visualize and imagine seeing your subtle body as it is separating from your physical body and is traveling where you want to go, do and see.

When you finally realize that you've managed to astral project, you may at first find yourself instantly back inside your physical body.

Note:

If you do this simple exercise you'll begin to consciously know when you are dreaming. By learning to remain conscious while dreaming you'll begin to feel the effects of your projectile. The vibrations that sometimes precede separation will serve as a signal that projection is occurring.

Remember:

Astral Projection is a natural phenomenon that occurs every time you sleep----the only difference is your ability to remain consciousness is enhanced and therefore directing your subtle body in the direction you want it to go, whether it be in the past, present or future, it can be achieved.

Nobody dreams of a life filled with mediocrity and regret, but for some reason, most people allow themselves to be chained to these weights.

As they ignore the spirit within them dying, along with their passion for life and the gifts that are their birthright.

To me, this is the cruelest way to allow yourself to live, because this is not living at all--- and I refuse to not live my life.

Thera Florann Sailor-Dill

My Life's Journey

When it came time to writing a chapter all about myself and how it suddenly dawned on me one day that the world that I thought I knew, was not at all the way it seemed, proved to be the most difficult. It has taken many years for me to over come my shyness, my habitual fear of worrying about what others think about me. One day I began to understand the actualization that reality is all about perceptions of the mind's ability to maintain a collective vision, ideology, and like frequency, a sort of base-line connection with its uncreated self. Although as human beings, we were created into the likeness and image of our maker, of which many hold that maker to be God.

The difficulty of this task initially rested in the ability to openly and honestly write about my myself and express my most inner thoughts and perspectives to total strangers. Even in the new age of openness and acceptance of others' point of view with out judgment, some people may still look at you as though you've just killed your mother.

In light of such revelations I really didn't know how or where to begin my story, or for that matter, this book. As a matter of fact, I've always found it somewhat difficult at various times, and a little bit uncomfortable when I was the topic. I've never been the type to brag or boast about the things I own, or the places where I've traveled. Basically, I'm a bit shy and quiet until I get to know you. But once that hurdle has cleared, I've been known to talk you to sleep. And that just might be a good description of my personality type: a bit quiet at first, and then, WHAM!

In relative reality, truth is always stranger than fiction, simply because I've never been that comfortable just being me. I have always known that there was something missing, I just couldn't put my hands on it. Growing up I daydreamed constantly during my high school years. And even long after that into adulthood. I would often find myself alone in a quiet place with my eyes closed, daydreaming, a lot. The things I lacked in reality; and at times this was a very extensive list; I more than made up for it in my dreams. Daydreaming about how I thought life should be and the material things I wanted to have had become my way of escaping the hardships of living in poverty and growing up black in the south. It (daydreaming) became my way of experiencing alternate realities and dimensions, and a means for achieving a natural state of high. My daydreaming activities kept me away from drugs, alcohol, cigarettes, and a life of crime.

I had seen the effects that drugs, alcohol and cigarettes had on my dad and uncles; and much later in life I witnessed my brother's struggle to overcome drug and alcohol addiction. In a sense, daydreaming was my salvation. At some moment in time I began noticing that a number of my dreams were in-fact, a sign of things to come. And even then, as some of those foreseen events began unfolding into reality right before my very eyes, it would still take awhile before realizing what was occurring and connecting all the dots together. I really didn't say too much about these events to anyone when I was growing up out of fear of being labeled a nut case.

For instance, I predicted that a teenage girlfriend of mine would turn to drugs and not live beyond age 25. Weeks before her 25th birthday she died of a drug over dose. This just wasn't the kind of thing I wanted people to know about me, but, for one reason or another, I did share this information with my former and late girlfriend in hopes that she would seek another direction in her life's choices. When I received word of her death I was saddened by it all even though I had seen this outcome years before.

There are many times well in advance where I receive information about what color and style of clothing a person would be wearing days ahead of any future meeting. One day as a teenager, I had had a visual image detailing exactly what my future wife would look like nearly 8 years before we actually met. When my wife and I had finally met in person, even though she didn't know who I was at the time, I told her in a non-threatening manner that we would get married. And six months later we did. That was nearly thirty-one years ago.

As an adult I would on occasion briefly mention a thing or two about my hidden abilities in comfort to my wife, and much later to our daughter. That was as far as I would go with such matter. Precognitive events reveling my future just kept on streaming into my conscious awareness as if my life had somehow become scripted. Sometimes I knew exactly what others were about to say even before they begin speaking to me, and to tell the truth, I still do. Many times I would tell them what they were about to say, sometimes cutting them off before they speak. I have since learned how to control the urge of letting people know that I know what they are about to say to me by being more patient and keeping my lips sealed long enough to let them talk. This approach makes my wife very pleased because she realizes that often I already know the outcome.

Even after all that I've written so far, it is still very difficult writing about my life. Beginning my story during times of the past when I worked as an independent financial stockbroker would certainly make a very good read for those who like stories about what goes on behind the scenes of the financial markets, but it would leave out some very important details of when, how, and why I suddenly became aware of the fact that God works through our minds to manifests reality (in terms of physical, metaphysical, supernatural and paranormal means).

After much thought and consideration during periods of extended meditations, I've decided that in order to tell a more complete and detailed version of my life's journey, one that is relevant to the topics discussed in this book, it would be a whole lot easier to use certain movie scenes as a metaphor from time to time. Besides, I've seen a number movies that are somewhat similar to my real life experiences, the difference being is that I didn't get paid for them. Also, some of you may even find this approach a bit more interesting, less boring. And, with that concept in mind, writing about my life's journey begins in the best way that only I know how to tell it, with a comparison to that of a popular movie. Thank you Hollywood for all of your help!

In many ways life is like a well scripted scene from a movie, you always know what's coming if you fast forward ahead...

Most people just love it when they read a real life story about how a nobody from nowhere, who somehow managed to overcome seemingly insurmountable odds, turning rags into riches, and then living out the rest of their life happily ever after. Such dramatic story lines seems to always capture our imagination as it invokes our strongest emotions. Such down-to-earth, life like movies are the staple of a well written Hollywood film script. And this, my friends, was the message of the movie: *'In Pursuit of Happiness'* featuring actor: Will Smith.

In Pursuit of Happiness is a film based upon real-life experiences of a once temporary, unemployed homeless man, who found himself down on luck and out of work until one day he managed to earn his way out of shame, and into the ranks of fame and fortune as a financial stockbroker on Wall Street. Eventually founding and running his own independent business, and then writing a book about it, which later became a movie. Not bad at all for a guy with only a high school's education.

Whenever I use the term *"Wall Street"* in this book; it does not necessarily indicate the actual place or location within New York City; which is famous for, and is well known for that name and businesses that operates at that location (Wall Street). Instead, it is a loosely used term for describing in general those who work in the financial industry as a whole, wherever they are located geographically.

Truth be told, even though I've traveled back and forth to New York City a number of times while employed as a stockbroker, needless to say I have never visited the actual location of the New York Stock Exchange located on Wall Street. The closest I have ever been to Wall Street were during my visits to Grand Central Station on Park Avenue; which happened to be the location of the firm that I once worked with as a stockbroker.

Watching the movie *In Pursuit of Happiness* brought forth many selective memories of my own struggles in the mid 1980s; for I too, overcame financial hardship to beat the odds and find success as a stockbroker with a New York Stock Exchange listed company. In fact, both of our (Gardner: portrayed by Will Smith's character, and myself) situations occurred at or near the same time. Although, becoming homeless was not a concern of mine, nevertheless there were many challenging issues to think about when I began searching for what I believed was rightly mine. Such as extreme battles with poverty. My wife and I were always struggling to pay the rent, and so on. Since I've never consumed any alcoholic beverages, nor, have I ever smoked a cigarette or any form of smoking. I believe that these habits have always made it possible for me to remain in good health. Additionally, I'm what you might call a freak of nature type, who's never been sick, at least, none that I can remember. Of course, I had had a few sports related injuries, but, I always seemed to healed naturally without help from any medicine or medical procedure.

And, in similar fashion to that of a movie, I climbed my way to the top of the mountain in terms of status, money and material things. At the peak of my career as a stockbroker, I held the title of vice president, and later became chief executive officer. I found a business and was majority shareholder of a publicly traded company. Unlike the character depicted by Will Smith in the film, I did not ride off into the sunset, living happily ever after, with a trophy wife and all the other spoils of success as the movies credits began to filled the screen. For me, the experience was simply a gateway, or a bridge leading to a place where I'd never been before. It was an amazingly new beginning, though. This gateway or bridge, moved me closer to a realm of truth and a path towards spiritual enlightenment that would take several years to navigate. I made numerous false-steps along the way. But in the mist of trying to mentally grasp its significance, meaning and beauty, somewhere along this unforeseen venture I began to see all that was transpiring.

In a sense, I was down right lucky. Despite throwing away almost everything that I had accumulated over the years and had held high in regards to material wealth and financial success. It was with a guilty conscience and my emotional feelings and self awareness that allowed me to realize the destructive negative thoughts in my mind and hold onto those things in life that means the most – the love of my family and true friends. You see, I soon discovered that after all that I had endured up to that point in my life, the only thing that truly mattered at all was love. And, when and where things really came to fruition, it was love, strength, affection, and emotion showed to me from my wife and our wonderful daughter; together they helped me to come to terms with what I was going through. Unlike many of those who have come before me, I didn't leave my family behind. Instead, my wife and daughter joined me in a search for meaning.

Although I didn't have a name for or know what was happening to me at the time, it was through patience and further research into my life changing experiences when I finally realized that my individual awakening, or transformation had begun.

In hindsight, I know that there are thousands, even millions of people worldwide who suddenly find themselves walking along a similar path only to realize in the end that they didn't have to part with the ones they love in the process. Love doesn't have to hurt, and, it shouldn't become a burden or cause any discomforts to you or those you love. If you are truly beginning to awaken to the spirit of the almighty god; which, by-the-way, dwells within and without, then you should remain committed to all those you love.

Although my personal search for meaning has ended, another internally assigned task begins anew for me without having any investment of how I once perceived reality to be. As the way things appear to me now, there is a better understanding of who and what I truly am. Basically, what this means is that I am no longer imprisoned by, nor, am I held hostage by society's programmed logic or illusions, anymore. Since becoming detached from it all within my mind, I am able to approach life philosophically because my heart is now filled with emotions of an indescribable love and dedication towards all things. I pride myself in helping others who are poor in spiritual knowledge, and wants to awaken from their own slumber. This new vision and objective, which occupies my mind and heart everyday, has become my life's purpose. I now know with certainty, that there is so much more to life than unknowingly sleep-walking inside a bubble of a collective dream, that we have throughout the various ages of life on earth, incorrectly identified as reality.

In life, I've been extremely fortunate, in that, I have had ample opportunities to travel abroad and meet people from almost every continent in the world. Once, I even lived in Europe just years before the Berlin wall was dismantled. While in Europe, I resided in a small town called Kornwestheim, a town in the Ludwigsburg, Baden-Wurttemberg, Germany, district, about 10 km north of Stuttgart, Germany. At the time Stuttgart was headquarters to the Mercedes Benz Corporation. Other countries where I've spent time visiting and getting to know people there are: Japan, Mexico, Panama, Peru, South Korea and Switzerland. In North America, I've traveled to every state except the following: Washington, Oregon, Colorado, Utah and Maine. I once turned down an all expense-paid trip to Canada because of its harsh winters. My travels to all the places I've visited has taught me a very important lesson, one that I'll never forget: "people are the same wherever you go."

As you read about '*My Life's Journey*,' bear in mind that all views and opinions expressed are solely mine from a global and spiritual perspective as it reflects on the past. And, if I unknowingly offend anyone, by race, religion, cultural, or national, please know that I am deeply and truly sorry for it is not the intent of this book to reach that far.

My Previous and Current Lives
(Reincarnation)

"If I think real hard, I'll bet I could remember way back to the time of my childhood," says Forest Gump. Well, the same holds true for me. I remember bits and pieces of two previous lives I had before the one I am currently living. The earliest I remember is that my name was Francois, I lived in Paris, France during the 1700s. As an adult I was what society now recognize as a pimp. I owned and ran a local whore house which included a staple of women that many aristocrats desired and paid good money for them. I was killed before the age of forty by a woman who was very close to me. She shot me once in the heart, and then I died.

I was born to an unwed couple, my mother was barely 14 years old, and my father was seventeen. At birth I had red skin and red hair and my eyes were blue, which was sort of a strange thing considering that neither of my parents had such traits. I also remember the day my parents brought me home from the hospital (Grady Memorial Hospital of Atlanta, Georgia) in the darkness of night. My father had the honor of carrying me from the car and into the apartment they called home as my mom walked alongside us. It was a bitter and cold night, as I remembered it so vividly. A thin layer of frost was layered in the walkway leading up to front door. Although the nights were cold, the days were unseasonably warm for that time of year, which was in mid January, 1958.

At the time of my birth, my parents lived in a cheap collection of rental apartments that were located on the northwest side of the city of Atlanta. Within a very short time from the day of my arrival, we moved away from what was then called Tipton place apartment homes, to live with my grandparents, because, at the time life was financially challenging for my very young parents, as a result we seemed to move around a lot, almost like Gypsies.

Both my parents were teenagers, and the circumstances surrounding my birth was not planned for or wanted, and obviously, it forced them into an early marriage that neither of them were mentally or fiscally prepared to handle. Nowadays, teens having babies are so commonplace, but for my parents, it was very uncommon, and getting married at such a young age was a very hard decision for them to make and to keep. Consider this scenario: my mother and her mother (my grandmother) were both pregnant at the same time. As a result my youngest uncle is only six months older than I am. You might say, that he was like a big-brother.

The ability to remember my early childhood at a time that conventional wisdom believes is impossible to do, is considered among those who have studied and researched traits in people who have demonstrated some sort of psychic phenomenon as a early sign of someone born with exceptionally intuitive skills. Research also reveals that one or several family members of an intuitive (psychic) most likely provided a venue for their psychic skills to be learned and developed at a young age. I won't argue with these researched findings because much to my dismay it was discovered that there were members within my immediate household who often displayed uncommon abilities of foreknowledge. So maybe, or maybe not, such research into the life of psychics holds some truth in many instances.

What I remember along the concept (of psychic research reports) is that my mother had often displayed certain abnormal traits of psychic powers but, she was never taken seriously by other members of our family. For instance, my mom has the ability of knowing which members of the family or close friends would be the next to die. So, in this case it is very understandable why many in the family went out of their way trying to avoid being around her. She also has the ability to talk to those who have moved on to the other side in her dreams.

Not that long ago while my wife was helping me to edit this book I spent quite a few weekends at my mom's place because of her health, plus she lives alone. On one particular Saturday morning upon waking up she said to me, I dreamed about Julia last night. At about noon she received a call from her brother telling her that Julia had past away Friday night. That's the way it is with my mom, and sometimes it is that way for me, too. And just like me, my mom has never asked for, nor has she ever received any monetary compensation in any form for what she can naturally do.

I was raised during a era of a great moral struggle and change among people all over the world. In America protesters were concerned about getting involved in the Vietnam War conflict which turned out to be a war that politicians still refuse to fully acknowledge today... as a war. Instead, they have coined the phrase "conflict" when referring to Vietnam. And then there was a constant reality of civil unrest and ugliness unleashed against unarmed marchers both black and white in several southern cities who's administrators were unwilling to end America's version of South African apartheid. While a global conflict of continued wars, rumors of wars, famine, and genocide was, and are still happening somewhere in the world, it was particularly a worse case scenario for certain people with dark skin color living in the home land. It didn't seem to matter where you lived in America during the Jim Crow era if you were born of dark skin, especially if you were considered to be a member of the Negro race, the treatment received from the average business in the south was inhuman. For black people, mulattoes and poor whites alike, life was already fiscally depressive. I'm using the words "fiscally depressive" to describe a general condition of immoral bankruptcy and bad behavior ingrained in the collective consciousness of a society that once harbored that such indifference towards its' minority and poor members were justified according to both biblical principles and constitutional laws that fostered a climate of separate and harsh treatment for these people.

In short, I'm referring to a mental condition, and a disease known as racism and bigotry which are still with us in some form or another today. In today's society, anyone of status who would openly admit to such beliefs stands a good chance of financial ruin by mainstream society, so many of these people who are still clinging onto such out-molded practices have chosen to hide their ill-fated ideals in the comfort of sympathizers and away from public scrutiny. These people are the most dangerous members of the human race simply because they are still holding on to such false and selfish beliefs. Although many of them have managed to dodge the public spotlight, they still tend to keep such hatred alive and valid by programming their young and totally innocent children into believing what the rest of the world's people know to be untrue.

From a certain perspective, I was very fortunate to be born and raised in an era of expanding human consciousness and the conditions that forced many of those in self appointed roles as gatekeepers of a false and jealous god, a god that favors the well being of a select few at the expense of so many others, to re-conceptualize.

I was reared in an area where people of various racial and social backgrounds became unified in a national movement that was an inspiration twenty years before my birth from a very successful blueprint that was created and used by Gandhi to bring the entire British Empire to its needs.

Also I give credit to the courage and stubbornness of a lone and spiritually awakened being known as Rosa Parks. She was the spark that ignited, then called into action a like minded post WWII generation known throughout society by the moniker 'baby boomers,' which later gave birth to people known as hippies around the world, who then focused their collective energetic powers and will towards a machine of world hypocrisy by a much hidden aristocracy of power, and their gatekeepers (governments, local and federal). And who in the world would've thought that such an unassuming, low waged black woman on her way to work, ridding a segregated bus system in Selma, Alabama, the deep of the deepest southern nastiness, would summoned enough inner strength and courage to just say "No." At the time, and history bears this out, just saying "no" became the most powerful weapon of the civil rights movement.

The power to change the machine of programmed hatred all came to an end the moment Rosa uttered this simple word: "NO!" Put it this way; without Rosa, no one would have ever known about Dr. Martin Luther King Jr., beyond black America, as well as, all other famed civil rights activist of that era. Rosa Parks was my heroin.

Growing up in a big southern city like Atlanta, Georgia, during the civil rights movement, which was home to so many of its' core strategists and foot soldiers, alike, at a time that might lead one to conclude that I had to have had a few horrible and personal experiences of my own to share with you about racism, especially in regards to a potential conflict or two, with white people. Well, I am very happy to disappoint you about such assumptions if you have them. Strange as it may seem, given the circumstances surrounding most news worthy events of the time, life for me was fairly normal for a kid of my upbringing and racial makeup. My genetic racial makeup is all over the place, it includes a mixture of African, native American, Latin and European bloodlines.

Living in the south I been mostly identified as a black man. I find it a bit strange that within the mindset of some black people, whom, because of where they were born, do not considered themselves as a part of the African race. Likewise, they are also a part of another racial makeup or two, and more times than not they'll make claims solely to that linage.

Although, my parents were almost always engaged in a constant battle with poverty, my siblings and I somehow managed to survive the horrors of growing up in the deep south within the shadows of the civil rights movement unscathed by its' ugliness. Considering the circumstances of our early years, we all turned out to be good people by any measure.

The reasons why my siblings and I didn't bear much witness to civil ugliness may never be fully known, especially since the civil rights movement was a fabric of our time and is now considered a relic of the past. Maybe it was the work of divine intervention by way of parental determination. Whatever it was, it provided a safe haven for us as it worked-out extremely well when taken into consideration that during most of that time we were the only non-white family to live in our community. Almost regularly, we played with our next door friends named Clifford, Lisa and Robert, who were each white.

My School Daze

In high school, I spent most of time and energy studying and practicing Chinese Kung Fu, Korean Tae kwon do, Japanese Judo, and karate, and American style boxing and wrestling. In those days physically training my body to a point of near perfection left very little time for dating girls or hanging out with friends. I day-dreamed often during school class hours about how to improve my skills in martial arts to the point of falling behind in my studies.

Eventually, as is the case with many high-profile celebrities, I took the easy way out of school by taking a written test which demonstrated my equivalency, so that I could complete high school requirements in less time, and then graduate from high school without ever leaving the house. Today, we call this path option: home schooling.

At some point in time, during the days and nights of constantly training to become the best martial arts master the world has ever known, that I began to meditate on my own. As I now recall such events, I would simply sit in a lotus posture for hours on end with nothing in particular on my mind. And, by the time of my 15th birthday, I had obtained a black belt level of efficiency in several martial arts disciplines. At some time later in my youth, I also developed a keen interested in music, singing and dancing. I am a publish song author, even though, I am no longer active in that arena. Along with a few friends of mine, we formed a singing group and called ourselves: the Newcomers. We spent a full year rehearsing our craft before we began performing at various high school talent shows and night clubs in the Atlanta area, and, we once managed to get a booking onto James Brown's weekly televised music show called: "Future Shock." After several years of performing and practicing as a musical act, the group suddenly split up.

Even though I had devoted a lot of time to the music business, I still kept my body in decent shape and continued practicing martial arts and then meditating late into the late night hours.

I didn't participate much into other sports such as basketball, football, nor, baseball, but when I did show an interest towards other sports outside of martial arts, I usually became very good at it. For instance, at age 18, I learned to play the game of basketball.

Typically for this sport, age 18 is considered a bit too late to develop a good game. But, I was beginning to learn how to defy logic by practicing on the fundamentals of the game. Eventually, I did extremely well at the game of basketball, but never played the sport in high school, but once I did play in a semi-pro basketball league. It was the same pattern for me with every other sport that I pursued outside of martial arts. If I really worked at it, I usually became very good at it in a relatively short period of time. Many years later, at age 37, I took up the game of golf with the same results. To this day, even though I am a professional golfer, I constantly rebuild my swing while always trying to get better.

Leaving on a Midnight Bus

At age 21, I decided to leave Atlanta, and I eventually moved across country to Monterey, California – thanks to an enlistment into the U.S. Army, all of my living expenses were provided for. It was a long-held goal of mine to leave Georgia and live on the west coast, where all the stars played and lived; at least the ones that I followed. After six weeks of basic training, and then, another four weeks of advanced training, all in Columbus, Georgia, I was on a jet, landing at the San Francisco, California Airport. This may sound like a fairy tale, but within eight months of arriving on the west coast, I literally met, and then married the first and only girl that I've ever asked out on a date – true story.

Suddenly, there I was, an enlistee in the U.S. Army, nearly 3,000 miles away from the southeast coast, living in another state, another city and with a wonderful family of my own to care for. For that reason, and that reason alone, is when my perspective on life and its' meaning began to shift.

Up until that moment in time, I had never thought about the well being of anyone other than, myself. With a wife and the birth of our daughter just weeks away, it suddenly became crystal clear and necessary that I at least investigate other ways of providing a better standard of living for my family. As a soldier, my monthly income was severely limited, and all potential increases in pay was subjected to a review by national politics and lawmakers living in the nations capital. There were annual small increases in pay called cola's (cost of living allowances) for all soldiers, but for the work each of us endured the pay was mediocre at best. I had a saying back then: "they love us during events of war, and hate us in times of peace." To make my point, just look at how the veterans of all America's conflicts are treated after they return home and the fighting ends. A great number of them become homeless, while others face post war related stress issues and many other mental disorders. I think this country owes its' veterans a lot more than they are receiving.

Don't get me wrong, here, the issues facing veterans are not just problems burdened by politicians, cause, we all play a major role in their post service treatment, too. As soon as the conflict of war ends, and people feel safe to go about their daily routines, soldiers and war veterans are soon forgotten. Worst of all offenders of veterans are the media. They use images of veterans along with the word patriotism, this is good boosting for ratings which equates into more advertising dollars. In the end the when stories vanish from the headlines of the media, veterans become out of sight, out of mind.

With thoughts of doing financially better, I readily accepted an invitation from a total stranger one day to attend a business meeting with an opportunity to learn ways of getting rich; which was being held at a local hotel. At that meeting (seminar), I was really impressed by the level of professionalism and presentations of all the speakers that night. Just hearing the stories of each person there that evening, about how some of them managed to overcome extreme levels of poverty, while living on meager monthly wages to eventually command a meaningful 6-figure income, was highly motivating and I was immediately sold on the idea of owning my own business. The name of the company that sponsored these opportunities to ordinary people like me and others, was the Amway Corporation.

Up until that moment I had never even heard of such a company as Amway. As the night went on, we suddenly reached the best part of the entire event. For anyone wanting to become a part of something bigger than themselves, with a real chance of becoming rich, all that is required of them to participate in the opportunity of a life time was to simply purchase a starter-kit for a minimum fee of $25.00. And with that I immediately began the process of learning how to sell soap, and how to recruit other soldiers who lived on post, to also sell soap to make more income for their families.

Within a very short time of working the business plan laid out before me by those in the Amway business, I had amassed a down-line of nearly 150 people. Back then, the way network marketing worked, is that a percentage of all sales generated by those you sponsored into the business, you would receive as a bonus from that distribution network each month as each person is instantly compensated. The only problem in such a system occurs when someone in the chain link fails to perform, or suddenly drops out of the program altogether. Accordingly, such actions tend to effect all of those in the down line of the system. This scenario is just what happened to my over-ride sales commissions one particular month with nearly $40,000.00 in orders on the line. In less time than it took to build a distribution network, my entire sales organization had collapsed because someone within the up link failed to fill their orders. And the money paid into the network suddenly vanished and no products were received for customer delivery as each member of the sales group became bitter at the prospect of not receiving products, nor a refund from the company.

Likewise, my plans for getting rich and obtaining the American dream as an Amway distributor suddenly went out-the-way it came, quickly. This was the first time in which I realized that the American dream is just that, an illusion.

Needless to say, one by one, members of my sales network would soon leave and seek opportunities elsewhere. As for me, the experience of thinking outside of my comfort zone had become highly intoxicating. For the first time in my life I felt empowered to achieve a certain degree of financial success because at that very moment I had become convinced that being rich was a matter of choice, not luck. People used to make jokes about me and other people going around selling soap in hopes of making it rich.

In retrospect, hindsight is always 20/20. While I didn't become rich selling Amway products, the founders of the company went on to become billionaires. They now own professional sports teams and other high profile interests around the world. And for a few people who helped to make the company a success story, they got rich too, all from selling something as simple as soap. So the moral of this aspect of my life's journey is quite clear, life is what you imagine it to be, every time....

Time of Miracles

In retrospect, the debacle and fallout from my experienced with the Amway Corporation as an independent sales contractor played a major role in preparing me to withstand the circumstances of series of events that turned out to be a course in miracles. In a slow, and deliberate way, I was beginning to learn ways to unleash the tremendous powers of belief in the face of seemingly insurmountable odds. And at a deeper state of awareness, I was subconsciously being introduced the awesome powers and intelligence of the infinite source, from within me, as me.

Manifestations of miracles are happening all the time, everywhere in the world, each moment. Just to exist as a human being is the greatest example of a miracle there is. But to understand the significance of what I consider as manifested miracles to effect my life, it is best that you to at least become somewhat familiar with events that led to what I consider as the first miracle. Somehow, when the focus is aimed at events that we believe qualifies as a miracle, we somehow seem to think only of those extraordinary events outlined in biblical times, for which modern versions of miracles become quite pale in comparison to something that is believed unlikely to occur, again. For the record, meeting and then marring my wife was a miracle, or a match made in heaven. On the day preceding our wedding, my wife made a statement so profound that still rings in my heart and mind to this day, she said: "now, I know that I am loved."

Miracle One

When I was in second or third grade, events of the first miracle occurred. My mother and some close friends of hers had decided to break the bored housewife syndrome and take the kids to a nearby community park. It was a very hot summer day, and what we all wanted and needed was a place with room to roam, where the kids could simply run wild and play. The park we visited on that day is named in honor of General Ulysses S. Grant. Locals simply call the place Grant's Park. During this particular time in Atlanta, Grant Park had had its' share of media coverage in the local press as it was an unwilling participant of several marches featuring men in white robes and hoods, with guns in their hands, known as the Ku-Klux-Klan. Things must have been resolved by the time that our mom and others decided to treat us to a day at the park, for if not, it is certain that such an adventure would not have been pursued.

The community where we lived at the time was predominantly white. In fact, from what I recall, we were the only non-white family on the block. I say this because of a constant reminder from one of our school teachers, who at the time, had made it her mission in life; as it seemed; to sort of drive by our home and spy on us each school day. From time to time she would openly comment in front of the entire classroom of students: "you folks don't know how to live around white folks". It is because of these unwanted outbursts, which was never told to my parents, that led me into believing, rightly or wrongly, that we were the only non-whites living in the community. And to this day, I still don't know if this was true.

Anyway, going to Grant Park was a big deal for us kids because of its' vast openness and spaces to play, and the fact that nobody would complain about a level of noise that we were bound to produce. On this particular outing at the park, all of us kids just scattered around to the various sections of trees and pathways, while our parents remained stationary in a picnic area. At sometime during the day, my second to the youngest brother, along with a few of his friends were given what we called "hot-ice" by some older teens, as a prank. Thinking that the ice was cold, my brother put some in his mouth to suck on. The hot-ice began to melt away at his inner mouth, and then it entered his throat were it continued to wreak havoc. My brother couldn't breathe or communicate with anyone about what was happening. Somewhere along the way he would become unconsciousness.

I became alerted to what was happening by the sound of my mother's very loud scream from nearly a mile away.

By the time I arrived at the scene to see what transpired, an ambulance had come and taken my brother and mom away to the hospital. Later that night, when my parents arrived home from the hospital, my mom sat quietly alone in a corner of the main room of the house. For a while, I assumed that all was fine in regards to my brother. There was no talking by anyone in the house. Everything seemed to be uncharacteristically, quiet. And that's when I heard my mom's loud scream, once again.

It was my mom's second scream of a very long and unforgettable day. Only this time though, I heard her say that the doctors who were treating my brother didn't expect him to live throughout the night. With that in mind, and the thought of losing my brother, I closed my eyes, and then I begin to visualize him (my brother) getting well. For the first time in my life, I prayed. I prayed nearly all that night. In my mind I could see my brother playing around with all the other kids in the neighborhood and having fun. And for no particular reason, and certainly without thinking, I released an image of my brother in a healthy state unto the universe.

At some point during the night, between all the activities of visualizations and prayer, I fell into a deep and soundless sleep. I was suddenly awakened early the next morning by another scream, but this time, the scream turned out to be a scream of joy as my dad came home with very good news of a miraculous recovery by my little brother. Not only did he survive – he was expected to be released from the hospital the very next day. My brother would grow to become the choreographer for the film produced by Dallas Austin named, "Drumline." Most all of the close up hand-shots of drum performances of that movie are the hands of my kid brother. He mentioned to me that he only recalls passing out during that dreadful moment in his life.

A Second Miracle

The nature of my second miracle did not involve a life or death situation. It may even qualify as case of synchronicity or LOA manifestation, or something alone those lines. Nonetheless, from my point of view, when reflecting back to what transpired over the course of a few short days in the spring of 1985, I'd say it was nothing short of a miracle.

It was during a time that my wife and I were expecting the birth of our only child. I was on active military duty at the time with the U.S. Army. My wife was experiencing complications of the birth of our daughter, and I had just received orders by the Department of Defense which had just reassigned the remainder of my tour of duty to the European Command in Germany. It became apparently clear to me, based upon this haste assignment, that I would not be around to help my wife in such a difficult time. Worse yet, it also meant that my wife would be left alone with no one to turn to for help in a time of need, I couldn't let that happen. Deep down inside of me, I knew that I wouldn't let that happen. The more I thought the situation over, there really were no valid reasons why the U.S. Army should not delay these reassignment orders until my family crisis was over. So, I made a formal request through the chain of command for a temporary deferment of orders for reassignment to Europe. The request was typed in a legal format on a form the military calls a DF. Which simply means a delay of duty of an assignment. In this case, for the undue hardship that this action would cause to my family. Considering that our country was not engaged in war at the time, this request should have been a slam dunk, one would think! But the request was promptly denied. So I did what any reasonable person would do in a similar situation, I submitted a second request, and it too was quickly denied. So I decided to make my request known in person to the company commander, who was my immediate supervisor, knowing that he had authority to approve or disapprove a hardship request on the spot, and that could have ended my crisis right then and there. But, much to my dismay, my request fell upon deaf ears once more.

The next option available to have my request approved would involve the help of a military lawyer which had to be assigned to me, but, this too required permission from the company commander in order for me to seek help through legal channels. It also meant that my reassignment deferment request would become effective immediately until an outcome was decided. This too, was also denied.

Next, I decided to make a request of deferment from my reassignment known directly to the battalion commander without my lower commanders' approval. As usual, I left a message with the commander's secretary. I made sure to tell the secretary the nature of my call, and that it was urgent that I received a reply. The battalion commander responded by asking the brigade chaplain to council me. A military Chaplin, I reasoned, is a man of faith, someone who answers to God, only. Surely, he'll see the situation from my point of view and then side with me. When I arrived at the chaplain's office that evening, I sensed that he and my company commander had talked about it, so the Chaplin had only these words to say: "come Friday, you'll be en-route to Germany, Soldier."

I then made my request known to the to the division commander, the highest authority on post; and to no avail, this too fell upon deaf ears. It was now Tuesday, and Friday was only days away. On the way home one day from the office I ran into a friend and used this moment to voice my frustration about the way I was being treated, and the way things were happening, or what was not happening. All he would say to me is that: "you can't beat the system, they don't care anything about you or your family – because you are property of Uncle Sam. My advice to you is to just suck it up and go to Germany."

After conferencing with several others about this situation, my resolve grew even stronger than before and I literally refused at that moment to give in. On Wednesday morning of that week I placed a direct phone call to my state senator in Georgia. At the time it was Sen. Sam Nunn, my effort to reach him was totally ignored. So, out of frustration and still determined, I placed a direct phone call to a local politician I'd seen many times on TV, and had read various articles about him in the local papers (Monterey Herald). His name was Congressman Leon Panetta. I couldn't talked to him directly, but I did get a chance to speak with a staff member, who then relayed the nature of my call to Congressman Panetta.

Later that Wednesday night, I did something that hadn't done in quite some time – I prayed and then meditated about my situation to GOD, and to anyone else who would listen. In a sense, I let my feelings and desires be known to the cosmos. All through the night I kept to my self, away from family and friends, in total silence and darkness. I soon began to see scalar waves of blue, yellow, red and green roll from left to right, popping in and out of view as they wished, all in my mind's eye. I kept on praying and asking for help, telepathically. I was too ignorant of the ways of consciousness at the time to fully understand and appreciate what I had stumbled onto, or if it would make any difference. It was the same scenario as when I had prayed as a kid to save the life of my brother. What's so ironic is that kids have a natural ability to limit all distractions from competing noise (frequencies) within their mind, therefore they are ready to effect things simply from praying or meditating about it.

Anyway, it seems like the older we become as humans on earth, the more systemic programming builds a strong signal which tends to dominate communications coming from your intuitive mind. We'll talk more at length about why this happens and how to correct it in "How to Develop Your Spiritual Powers." If I had truly known the significance of what the universe had revealed to me earlier, my life would have evolved spiritually that much sooner. Even though I was beginning to witness some of the awesome powers from within, I was still too blind and stuck in logic to embrace it at the time.

A Prayer Answered (Manifested)

Anyway, early that Thursday morning, before most people would find time to eat, the Brigade Chaplin made a special visit to the office where I worked, unannounced. When I saw him, immediately, I knew in my mind that things had changed virtually overnight, and that it had a lot to do with leaving a message at Congressman Leon Panetta's office. As it turned-out, the Congressman brought forth an immediate inquiry to the post commander and things rolled down the chain of command from there. On that day, what the chaplain said to me was similar to this: "Mr. Sailor, what is it that you want?" I replied: "that given the way I was treated by almost everyone in the chain of command about this situation, I want out of the Army." And with that the Chaplin said to me: " you'll have your honorable discharge papers drawn up and ready tomorrow, is that quick enough, for you?"

And so, on the following Friday, instead of traveling to Germany, a miraculous turn of events had given me the choice to exit military service one year ahead of my scheduled date of termination, and with full honors. And when I finally had time for reflecting on the way things had transpired, I couldn't help but to think back to the times I had spent listening those Amway sales-recruit meetings and learning how to communicate with people outside of my comfort zone. Instinctively I knew that I could do much more from an economical point of view. And that this was a beginning to awakening from my self imposed limits of what life could be.

In hindsight, it was during one of those rah-rah meetings of becoming rich, that I was introduced to a book that would become the first, of many, that would help my awareness to deepen, and to begin the process of listening to the universe, from within. The book was titled: *Think and Grow Rich*, by Napoleon Hill. Never, before reading this book, had I ever been exposed to such a positive and awe inspiring message, such as the one featured in this book. The universe conspires to give you what you ask for, you just have to learn not to get in the way.

The problem which arose while I was an independent contractor with Amway was truly a blessing in disguise because the positive words within that book kept resonating in mind. And while faced with seemingly insurmountable odds that were placed before me in trying to amicably resolve the situation with the Army. I was filled with confidence from reading the messages of *"Think and Grow Rich."* I quickly landed a job as a car salesman the following Sunday after my honorable discharge from the Army was approved. Working as a car salesman of a local dealership, I almost immediately earned in commission dollars more money than I had earned all year as a soldier, in one month. As a soldier, I made only about $8,500.00 a year. When I began selling cars it grew into $5,000 - $10,000.00 a month.

Financially, times had become good for me, but the good times didn't last. After selling cars for nearly two years at the car plaza of Monterey, California, the auto industry as a whole went into an economic slump and has never fully recovered. I made a bold move employment wise and seemingly rebounded quickly after becoming a licensed life insurance representative in the state of California. At first, I did good selling life insurance and actually brought home a larger paycheck than I had as a car salesman. But the good times would become interrupted once again shortly after a year in the business of selling life insurance policies.

All of my sales at the time were mostly to former friends in the Army who were still stationed at the local military post. One day, the post commander got hung-up in politics of business with the urging of a few traditional insurance companies that were clearly selling inferior products to the troops that could not stand-up side by side to the products offered by my company, decided to ban from post, the insurance agents working with a then controversial company based out of Duluth, Georgia by the name of A.L. Williams Company. The A.L Williams Company would go on to becoming the nations largest insurance company when it later merge with the Travelers Group. There were many common folks inside the agent ranks of that company who made millions over the years from selling life insurance products, alone. But not me.

However, I did make a substantial sum of money working with the company, but not enough to say that I was rich, although comfortable could be a better description.

With the post commander's decision to ban all A.L Williams agents, it killed my business in the town of Monterey, California. Anyone familiar with the Monterey Peninsula area and economy knows that there were only two industries in that area: tourism and military. And of the two the military was by far the largest employer and spender in town. If you can't sell to the soldiers, you simply could not make a living there. Once again, for the third time in 3 years, I was faced with the prospect of an uncertain future in regards to income. With that in mind, and unclear about what decisions I would have to make, I return to meditating about my situation once more.

Silent, Still, Subtle Voice

When I began meditating some time ago, it became quite evident that I was not alone, for an inner voice within my mind began talking, guiding me toward answers I was seeking. In fact, this inner voice, or my intuitive mind, had always been there to assist me, if only I had known about it much earlier in life. But once I realized what this phenomenon was, I began testing it for accuracy, I almost immediately found that this new power could be used to help me decide things in my life. For instance, would it be best to stick it out in Monterey, Ca., in case the banning of agents from conducting business on the military post was lifted? This meant that I could resume creating leads and making sales. Or, should I move to Hawaii where I had a standing offer to sell cars again. Eventually I chose to move back east to the place of my birth, a place where I had built-in support among family and friends should I need it. And most of all, I could start over. One things for certain, a choice had to be made.

As young as my family and I were at the time, Hawaii seemed like a very attractive choice but, it certainly was not the most reasonable choice to make of all the options available. Also, it would have been so much easier to remain in Monterey where where my wife and I had connections and were already established in the community. But a small, still, subtle, voice kept saying in the back of my mind that any of the first two options would be a very bad decision. Instead, the voice showed me by way of visualizations and imaginations in my mind that life in Atlanta would fare much better than all other options.

With much logical thought, and anticipation, we moved to the southeast, and back to the city of my birth. But this decision would not be without some reservations at the fore front of my mind. For one, I finally realized that my family might not feel comfortable in the south since we were a racially mixed family. And secondly, I feared that our daughter would develop a southern accent, one of which not even I carried around. In the end, though, all concerns were brushed aside.

Going Home, Again

Relocating to the area of Atlanta, Georgia turned out to be a good decision for us, overall. My wife and I were able to find work within weeks of arriving there, and within a year, I had become a stockbroker with a small OTC brokerage. The stockbroker gig lasted only a few months before being shut down by the Securities and Exchange Commission for committing fraud, and once again I was seeking another place to work. I quickly found another job in the same business.

The year was now 1987, and the financial markets were in turmoil as a result of a huge sell-off from what is known as 'Black Monday.' Anyway, I consulted with the voice inside of me and decided to keep seeking opportunities in the same industry even though experts were all saying that the end was near. A few people poor in heart committed suicide in New York by jumping out of windows of skyscrapers. In Miami, Florida, a local broker's customer decided to have his lunch while shooting and killing his broker and others in the office of the business, and then turning the gun upon himself. Amongst all the doom and gloom news coverage about wall street that were filling the front pages of almost every major newspaper of the time, the genie within said to stay the course and that things will be alright. So I did.

Eventually I landed a job as a stockbroker with a regional N.Y.S.E. member firm. Several years later I had become the top producing broker and a vice president at the firm. What at first, may sound like the end of a story was only a continuation of a process that I call "my awakening." In fact, every event in my life that had evolved up to that moment in time was simply more of a new way of seeing the world, the way it really is. I just did not realize it at the time. My process of awakening just sort of, happened.

Confessions of a Psychic Stockbroker

As a stockbroker, my income was based solely on commissions received as a percentage of funds coming into accounts that I brought to the firm, and then again, as funds moved laterally from one investment vehicle and into that of another, and yet again when ever funds were withdrawn or moved, commission dollars were generated. With this kind of arrangement, investment brokers and their firms have put themselves in a unique position to make money on the virtual movement of other people's money, without ever risking any of their own. Take for instance, a $10,000.00 initial investment received from a client, a stockbroker would on average earn approximately $1,000.00 or more in total payout whether or not the client makes or lose any money. This is why stockbrokers (and brokerage firms) are always prospecting for more investors. It's all about the numbers, and this is only the retail side of the business.

There are so many ways for people to make money in Wall Street's financial industry that it could make your head spin. In a sense, the street is allowed to gamble with your money and none of its own, and still get paid for it. And as many have discovered, when push comes to shove the entire industry is bailed-out at taxpayers' expense.

Almost from the very beginning of my career as a stockbroker, I understood the mechanics of the business with complete clarity. I knew that if I were to simply focus my mind on doing a good job, that my efforts and beliefs about making money for investors who trusted me enough to part ways with some of their money, that things would work out for me and them (investors) more times than not. I had a saying with each new client that came on board with me as their stockbroker: "my job is to create a tax problem for you." I meant that in a good way. If I made money for them, and lots of it, they would have to pay more in taxes on their capital gains. Most people don't mind paying more in taxes if they earn substantially more in capital gains. They understand that this was the trade-off for winning in the stock markets. Not only does an investor make money when the bet pays off, but the entire country makes money every time an investor wins, and likewise when they lose money, too.

In a flash of genius, it was decided then and there, that I would do things my own way after noticing that nearly almost all brokers working the retail side of the business, never made any money for their clients. Every month these brokers were constantly under pressure from the firm to continuously open at least ten new accounts a month with at least $10,000 minimum per investor. In addition, they had to produce $10,000 gross income every month out of fear of losing their job. In the stock brokerage business, this is known as meeting quotas, which is the standard operating procedures for all firms that creates a cut-throat environment where some people would steal from their grannies just to survive the cut at the end of the month. Stealing was so epidemic that I once considered leaving the business simply because I didn't want to be associated with thieves. Once I realized that not everyone working in the brokerage business were crooks, I began watching shares of stocks as they were being traded all day long for days on end, and suddenly I knew which stocks to buy and which ones to stay away from. It didn't matter to me at all about which stock exchange the shares were trading on, or which firms were backing them. I had seen enough of the business to know that you could lose money anywhere in the markets on any investment product at any given moment.

The fact that companies have in house traders, who trade against their own customers, is in itself a conflict of interest. But, based upon the structure of rules that were set forth by lawyers of the firms along with the government when the SEC agency was set-up, these apparent conflicts of interests are legal. So, I decided to focus my intuitiveness mainly on in-house stocks that were thinly traded because, I knew were they were coming from. Using my god given talents of psychic phenomena, I was able to sense a good stock opportunity, intuitively. Also, knowing what a stock would do in terms of moving higher or lower before the general public knows, is to know what people will do in advance, before they do it. And I had become very good at predicting what other people would do, the way that I selected almost every stock that I sold to my clients. You can say in hindsight that my system was very effective and the results have stood the test of time.

The credit for the incredible amount of success that my clients and I earned when I was a stockbroker was my ability of knowing intuitively what was likely to happen in advance. I didn't know what time frame certain things would happen, but I knew what the eventual outcome the investments would amount to.

The rest was up to my clients, for they had to constantly be patient at a time of turmoil in the financial markets. One of the first things that I would say to them (my clients) was that they must learn to have more patients.

Those who study psychic abilities call this aspect of PSI, precognition. But precognition is just one attribute of PSI, the real power lies in the knowledge of how to tap into this infinite source at will. Back then, my use of the power of the source was mostly instinctive and coincidental without really knowing that such abilities were possible. Nowadays its mostly intentional. While the instincts are still there, my intuitive abilities have greatly evolved overtime into a much deeper level of awareness that seems to have no boundaries of space or time.

Ask and You Shall Receive

Ask and you shall receive is a lesson that I accidentally stumbled into. During the mid-summer of 1992, shortly before hurricane Andrew wreaked havoc onto south Florida, I was vacationing with family and friends along the beaches of Panama City, Florida. We had managed to lease a luxury duplex on the beach front for an entire week. It had been awhile since I last spent any considerable time on a beach, especially since relocating to the Atlanta area to live. Anyone who've spent some time in the city of Atlanta has but one common gripe, the city has no beaches or water front resorts to boost about. So we traveled Panama City Beach, Florida with the full intent of enjoying a week's long, relaxed vacation away from the hustle and bustle of the concrete jungle that we called home. At the time, I had a standing policy that says, where ever my wife and I would travel, our daughter would come right alongside us no matter what, simply because I didn't want my little girl to miss-out on any adventures as a child due to parental selfishness of not wanting to bring along their kids. I wanted my daughter to be able to say that she had experienced things and traveled to many destinations while growing up. And indeed, my daughter traveled alongside my wife and I where ever we went. You name the place, and chances are good that my daughter's been there before.

There we were, sleeping late into the morning hours and simply being lazy. Eating out every day and walking along the shores of Panama Beach, spending money at nearly all stores we walked into, and contributing to the local economy.

Early one morning, when I was alone on the balcony, watching the vast ocean waves slam into the shoreline, I asked a direct question to God telepathically---I asked: who am I? Shortly thereafter, something very strange and mystical began to fill the inner regions of my mind and body simultaneously. Whatever it was, I couldn't say but, it felt like a mix of calmness, a sort of cool and gentle breeze surrounding me and touching my body. While this was happening, I really didn't know how to react, or what to do about it, or if I should do anything at all--except experience the moment for what it was.

There was no pain from this event, but there was a smooth hint of vibrations, and I felt temporarily weak in the knees as goose bumps begin appearing up and down my arms. And for a while, after overcoming the fear of dying, I finally decided to sit down and rest on one of several lawn chairs on the balcony. Unsure of what would happen next, I eventually conjured up the will to go back inside the beach-house, lay back in bed---in between the comfort and warmth of sheets and covers, next to my beautiful wife, who was still sleeping. I remained fully awake and began meditating on the whole event.

Later, I remembered earlier during the year that I had spoken directly to God while meditating but, received no response. But this time was very different, because on this occasion I closed my eyes, and mentally repeated the same question again and again: "who am I?"

To say that I expected a response to my question, well, that was not part of my thought process, nor intention. At the time, I didn't know that God would respond to direct questions if they were asked telepathically but, I soon found out that this was the case, and this accidental discovery of mine became the beginning of my understanding the values of meditating with the express purpose of communicating with God. And later it to helped unleash and enhance the psychic abilities within me. It also explained why some prayers seem to go unanswered.

Within a few short moments later, there I was again, half awake, half asleep, showing signs of drifting off into borderland. And, as if watching a well-scripted movie, a scene began playing in on my mental screen. I was showing me things that I had long forgotten, until I realized that this was the same dream that I had had about my office in Buckhead.

Inside this dream of mine, all the key people of the company were working at their assigned areas of responsibility, and I had just walked onto the trading floor; which was directly behind the wall of the main entrance; when all of a sudden, John Clark, a manager with the firm, called out to me, saying: "Rod, did you see PJTV this morning?" He then continued: "it's at 76 a share!" This dream turned out to be a precognitive event (seeing into the future), within a few months later the entire dream, every aspect of it literally manifested into reality.

Dream Manifestation

In January 1993, PJTV had reached an all time historical high of $74.00 per share. To understand the significance of this – a brief background of this stock is warranted. I began selling PJTV stock to most of my clients when a young man named David Cowherd, mentioned that I should take a look at this company in the fall of 1991. This happened shortly after a few of my clients had made out big on an investment in the Image Bank, which was purchased by the Eastman Kodak company at a premium. David approached me about PJTV because he and a couple of office managers had been buying the shares for quite some time and they wanted to dump the stock off to someone else and move their clients' money around. At the time PJTV was a very thinly traded issue, in order to sell a position, you had to find a willing stockbroker to buy it for the same amount of money you hoped to move. In other words, what they needed was a place to dump their bad investment decision before their clients began to lose faith. Since they also worked as stockbrokers and managers, they had a wealth of inside information on every stockbroker's book in the office. Basically all the had to do was look it up on the computer print-outs. And yes, that is insiders trading but, it is the kind that no one gets punished for.

Anyway, it really didn't matter to me because I also had possession of inside information: intuitive knowledge, which is the ultimate form of insiders information when you know how to access it.

So, when David came to me and asked if I wanted buy into the PJTV stock, I knew immediately what he and the others were up to. But, I also knew in advance that this particular stock would pay handsomely in the future.

One particular client of mine from Cottonport, LA., would be the first of many of my clients that purchased shares into this company. The client from Cottonport went against the advice of his brother; a high-level insurance company executive; and invested his life's savings of nearly $6,000.00 into an unknown and virtually bankrupt company that I recommended. There were approximately 500 more investors who would follow my advice and put up most, if not all of their money into this stock.

For years, this was essentially the only stock I would offer to anyone brave enough to invest money with me. In the fall of 1992, with my clients' hard earned life savings, we collectively controlled 75 percent of all PJTV shares that were outstanding. When I began buying it on behalf of my clients, the stock was trading at .34 cents per unit. This meant that not only did an investor receive one share of common stock, they also received two common shares and a warrant. This was an incredible three for the price of one deal. But then again, the hucksters on wall Street didn't expect this deal to amount to anything. Consider this: the company had no money in the bank, nor revenues to talk about. The only thing nearing intangible value they had to show was an office space that was leased at Madison Square Gardens, in New York city, and a shoe box, that's right, a shoe box was used to demonstrate the potential of their theoretical product. That was it!

Needless to say, I went against the advice of company managers, and the chairman and CEO of the board of directors by sticking to my guns. I steadfastly refused to encourage my clients into selling or diversify into other stocks that were offered by the firm. For this, I was branded an outsider, a maverick. Later I picked up the nickname, "Stealth." Mike D, the first client I put into PJTV, ended up becoming a millionaire in January 1993, as his holdings were cashed out at more than $1.3 million. Virtually every client that trusted my advice with their hard-earned money, and invested it all into PJTV, became rich that year.

Understandably, I had become an overnight success in the financial business. Within a few months of January 1993, I had accumulated enough personal income to live anywhere in the country without asking about price. Eventually I purchased a mansion for my family that was once owned by R&B recording artist Teddy Reilly. My neighbors included members of the NFL's Atlanta Falcons, and numerous doctors and local statesmen.

My personal fortune had changed so fast and drastically that many of my neighbors, and some family members believed that I had become involved in something illegal, or that I was a drug dealer. It was hard for any of them to realize that I had earned – the amount of money I had coming in legally and paid hundreds of thousands in taxes.

In 1995, I had had enough of the financial industry decided to leave the brokerage business altogether to become an entrepreneur. The internet boom was just beginning to heat up with the wildly successful release of the first commercial web browser called the Netscape Navigator. At the same time I opened a mortgage brokerage company, the business was growing so rapidly that I couldn't control the agents who were working with me. I was deeply concerned about fraudulent applications being filed under my company's license. So, listening to my inner voice of reason and intelligence, I decided to close the company down and at the same time began experimenting with the internet.

For several years I hacked away late into the night and early mornings, I was very motivated and wanted to learn everything I could about computers, including how to write code in a variety of languages. Eventually I became quite efficient as a programmer in the following languages: Basic, Java, C, C+, PHP, SQL, HTML, DHTML and COBOL. I then programmed and constructed a business news and information web site with more than 100,000 coded web pages and nearly 300,000 links to other sites. Overtime there were several unsolicited buyout offers from various internet companies, including one with close ties former president H.W Bush, and members of the family who owns an NFL franchise. All offers were declined.

Many of these companies were well funded, and within a very short time many of them simply duplicated parts of my website business as their own. The things offered on my website were a first in many areas of the growing internet business: such as online mortgages, online tax filling, online legal filling of corporation papers with links to each state that allowed online corporate document filling.

My internet venture became a publicly traded stock company in December 1998, and became listed on the NASDAQ electronic exchange under the ticker symbol: bibn. For most of 1999, I was a stock market multi-millionaire on paper as my personal ownership in the company reached a market value in excess of $50,000,000.00. However, after the events of 911, like many people who were invested in the markets, I lost almost all of the $50 million in value as the company's stock was adversely affected by the New York WTC bombings.

Voice within Reemerges

One day shortly after selling what was left of the company, I founded to a group of private investors for cash and stock, I began to hear an inner voice within me once again. "Move to Florida, do the book," kept resonating in my mind, over and over and over, again. At the time what I wanted to do was just play golf and be left alone. I wanted nothing else to do with a business of any kind. I planned on improving my golf game and at some time in the future, I would also try out for the Senior PGA Tour. Earlier I had joined a mini-pro tour organization named Adam Tight Lies Tour. I played a couple events in Mississippi and the reach the finals as a member of the World Golf league, which was held in Myrtle Beach, South Carolina. Playing mini-tours was a tool for me to learn about golf on the road. While I was mentally ready to play out there, my physical game was not.

Nevertheless I went out on tour anyway. Getting my game ready for the senior tour cost a lot of money. I had spent nearly several thousands of dollars on equipment and a place to work on my game over the years. In the process I met several pros and became close friends with some. In the game of golf there are many spirits on the golf course and they truly recognize and appreciate it when they meet other spirits in pursuit of knowledge, and is quickly available to help you with mental techniques and the mechanics of the swing. I broke par for the first time in golf as a professional, I carded for 4 under par. Eventually I ran short of self funding and had to reluctantly return to the act of generating a source of income. So, I put golf on hold and went back to work.

Over the next several years, I would become involved in several businesses – just to make money, but the words from the inner voice kept flowing into my mind, "do the book." I had no idea of what to write about, I just knew that I had to start writing something.

To say that I became totally engulfed and consumed by the voice is an understatement. At one point, I thought that I was losing my mind, until early one morning, the voice appeared to come from somewhere else, outside of my head, but inside the room, where I slept.

"Wake up!" I heard the voice say, "it's time to get up, do the book." What should I write about? "You should write about the truth as you know it to be." The voice continued; "there is only one of us here, we are but one consciousness, there is only one soul, and many spirits. But still, we are just one. You resonate from a single source of intelligence, an awareness that encompasses all realms of existence, including that which you call the universe. Within every human being are attributes of the source. Human beings has the ability to create, to manifest, to change things. You have become lost in total awareness of that which I AM, as a result, you believe that you are separate from the cause, from me, that I AM. You have created overtime, that I am, that what I am not. I AM the cause of everything that is. Humanity has become confused by illusions of opposites, which are the same, of competition – instead of cooperation, of ownership - instead of sharing, of good and evil, of heaven and hell, of god and Satan." These thought-forms are all manifested in the collective consciousness of humankind."

"There is only that which you take into your imagination and with the strength of frequencies within your mind, that these things are made real. When mankind collectively seek and know this truth from within, these problems will exist no more. Because your awareness of the spirit that you are, and love of truth will become your known reality. This is the truth of revelation, not wars, famine, and disasters. All these things are of your own makings. When the truth that I Am becomes known by all, is when the shift into global enlightenment takes place. Because this has not yet taken hold, all of those things brought to you in the light of the past, shall repeat themselves, again and again, until all are enlightened. This is the path, each of you must take – one at a time – until all have chosen to live as one. True power comes from within you, not from without. This is the only reality."

For several years the voice guided me towards all the information I would need to write this book. But, I still had many questions lingering in my mind. Strangely, one by one, these answers would slowly come. The title of this book jumped out at me in my half awake state of mind. I kept hearing these words: "this book should be called The BOAT, and it should be about the attributes of human beings, what they are capable of doing." And with that, I began to write.

Later I began experiencing more attributes of psychic phenomena within days of working on the first chapter of this book. In hindsight, I had already – experienced spontaneous events of ESP senses many times before, but never did it occur to me at the time that I would ever consider myself as being physic – having the ability to access psychic powers intentionally. Since that time, I have learned more about my own psychic abilities. Nowadays, I often perform telepathic healing on people in need without charge. And from time to time I teach remote viewing and other psychic techniques (see Tapping the source for more).

Spiritual ignorance is the mark of the beast...

TELEPATHY

This chapter alone is worth the price of admission. What you are about to discover in this reading is a true and accurate account of all the mechanisms involved in the art of telepathy. And since telepathy is an art implies that you too can do this in a matter of minutes once you become familiar with how and why it exists. (You can do this is in a matter of minutes, once you become familiar with how and why it exists.)

First things first, I must answer any preconceived notions of what telepathy is and is not. As with all other psychic powers mentioned in this book, telepathy exists simply because it is a natural phenomenon and aspect of the subjective level of the mind. With that being said you should realize by now that everything within the physical realm is a manifestation of the subjective mind, and in all instances the art of telepathy is the primary method of delivery which the subject mind uses to carry out all of it functions. In short there is nothing in reality that did not come about as a result of telepathic power.

For instance, almost everybody has prayed at least once in their lifetime. You should know that telepathy is the vehicle that delivers your prayer to its intended destination (God). And since the prayer was originated by yourself means that you were its transmitter.

Here are a few key things you should know at this point before advancing further into the art of telepathy. And I promise these things are quite painless and can be remembered easily:

1. the preferred language of telepathy and the subjective mind are images,

2. thought vibrations and visualizations are used to animate images of the subjective mind and the art of telepathy,

3. telepathic messages must have a transmitter and receiver,

4. distances, time and space does not matter,

5. telepathy allows psychics to speak to the dead,

6. telepathy allows you to foresee future events,

7. it also allows you to access information from the past,

8. and present, (access present information)

9. it allows you to know what other people are thinking (mind reading),

10. it can also be used to heal yourself or others,

11. telepathy can be used to manifest your life's daily events,

12. it can also allow you to become more knowledgeable than you are now,

13. it can also be used to warn you of impending danger,

14. it can be used to channel energy, especially chi,

15. it enables you to accurately tell time without a timepiece,

16. belief is essential as it is for all things.

With all of the aforementioned attributes of telepathy it should be clear by now that nothing exists without it. And yes, it can be used for mind-control if the intended receiver is unaware of how it works. In fact this is the sole reason hypnosis works the way it does. Without the subjective level of mind, along with the transmission power of telepathy, hypnosis would not exist.

How did I come upon this powerful telepathic knowledge?

While living in the Central Florida area some years ago, my cash reserves ran very low, which meant that I had to find away to generate cash. Eventually I answered an ad in search of limo and taxis drivers. After attending a two-day presentation I quickly got licensed and began working part-time. I used the Law of Attraction and telepathy at the onset, immediately I began raking in $500.00 - $900.00 per day. Besides learning to ask questions to my inner core of wisdom and knowledge, I accidentally stumbled upon magic one evening while watching a live PGA Tour event on TV.

Here's what happened: during the 2008 annual tour championship tournament held each year in Atlanta, Ga. at the East Lake Country Club, on the back nine Sunday evening. Sergio Garcia and Anthony Kim were ahead of the field by 10 strokes, and tied for the lead with 9 holes remaining. A fellow golf fan whom I befriended in Florida had placed bets on Anthony Kim winning it all. Then he asked me what my thoughts were. I closed my eyes and then asked telepathically: show me or tell me who wins this tournament? I froze in silence for an undetermined amount of minutes, and then, much to my surprise, a name appeared onto my mental video screen: CAMILO VILLEGAS!

The first thoughts that came across my logical thinking mind was this: there is no way Camilo could win this game, he was at least 10 strokes back with 8 holes to go. So I went against my logical thinking and told my friend that neither Sergio nor Anthony will win this game. I said the winner was going to be Camilo Villegas. He looked at the score board and then placed a bet against my pick.

Low and behold, Camilo made an incredible run, picking up 10 birdies to close out the round tied neck and neck with Sergio and Anthony, who both struggle to hold onto a tie at the close of regulation. Later the three players entered a sudden death play-off, PGA Tour style, to determine who the winner would be. Needless to say Camilo did win! I learned a lot from that event, it actually opened the gates of non-traditional intelligence unlike anything I'd ever known before. And the thing is that I had no prior expectations when I invoked this great power within me. In my view it was totally incidental.

It didn't just end there. Later I wanted to know how best to send a telepathic message to someone and have them receive it. So (add coma after So) I asked my inner core to reveal to me how this could be done. And the answer was given to me, it said telepathically: "images are the language of telepathy." With that response I decided to conduct my own independent research to see if the information I received from my inner core was correct.

I enlisted the help of twenty hotel staff workers, and 10 total

305

strangers to participate in this experiment. In all but one instance did the experiment not work. Each hotel staff member reported hearing my voice and seeing my face during the prearranged time of the experiment. And the most interesting aspect of these experiments were that in each case, not only did they receive my telepathic messages, but that they felt compelled to follow a different set of instructions that were only given to them telepathically. You see in each case, I gave a verbal set of instructions to each person, and later during the actual transmission of telepathic messaging I gave a completely new set of instructions. Each person followed the new set of instructions without delay.

Here's what I learned from the telepathy experiments:

1. images are the most powerful way to send telepathy messages,

2. the receiver must know how to open up their senses to receive telepathy signals,

3. telepathy messages takes precedence over any other instruction given verbally prior to receiving telepathic message,

4. telepathic messages can be broadcast to millions of people at the same time from one sender under the right circumstances,

5. even if a person is unsuspecting, telepathy signals can still affect them if received,

6. telepathy is the language of animals and insects.

So then, you might be wondering at this time, why do I say that telepathy is the language of animals and insects? Here's why: my wife and I were walking together one day getting some much needed exercise. As we approached our home on a straight and hilly road, my wife could see the cat she adopted from the wild about 10 rows of houses ahead of us. She called out the cats name and received no response. She stated that we were to far away for the cat (Spooky) to here her. I then suggested that she use telepathy to send a message to the cat. She relented, saying that it won't work. I then told my wife that I'll do it for her. Briefly I closed my eyes and imagined seeing the cat face to face. I then sent a message to the cat telepathically, when the cat suddenly turned around and looked at us, my wife was very amazed that my little experiment of the moment in telepathy actually worked. The cat turned and waited for us to catch up to it. Later that night, I over heard my wife retelling the story to a friend.

These situation with the cat was not the only time I've had the opportunity to display my knowledge of how telepathy works. There was the one time when my wife and her step-mother called me into the living room of the house, said the wanted to discuss something with me. Immediately, without hesitation, I knew exactly what they wanted to say, and before they could speak, I told them what the nature of the discussion was all about. The first thing my wife asked me was: "Did Shaun tell you?" Of course not, I replied! To this very day neither my wife nor her step-mother can recall this event.

By the way, the ability to know what other people are thinking has been a trait of mine for as long as I can remember. In fact, I've had to tone it down a bit. People sometimes become a bit unnerved when they realize you know what they are about to say, before they speak it. In fact this phenomenon is more common than you think. Everyone has had some sort of preview about events to come, whether it be audible, visual or both due to telepathy.

Testing Your Telepathy Skills

This section is designed to help you bring out your telepathic skills and begin the task of evaluating and improvement. As I mentioned before, you already have the gift, you were born with it. Now is time for it to be unleashed.

Exercise One

This first exercise should be fun to do. It will add life to any party. Here's what you must do:

1. get a sheet of paper and a pen,

2. ask for a volunteer. Then have them think of a basic color in their mind, but not to tell anyone what color it is,

3. give the following instructions to your volunteer,

4. see this color in your mind with your eyes closed, you must see this color across your mental screen,

5. now, this is what you must do in order to see what color this person is seeing in his/her mind,

6. look closely at his/her facial features, look real good, and imagine seeing them with your eyes closed, now, you must ask: what color does he/she see?

7. be patient calm, wait for the answer to come to you from your inner sense, it will come,

8. to get it right, you must not let logic intervene, if it does you could be wrong,

9. now, write down the color that comes to your mind (what you hear) from a subtle, silent voice,

10. then ask your volunteer to state out loud his/her color,

11. now reveal what you've written down on paper before hand.

Practice this technique until you are able to hear clearly with distinction, the silent voice within, from what is called mental noise. Once you have the hang of this simple, yet very entertaining exercise it is time to move onto the next one.

Exercise Two

As mentioned before, distance has no barrier on telepathy performance none whatsoever. This next exercise will prove this point to you. This next exercise combines the first exercise, with one slight change! Do everything you learned from exercise one, but this time do it over the internet. That's right! You can do it two ways: 1. Use skype or some other online video conference service, and simply repeat the first exercise. 2. You can use any online instant messaging to perform this task. The only issue is that you should do this only with someone you trust.

Exercise Three

In this exercise you don't need any volunteers at all. In fact once you become proficient you might run off to Vegas and play poker. As I mentioned before, telepathy becomes stronger within you when used on a more frequent basis. This exercise will sharpen your insight by successfully showing you how to see (no predict) what cards a person is holding in their hands at any given moment.

I do this sort of thing a lot, in that I can see what cards a person has in their hand before they are revealed. But a word of warning! This ability has caused my family members to accuse me of cheating when we play a card game. You see, in their mind, since I win so much, I must be cheating. To them no one is that lucky! In a sense, they are right. I am not that lucky...

Here how it is done: 1. Get any deck of cards. 2. turn the deck backside up, and pull one card from any place in the deck. 3. Focus on the backside of the card, imagine it in your mind's eye, and ask the question: what card is this? Repeat this exercise until you are right nine of ten times in a row. Then you are ready for Vegas...

Exercise Four

Now for this final exercise to help you unleash your telepathy skills is one that many would die for: reading other people's thoughts. You see, this is very much a reality once you get the hang of it. But, as in anything you pursue in life, you must practice until you become good at it. This ability can not only help you make good decisions, it could very well save your life.

Here's how its done: 1. You have come to realize by now that imagination plays a vital role in telepathy skills. Visualization simply adds animation to an otherwise inanimate image. 2. The art of reading the thoughts of others is to maintain an image of their face within your mental screen, and then ask: what are they thinking? With patients and time the answer will come to you. The more you practice, the better you become...

In closing, you should know by now that telepathy is the way the mind delivers all questions and answers asked of it. All energy healing sessions, remote viewing, astral projections, are a form of telepathy as well as all other psychic phenomena. Telepathy works simply because you and I, along with everyone else is connected at the subjective level of mind. And there is only one subjective level of mind in all of existence, we share it.

The Last Words

This is where I get the chance to connect all the chapters within this book together. As disparaging as it may seem each topic is interrelated to all others in that the root causation is the mind, and more specifically the subjective level of mind.

Society has fostered a separatist's point of view for everything material. Since non-physical matter can't be seen with the naked eye alone, the notion that you'll accept precedence without questions has become the norm. For instance, what would your reactions be if all of a sudden you stumble upon a pyramid hidden deep within a forest, barely explored by folks close-by in your home town? As hypothetical as this may sound at first, it is exactly what happened to native North Americans. Hidden within barren lands of New Mexico, and again in the deserts of Nevada and Utah, lie the remnants of north America's unacknowledged pyramids. And similar to their well known counter parts found in Egypt and South America, no one knows who built them, and how they were built.

There are so many unknowns to our existence and the questions are still growing in numbers. Take for instance, no one in the science community talks much about the continent of Antarctica. Could this overlooked entity hold the key to unraveling the mysterious lost continent of Atlantis? Or could Antarctica be Atlantis?

What if there is a known cure for cancer, diabetes, and any disease believed incurable being withheld from you by powerful interest groups' intent on making a buck....what would you do? Better still, what if I told you that you are the cure for all of these situations, would you believe it?

For those of you content enough in letting others think for you, here's something to consider: Antarctica is nearly twice the size of Australia. According to a theory by Dr. Charles Hapgood, and supported by Albert Einstein, Antarctica was once a habitable place that supported life until the poles of the planet shifted nearly 26,000 years ago. Dr. Hapgood's assertion that Antarctica is the lost continent is supported by fossils discovered beneath the sheet of ice, animals that were indigenous of warm climates. And what if a pyramid is ever discovered on this continent, will the public at large be informed?

With so much at stake about the true nature of human abilities and history, reality suggests that those in possession of truth will continue the policies of old...Keeping the bulk of humanity in the dark for as long as they can, why? Because they get away with it!

You might asked, as a dear close friend of mine did....Rodh where are you going with this? And with that I'll fall back onto the main theme of this book.....Everything is connected.

Glossary

Agnosis:

An enlightened Human being with hidden and special knowledge. It simply means to have knowledge.

Astral Projection (OBE):

The ability of the mind (or astral body) to separate from the physical body and travel while maintaining full consciousness of the event, during which, there is no limit of space or time.

Astral Rape (PSI):

Is the act of a psychic who engages into having sexual intercourse with someone while they sleep, without prior permission. An incubus or succubus are spiritual demons or angels that do the same.

Awareness:

Knowledge of self and sense of whats happening elsewhere in the world with powers of mind.

Being:

A spiritual entity or human of some intelligence.

Big-Bang:

A theory, that everything that exists is the result of an explosion that occurred out of nothingness, caused by premordial matter. This theory is held by a number scientists and universities as to how the universe, and eventually human beings came into being. In short, it argues that life itself is purely accidental in nature. Some may consider this a materialistic view, which leads many into thinking that there is lack of substances for life to continue as is.

Causation:

Usually refers to GOD. Produces a result from which everything proceeds.

Clairaudience:

The ability to hear mentally, a subtle signal from spirit source.

Clairvoyance:

Psychic ability to see objects and visions. To see someones Past, Present and Future. Sometimes known as Sixth Sense.

Collective Conscious:

Refers to the mind of everyone, the universe and God.

Consciousness:

Refers to the mind a human or an awareness of self, as a spirit.

Cosmic Energy:

Any form or source of energy received from the Universe or any planets, stars, etc.

Cosmic Soup:

A mixter of early particles, atoms and plasma formed from the early formation of universe; theorized to set the conditions for all matter, including life.

Creation:

The construction or manifestation of everything that exist by GOD.

Energy:

The force used to contruct or create all matter, including life forms. The ability to do work. That which cannot be created or destroyed, it can only be transformed and put to use repeatedly.

Enlightenment:

A state of being, and knowledge of truth. A person no longer goverened by illusory of reality or programmed logic.

Esoteric:

From within. Understood by or meant for a select few who special knowledge or interests in metaphysics. Intended to be revealed only to initiates of a group: such as the esoteric doctrines of Pythagoras.

ESP:

Extra Sensory Perceptions (also see PSI).

Force Field:

Energy or aura that surrounds all human beings and all living things, such as plant life.

Higher Self:

The mind of a person, or their spiritual being.

Impressions:

Images received in alpha state or lower brainwaves while in altered state of mind.

Knowing:

Knowledge of things beyond logic or reason. A tool for those adapt at using ESP to help with everyday life.

Metaphysics:

Unseen matter, transcending physical matter. A branch of philosophy that deals with the first (unseen) existence of all things. Spirituality consists of things unseen.

NDE:

Experience that people had while dead for a short time. That are revived and explain what they had seen.

OBE:

See Astral projection.

Oneness:

A reference to everybody as one being with GOD.

Prime Creator (or Causation):

Reference to GOD.

Physic:

The study and principles of how things work in the physical.

P.O.S. (Power of Suggestion):

The ability to mentally suggest an idea or action into the mind of another, and have them act upon it as if it were there own. A form of mind-control. It also demonstrates power of the mind to manifest or create according to core beliefs.

Precognition:

The ability to see the future.

Premonition:

A dream, or flash of insight of an immediate event, sometimes warning of impending danger in the future.

Protocol:

A set of guidelines or procedures for a particular method, system or technology, so the outcome would result in a manner already known.

PSI:

Means psychic, as in the ability to see, hear, or sense things beyond the matrix of reality. Also, represents the 23rd letter in the Greek alphabet (pronounced as: Sigh).

Psychic:

A person with a set of nontraditional skills in perception that are not governed by space or time.

Quantum Physics:

The study of sub-atomic matter (particles).

Quantum Theory:

The theory of how sub-atomic matter and probabilies (chaos) effects and affects physical matter.

Remote Viewing:

The Ability to psychically project the mind anywhere in time or space. To find targets and/or retrieve information.

Spirit:

Life force of all beings, seen or unseen. The animater of the physical body (See Force Field).

Subconscious Mind:

An aspect of the mental being of a human that keeps all bodily functions working. It acts as on interpreter between the collective unconscious (God) and the conscious-mind of each individual. It is at times referred to as higher intelligence or self. It facilitates psychic powers in humans. It is the spirit of humans.

Superconscious/collective unconscious:

See God.

Telekinesis:

Mind over matter. The ability to move things without ever touching.

Telepathy:

Mind to mind talk at a distance. There is known limits to telepathy, which also includes images and feelings of other people. Often used in distant healing sections.

Temporal:

Pertaining to time or concerned with the shortness of life.

Third Eye:

Pineal Gland. Located about an inch inside of forehead, between left and right hemispheres of brain, suspended in bio-fluid. Also known as the first sight. On the surface this area is located between eyes and top center of brow. It is used by meditators, psychics and mediums to visualize mentally.

Whole:

A referrence to all.

www.ingramcontent.com/pod-product-compliance
Lightning Source LLC
Chambersburg PA
CBHW021217090426
42740CB00006B/255